Unpuzzling Your *Past*

A Basic Guide to Genealogy

Third Edition

Unpuzzling Your Past

A Basic Guide to Genealogy

Third Edition

Emily Anne Croom

BETTERWAY BOOKS
CINCINNATI, OHIO

 Published by Betterway Books, an imprint of F&W Publications, Inc., 1507 Dana Avenue, Cincinnati, Ohio 45207. (800) 289-0963. Third edition.

Other fine Betterway Books are available from your local bookstore or direct from the publisher.

99 98 97 96 5 4 3 2

Library of Congress Cataloging-in-Publication Data

Croom, Emily Anne
Unpuzzling your past : a basic guide to genealogy / by Emily Anne Croom — 3rd ed.
p. cm.
Includes bibliographical references and index.
ISBN 1-55870-396-9 (alk. paper)
1. United States—Genealogy—Handbooks, manuals, etc. 2. Genealogy. I. Title.
CS47.C76 1995
929'.1'072073—dc20 95-18210
CIP

Edited by Argie Manolis
Designed by Leslie Meaux-Druley
Cover designed by Stephanie Redman

ABOUT THE AUTHOR

Emily Anne Croom has written five privately printed family genealogies and the widely acclaimed *The Genealogist's Companion & Sourcebook*. A Houston, Texas, resident and former high school history teacher, she conducts genealogy workshops and is an active researcher and writer on the subject.

TABLE OF CONTENTS

FOREWORD, viii

CHAPTER ONE

In the Beginning 1

Inexpensive materials and consistent organizations are the first steps toward successful unpuzzling. The objects of the search are families, not isolated individuals.

CHAPTER TWO

Strategies for Winning 4

Being part game-player and part detective, the successful genealogist will follow certain rules: (1) be scientific, thorough, resourceful, cautious, systematic, and courteous; (2) look for ancestors as part of a cluster of friends, relatives, and neighbors.

CHAPTER THREE

Charting Your Course 7

Five-generation charts and family group sheets provide space for recording basic information about each person's life.

CHAPTER FOUR

How to Begin the Puzzle: The Outside Edges 12

Gathering family history is like working a jigsaw puzzle. Begin with what you know (the straight edges of the puzzle) and work backward toward the middle. The best way to begin is talking with other family members.

CHAPTER FIVE

What's In a Name? 17

Spelling, nicknames, and abbreviations of names can present special challenges to the genealogist. Understanding the patterns and habits of naming may give you clues for solving some pieces of the puzzle.

CHAPTER SIX

Hand-Me-Downs: Family Traditions 21

Family traditions are both interesting and informative, but the genealogist must be cautious in accepting these stories as fact.

CHAPTER SEVEN

Life History: Beginning to End 24

Family history is more than lists of names and dates. Suggested interview questions help the genealogist gather interesting biographical information.

CHAPTER EIGHT

History as the Family Lived It 27

The family historian seeks to fit the family into the history of the city, county, state, and nation. Suggested questions help the genealogist interview for this information.

CHAPTER NINE

What Were They Like? 34

Suggested questions help the genealogist discover the personality traits, physical features, and medical history of family members.

CHAPTER TEN

Checklist of Family Sources 36

Gathering information from family papers and living relatives is a logical way to begin a genealogical search. Interviews, family Bibles, letters, scrapbooks, photographs, and other memorabilia add depth and character to the project.

CHAPTER ELEVEN
Beyond the Family: Local Sources 45

After family sources, researchers often turn next to censuses and such local sources as cemeteries, community elders, newspapers, county courthouse records, public libraries, schools, and churches. Interlibrary loan may provide access to local history and records.

CHAPTER TWELVE
Beyond the Family: State and Federal Sources 62

State archives, libraries, and historical societies hold state census, land, pension, and other records that contain genealogical data. Important federal sources include census, military, public land, immigration, and naturalization records. Certain specialized records contain information for African-American or Native American searches.

CHAPTER THIRTEEN
Where Do I Look for That? 75

Suggested sources and specific examples help the reader in search of birth, marriage, and death information, parents' names, maiden names, former residences, and other details about ancestors.

CHAPTER FOURTEEN
What's In a Date? 88

Writing, reading, and using dates present special cautions for the genealogist. Examples from actual cases show how to use dates as tools to fit together other pieces of the puzzle.

CHAPTER FIFTEEN
Fitting the Pieces Together 95

The beginning of an actual search illustrates the combining of public and family sources to put together pieces of the puzzle.

CHAPTER SIXTEEN
Read It Right 99

Being aware of the characteristics of early American handwriting helps the genealogist read original documents accurately.

CHAPTER SEVENTEEN
What About Computers? 103

Both genealogy and word processing software can help researchers keep track of ancestral families. For both home users and on-site users, comuter research opportunities are increasing, including searches into certain federal land, military, and immigration records.

CHAPTER EIGHTEEN
Sharing Your Family History 109

Regardless of how the family history is shared, it can have meaning for the family only when it is shared.

APPENDIX A
Glossary, Abbreviations, Relationship Chart 116

APPENDIX B
Additional References 121

APPENDIX C
Libraries and Archives 125

APPENDIX D
National Archives 146

APPENDIX E
Territorial and State Census Records 147

APPENDIX F
Charts and Forms 155

INDEX, 177

FOREWORD

Friends often have said, "I'd like to work on my family tree, but I wouldn't know where to begin." Or, as they head for a visit with elderly relatives and I advise them to ask lots of questions about their family history, they usually answer, "I wouldn't know what to ask." Or a young friend calls me on the telephone, "I've got a history assignment to do a family tree, and I don't know how to do it." Or I see a family eagerly enter the library thirty minutes before closing time and tell the librarian they want to "look up their family tree."

So, this book is the result of prodding by friends and relatives who wanted very basic information, the kind that is obvious to the experienced searcher or professional historian but not at all obvious to the novice.

Many books are available to help family historians with more specialized problems of looking for Civil War or Revolutionary War ancestors, immigrant ancestors, or early settlers of the colonies. This book, however, is intended to help the family get started, by answering their most basic questions and by emphasizing the use of family sources, especially the living ones.

Relatively speaking, we have plenty of time to search for the distant past, but preserving the more recent past, the last eighty to one hundred years, should take place while the best sources are available: the family members and friends who experienced those years, who knew the great- or great-great-grandparents, who can relate a treasury of family stories and describe the family homes and weddings and Christmas celebrations. I knew only one of my own great-grandparents, and it never occurred to me to sit down and talk with her—until it was too late.

Most families, extended to include cousins, have one or more elders who remember rather clearly events of the early twentieth century and who knew family members whose lives and the stories they told reached back to the mid-nineteenth century. No amount of library research can duplicate or replace what these people can tell us.

Even my own generation lived what many students consider rather ancient history. They find it hard to believe that life existed without television or air-conditioning, just as some of us wonder at "the way it was" before cars or electricity. Probably we ought to record, as part of our family history, our own reminiscences and reactions to what happened around us.

If it is to have meaning, family history cannot be separated from the nation's history and culture. Therefore, to give our family history perspective as well as interest, we must eventually try to put the family into the society and culture in which it lived and worked. This book is intended to help the beginner gather this kind of information, especially for the more recent past.

Finding the family is, of course, the first step. This process is called genealogy, a fascinating, rather addictive hobby which quite naturally begins at home. It can involve one person or the entire family. Genealogy is like working a jigsaw puzzle. You will find pleasure and satisfaction as more and more pieces fit into place. The rule of thumb "begin with what you know and go from there" is certainly appropriate to genealogy. I like to compare the process to putting together the easily recognized straight-edged pieces of a jigsaw puzzle first to form the frame and then trying the other pieces to find where they belong. In genealogy the straight-edged pieces are the most recent names, dates and stories that we know or can find easily. Once those are recorded, we have some framework from which to look for more and in which to fit "missing pieces" as we find them. The middle of the puzzle is divided into families, some of which "fall into place" more quickly and easily than others. Working backward in time, or toward the middle of the puzzle, the family historian may complete some sections of the puzzle but may never really finish the whole—and may never really want it to be finished.

If you have wanted to work on your own family tree but never knew just what to do first, this book is for you. If you have done some searching but have not tapped the sources closest to you or in "ancestral" hometowns, this book is for you, too. However you use it, enjoy yourself and have fun working your own special puzzle.

I'd like to thank those who have pushed me hardest, encouraged me most, and asked many of the basic questions: my sister Judith King; my parents P.B. and Fletcher Croom; and my friends Charlotte Metcalf, Ruth Galey, Lorine Brinley, and Ann and Steve Hudson. And a big thank-you to Mrs. Nettie Barnes, my former junior high school teacher, who introduced me to genealogy in the first place.

Emily Croom
Bellaire, Texas, 1983

FOREWORD TO THIRD EDITION

Since the first edition of this book in 1983 and the second edition in 1989, many new genealogists have begun unpuzzling their pasts. I am grateful for the very positive response the book has received and the expressions of thanks that have come from readers all over the country. Because of such a positive reception and because genealogy is bigger than ever in this country, we can now offer a third edition.

Many features of the book remain the same; the sections on public records and computers have been expanded and updated. The aim of the book also is the same: (1) to give beginning genealogists a good foundation on which to build their research and organize their findings and (2) to provide genealogists of any level of experience with valuable reference materials in the bibliographies, appendices, examples, and case studies. All examples and case studies are from actual research, sometimes on my own families, but often from research I've done for other people.

A word of appreciation to Terri Mote, reference librarian of the Bellaire City Library, and to Norma Chudleigh for consultation on the computer chapter. I am especially grateful to Gay E. Carter, reference librarian at the University of Houston-Clear Lake, and Robert T. Shelby for their consulting, encouraging, answering questions, listening, reading, and offering constructive suggestions.

Emily Croom
Bellaire, Texas, 1995

CHAPTER ONE

In the Beginning

Has anyone ever asked you where your "people" came from? Your parents? Your grandparents? Your immigrant ancestors? Can you answer?

Or try the question, "Who were your great-grandparents?" That's the question that launched my search for family history. I was in the seventh grade. I thought I could answer easily because I had known one of my great-grandmothers. Well, I couldn't. With great confidence I started naming names. When I stopped at four, I was jolted into reality. "What do you mean I've got eight great-grandparents! I've only heard of four." Yes, I have two parents; yes, they each had two parents; yes, those each had two parents. Alas, I really did have eight great-grandparents, but my father's side of the family was one giant blank. Those people were hiding somewhere, and I had to find them.

I took to letter-writing. My dad knew only one older relative. So I wrote to that great-uncle in Tennessee. We corresponded until his death. From him I got a few answers, a few erroneous traditions, and a bunch of cousins. I was on my way! After several visits to Tennessee and a number of years, I feel that I know three of those four "missing persons." For example, Isaac was an asthmatic farmer with thirteen kids; he created a few problems by not requiring them to go to school. Pitser was a Methodist farmer who owned a mill and got up at three in the morning to go to work. Mary Catherine hated housework, so she raised peacocks and lambs while her daughter kept house. The fourth? Well, her name was Ann Marie. . . .

Thus, the search goes on. And it goes beyond these four. It reaches as far back as there are records available. It is like working a jigsaw puzzle. Once you have the outside edges put together, the challenge is to find and sort the inside pieces. Some are easy to put in place; some take fine discrimination and careful testing. Sometimes, no amount of searching can turn up evidence of people you know have lived. The puzzle never really gets finished, and you never really want it to.

How many of your great-grandparents can you name?

1. ______________________________
2. ______________________________
3. ______________________________
4. ______________________________
5. ______________________________
6. ______________________________
7. ______________________________
8. ______________________________

THINGS YOU NEED

The tools for working this puzzle are simple and inexpensive. There are many ways to organize your work There is no right or wrong way. The only requirement is consistent organization. Having tried several systems, I have found the following to be the most efficient and effective.

1. Three-ring, loose-leaf notebook binders and three-hole notebook paper. These are preferable to spiral notebooks because they allow easy additions of notes, clippings, letters, and photographs. Also, a hole punch is a handy tool when you add these items.

2. Three-hole dividers, one for each surname. As you gather more information, you can add dividers. Eventually you may divide into new notebooks. My Metcalf-Campbell book has these divisions:
   a. Metcalf-Texas, which covers the most recent four generations;
   b. Metcalf-Alabama, added when I discovered that they came from Alabama;
   c. Metcalf-Georgia, representing the earliest information yet gathered;

d. Campbell-Texas, covering the wife's family;
e. Campbell-Alabama, since the two families moved together to Texas from the same Alabama county;
f. Godwin, a grandmother's maiden name.

As more information on the Godwin line surfaces, I will divide that section of the notebook.

Begin with your surname or maiden name, and that name becomes a notebook. However, other surnames immediately enter the picture because each generation adds a wife-and-mother and her mother and her grandmother, and so on. You must decide for yourself whether to concentrate on only one line at a time. I could never do that.

In the days before computer-made indexes, I was reading the 1850 Tennessee census, hoping to find my last nameless great-grandparent with her husband and children. I was reading family by family the entire Madison County census looking for my Isaac Croom. Fortunately, the census taker saved Isaac's part of the county for the latter part of his duties and enabled me to experience one of those electrifying moments of which every genealogist dreams. I came across a man named Sterling Orgain—not your common, ordinary name, but the same name as one of my maternal ancestors whom I had not been able to find anywhere. Glancing quickly down the list of children, I found my very own great-great-grandmother and the brothers and sisters my grandmother had told me about! No one had had any idea (at least any that proved correct) of their pre-Texas whereabouts, but here they were in Madison County, Tennessee. So my search in Madison County *had* to include Crooms *and* Orgains.

Why divide the notebooks by state? Frequently families migrated in groups. Elliott Coleman moved from Virginia to Tennessee in 1845 because an aunt and some family friends had moved there and had written back glowing reports. He and a friend decided to try it. Soon three of his younger brothers joined them, and a sister moved just across the border into Mississippi. My search for them was centered in that one county, where I found records on all four Coleman brothers. When they witnessed each other's deeds, acted as surety on each other's marriage bonds, bought dry goods from the same merchant, subscribed to the same newspaper, attended the same church and civic functions, and conducted business in the same town, their descendants have reams of notes to copy. There is no point in copying each source two or three times and filing under each brother's name. Keeping it all together under "Coleman-Tennessee" gives a good *family* picture. Elliott was not an isolated individual but the oldest brother of a family group.

Elliott married a Patton girl from the next-door county, which was full of her relatives, and now mine, too. This marriage added the Patton section to the notebook. As I read the records of both counties, I made all my notes with a carbon copy, one for the Coleman section and one for the Patton section, if both names appeared in the same record. Otherwise, I kept each page of notes for one family only and marked in the top right-hand corner the surname under which the page was to be filed. (See Figure 1.)

What about using computers instead of notebooks? (See chapter seventeen for further discussion of computers.) First, you can "do genealogy" quite effectively without a computer. Second, unless you use a laptop or notebook computer to take and store all notes, you will need an organized way of recording and filing the information you gather at interviews, libraries, and courthouses and from correspondence. Once I have taken my notes, I do not have the time or inclination to transfer them all from notebooks into the computer. Besides, I find it easier to study and evaluate data on people of the same surname or from the same county if I see it spread out around me on paper. For example, you may find multiple marriage records, deeds, wills, and cemetery inscriptions in one county for people of your surname. Are they related to each other? Are they related to you? You may not know at the time you write down the information. I prefer to keep this information in a notebook until I know which individuals fit into which families. Then I can choose which ones to add into my genealogy program or word processing documents.

Choose one or two of your surnames to begin with. Remember, you may have at least eight to choose from, with your eight great-grandparents. Set up your notebook, and you are ready to begin one of the most fascinating, rewarding, never-ending, mystifying, and addictive hobbies available to humankind.

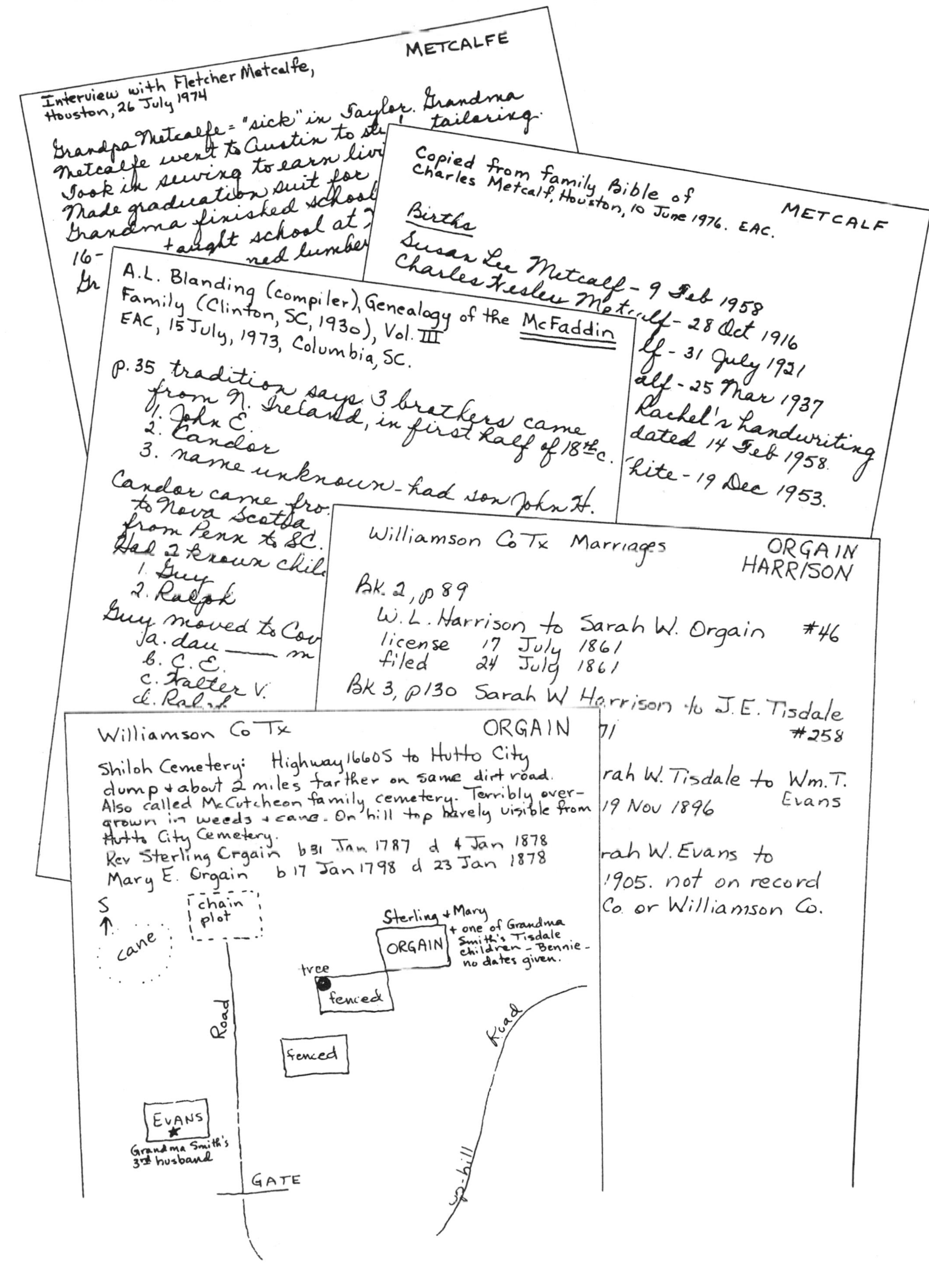

FIG. 1: EXAMPLES OF NOTE TAKING

CHAPTER TWO

Strategies for Winning

Games have rules, and successful game players—like detectives—have strategies for winning. The genealogy jigsaw puzzle has a few of its own rules. The successful genealogist, being both game player and detective, develops and uses the strategies that get the best results. What are the special rules and strategies of this game?

Be scientific. Write down your sources of information: who told you or where you read it. This process is called documenting. In doing this, the historian has the same purpose as the scientist. Both are trying to prove something. People will ask, "How do you *know* Great-grandpa was from North Carolina? Papa always said he was from Alabama." What documents or sources can you point to that prove, or even suggest, his North Carolina origin?

To document your notes, title each page with a heading that contains the source information. (See Figure 1.) For an interview, write down the name of the person you are interviewing, the location of the interview, and the date. When copying data from family Bibles or cemeteries, write down who copied the information, where it can be found if needed again, and the date. For published books, give the author, title, publisher, date of publication, volume and page numbers. The process is a simple one if you ask yourself, "Where can I find this exact information again if I need it?"

Be thorough. Approach your subject from several angles. Write down as much information as you can. Evaluate all your information. A good historian will try to learn who, what, when, where, how, why, and with what results. The family historian wants to know where and how just as much as who and when. Perhaps you talk with several people who knew your Great-grandmother Metcalfe. Each one may give you something different in your effort to "know" her. One talks about her church activities. Another remembers her sewing and knitting. Still another describes her house in Taylor. One saved her favorite recipe. Your puzzle needs all of these parts to be complete.

Be resourceful. Strive to investigate many sources. It may take multiple documents to determine a correct date, place, name, or relationship. Firsthand, or primary, sources are usually the most reliable—documents made at the time of the event. These include information a person told or wrote about his or her own life and family. For instance, a man records his birth date and place on his Masonic Lodge membership application; a grandmother writes to her grandchildren giving the names of her parents and grandparents, whom she knew; a bridesmaid describes the wedding in her diary. Other primary sources, although often written by someone else, include wills, deeds, tax lists, marriage licenses, church registers, newspaper reports at the time of the event, census records, some Bible records, some information on birth and death certificates, people who took part in the event you are investigating, and people who knew your ancestor personally. Not all of these sources will be available for each ancestor, but the genealogist strives to find as many as possible.

Be cautious. We cannot believe everything we read, even in public and family documents. Genealogists, like scientists and detectives, must not jump to conclusions but must be ready to question what they are told and what they read. They must evaluate, guess, ask another way, try another source. Even primary sources can contain mistakes. For example, Alfred, filling out his father's death certificate, furnished for public record his father's birth date and place. (This document could be considered a primary source on the death information but would be a secondary source, one not produced at the time of the event or by someone who participated in the event, for the birth information.) Years later, we discovered the father's church confirmation record, which gave a different birthplace. This led to a search for documents for which the father himself had provided the birthplace information. Because this was a late-nineteenth-century birth and the father lived into the 1940s, his Social Security and Masonic Lodge applications became the documents which confirmed his birthplace. Their information agreed with the church record, not the death certificate.

The following is a case study using interviews instead of documents to illustrate these strategies.

In a client's family, we were trying to identify Uncle George's wife. Sister said that Uncle George's wife was Aunt Tella but could not remember her real name. A cousin said she called George's wife Aunt Stella. Hearing both names, these two relatives remembered that Tella and Stella were both short for Costella, but neither could remember Aunt Tella/Stella's maiden name. The 1880 census shows her given name as Euphima, but no relative present had ever heard of anyone by that name. We asked whether George might have married twice, first to Euphima and then to Costella. No one remembered, and the county marriage records and the family Bible, both of which might have answered the question, were destroyed by fire years ago.

We continued down the list to other aunts and uncles and their spouses. Everyone agreed that Uncle Walter married Sally Campbell and Papa married Emma Campbell. Two Campbell girls? Were they sisters? Then it clicked. Mama always said she and Aunt Tella were sisters. That made Aunt Tella a Campbell too. Three sisters married three brothers? Then we read the 1870 census of Mama's family, and Aunt Tella was there: E C or Euphima Costella Campbell. Then someone remembered, "Oh, yes, that *was* her name."

A new question had appeared in answering the original one: What about the third girl, Sally, who married Uncle Walter? The marriage record proves that she was a Campbell. Costella and Mama had a sister Sarah, or Sally; but if their sister Sally had married Walter, she would have been 25 years older than her husband. We asked again, "Were Aunt Sally and Mama related?" The response was noncommittal. We approached it from a different angle: "Did you know any of Aunt Sally's relatives?" Answer: Aunt Sally's mother was called Aunt Cindy. Okay, part of the dilemma was solved. Mama's mother was Emily, not Cindy. So, Aunt Sally was not Mama's sister. The new question arising was "What Campbell family *was* she part of?" Additional searching and asking may answer this question and raise still others.

Another caution for genealogists concerns copying. Handwritten or typed copies of originals can contain errors, so it is wisest to consult the original whenever possible. Microfilm and photocopies of an original preserve its accuracy. They are good substitutes when the original is not available.

Copied records are secondhand sources. They may contain valuable information, but human error is more likely in copying, especially when researchers read handwriting of a century or two ago. When you do your own copying, be as accurate as possible.

When I was searching for my great-grandfather Isaac's first marriage record, I found a typed copy of the marriage book in a library. Eagerly I copied the name of the bride as given: Elizabeth Steer. Months later, I had an opportunity to see the original marriage record and discovered that her name was not Steer. The name had been hyphenated in the original; and the copier had taken down only the first syllable, and that incorrectly. Her name was Sturdivant.

For accuracy and detail, it is helpful to photocopy records and photograph tombstones and houses if the information is likely to be questioned or is of major importance.

Be systematic. Keep all information about one family together. This practice makes your search and the use of your findings much easier. Organize your search before you go on an interview or to look at public records. Know what you are looking for. File your notes in the proper section of your notebook. As you see in Figure 1, your filing and note-keeping can be quick and easy if you write at the top of each page the surname or section to which the notes pertain.

Be considerate. In interviewing people, you will get more cooperation when you are on time, tactful, polite, to the point, and appreciative—and when you don't stay too long. Usually 45 minutes to an hour is long enough for such a visit. Repeated but shorter visits are usually more effective than one long, and therefore tiring, visit of several hours.

In libraries and public buildings, observe their particular rules as well as common courtesies. When you go into a county courthouse to look at public records, introduce yourself to the clerk and ask for permission to see, or for the location of, the particular documents you are interested in. It is helpful to explain that you are working on family history. You need not go into detail about your search. The employees are not usually research experts and are not being paid to listen to a visitor's family tales or history. If you have a question about using a particular document, ask for help. You may find it beneficial to ask the clerk to give you the name of a local historian, genealogist or society to contact in your search.

Use a cluster approach. A valuable strategy for genealogists is to study each ancestor as part of a cluster of friends, relatives, and neighbors. By gathering information on these people, you often learn more about your own family, for ancestors did not live in a vacuum. They witnessed deeds and wills of family members or close friends. They were bondsmen for the marriages of brothers, sisters, cousins, or close friends. They moved or went to war with classmates, fellow church members, lodge brothers, or relatives. Elderly parents often migrated with one or more of their grown children. Uncles and nephews combined their families into wagon trains or ships bound for new homes far away. They lived next door to or across the road from other family members, including in-laws or married sisters, and thus appear close to each other in the census records and some tax rolls, even when their surnames were not the same. For example, the W.M. McAlpin of Mississippi who testified on George M. Shelby's Texas Confederate pension application, saying that George had indeed served when and where he said he had, for they were together, turned out to be the husband of George's first cousin Emeline Shelby. The Annie Oldham who, with her husband, Lafayette, lived next to John and Jane Shelby in 1900 in Robertson County, Texas, turned out to be John's sister. The census record did not tell us this, but records found later in the search did. The Alfred Moore who was in business with Sterling Organ when they petitioned Congress in the 1820s was also Orgain's brother-in-law. Your picture of the family is more complete when you work on the cluster, and sometimes you find clues, evidence, or proof you could not have found by working only on one individual.

CHAPTER THREE

Charting Your Course

Several kinds of charts provide good worksheets for your family history puzzle. The first two, the five-generation chart and the family group sheet, represent the outside edges of your puzzle, the basic information that you gather on each person's life. This information is called vital statistics. It includes

when and where (county and state or location in foreign country) he was born
when, where, and whom he married
when and where he died
where he is buried (cemetery, city or county, state)

This information is identified by abbreviations on most charts to save space:

b—born
m—married
d—died

The five-generation chart shows you and your ancestors, or your "family tree." The chart shows each person as a child of his parents, a line coming from the union of two people. The chart is a handy reference for "who fits in where."

The five-generation chart shown in Figure 2 shows Ferdinand G. Coleman as #1. He was born about 1794. The *c* stands for the Latin word *circa* which means *around* or *about*. He married Elizabeth A. Phillips on 3 January 1822. He died in 1867. All of these events took place in Cumberland County, Virginia.

Ferdinand's father, Elliott, is #2 on the chart. Elliott's birth date is not known but has been estimated from available evidence, which can be listed or explained on the back of the chart. His wife (and Ferdinand's mother) is listed as #3. Her birth and death dates are approximated from available information and therefore are shown as "about 1773" and "about 1853."

Elliott's parents are #4 and #5, although nothing is known of his mother or her family. William was Elliott's father; William's father is #8, Thomas, whose parents were Daniel and Patience, #16 and #17. The blanks indicate that nothing is known, or has yet been gathered, about those people.

Notice that each mother in Figure 2 is listed by her maiden name, her name before she married. Elizabeth's mother, Patty, is shown by her nickname as well as by her given name. Elizabeth is #13, and her maiden name is shown with a question mark to indicate that evidence points to Watkins as her maiden name or that some searchers feel that was her maiden name, although nothing has been proved at this time.

As more information is gathered and additional charts are needed to go farther back in time, write in the number of the next chart on which you can find that person. In Figure 2, Ferdinand's maternal line, through his great great-grandfather John Archer, is continued on chart 12. As you see, Ferdinand himself was a continuation of chart 27. Any person can be #1 on such a chart.

On the five-generation chart, each column represents a generation. On your own chart, you will be the first generation, #1. Your parents are in the second column and are the second generation going back in time. Your four grandparents make up the third generation and third column; your eight great-grandparents are the fourth column. Your sixteen great-great-grandparents will occupy the fifth column. The father's name is listed first in each set of parents.

Begin your own chart with yourself as #1. Fill in the vital statistics which pertain to you. Your father is #2, and your mother is #3, shown by her maiden name. Fill in their vital statistics as well as you can using information you have at home that is known to be accurate. Your father's father will be #4; your father's mother, #5. Your mother's father will be #6; your mother's mother, #7. List their names and as much information as you have now. It may be helpful to list below #1, #2, #4, and #6 their children's names, as in Figure 2. File the chart in your notebook so that you can add

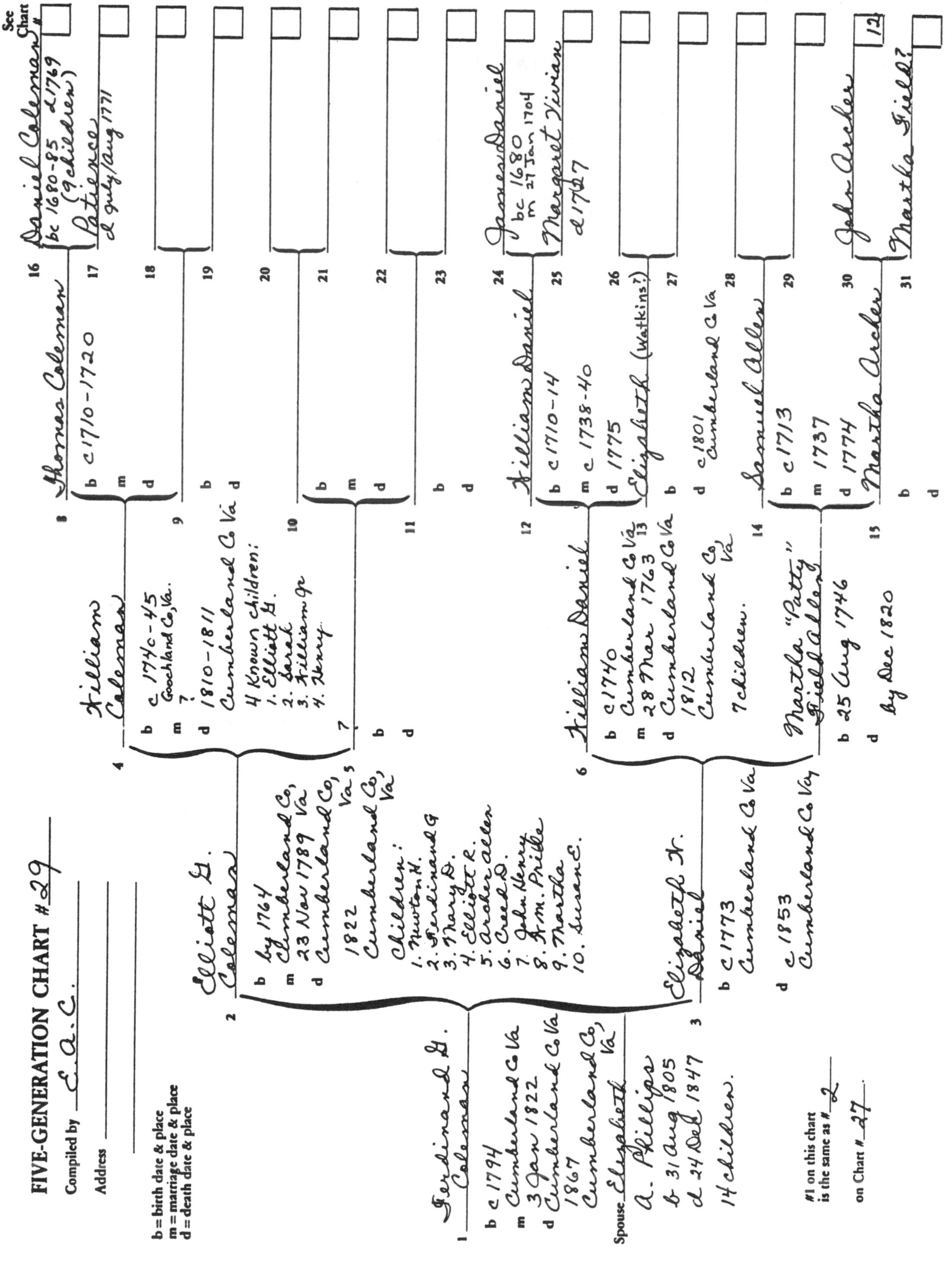

FIVE-GENERATION CHART #29

Compiled by E. A. C.

Address

b = birth date & place
m = marriage date & place
d = death date & place

1 Ferdinand G. Coleman
b c 1794
Cumberland Co Va
m 3 Jan 1822
Cumberland Co Va
d 1867
Cumberland Co, Va

Spouse Elizabeth A. Phillips
b 31 Aug 1805
d 24 Dec 1847
14 children.

2 Elliott G. Coleman
b by 1764
Cumberland Co,
m 23 Nov 1789 Va
Cumberland Co, Va
d 1822
Cumberland Co, Va
Children:
1. Newton H.
2. Ferdinand G
3. Mary D.
4. Elliott R.
5. Archer Allen
6. Creed D.
7. John Henry
8. Wm. Prille
9. Martha
10. Susan E.

3 Elizabeth W. Daniel
b c 1773
Cumberland Co Va
d c 1853
Cumberland Co Va

4 William Coleman
b c 1740-45
Goochland Co, Va.
m ?
d 1810-1811
Cumberland Co Va
4 Known children:
1. Elliott G.
2. Sarah
3. William Jr
4. Henry

5 ?
b
d

6 William Daniel
b c 1740
Cumberland Co Va
m 28 Mar 1763
Cumberland Co Va
d 1812
Cumberland Co, Va
7 children.

7 Martha "Patty" Field Allen
b 25 Aug 1746
d by Dec 1820

8 Thomas Coleman
b c 1710-1720
m
d

9
b
d

10
b
m
d

11
b
d

12 William Daniel
b c 1710-14
m c 1738-40
d 1775

13 Elizabeth (Watkins?)
b
d c 1801
Cumberland Co Va

14 Samuel Allen
b c 1713
m 1737
d 1774

15 Martha Archer
b
d

16 Daniel Coleman
bc 1680-85 d 1769
(9 children)

17 Patience
d July/Aug 1771

18

19

20

21

22

23

24 James Daniel
bc 1680
m 27 Jan 1704

25 Margaret Vivian
d 1727

26

27

28

29

30 John Archer — See Chart # 12

31 Martha Field?

#1 on this chart is the same as # 2 on Chart # 27.

FIG. 2: COLEMAN FIVE-GENERATION CHART

information as you find it. Some family historians prefer to keep all their five-generation charts together in a separate notebook. Others prefer to keep one in each notebook illustrating the families in that particular notebook.

The family group sheet is very useful. It contains one family, a mother and father and their children. A sample is shown in Figure 3. The husband's full name and the wife's maiden name head the sheet. The *II* added to Elliott's name distinguishes him from his grandfather for whom he was named. Elliott's birth date is not known. Only the approximate year of his birth is given. His death date also is not known but has been narrowed down by existing evidence to be between 3 February and 17 February 1892. The sources used to estimate these dates can be listed on the back of the chart.

The wife's birth date is given one way on her tombstone and another way in the Bible record, so both years are listed: 1828/29. These differing sources can be listed and explained on the back of the chart. Because her exact birthplace has not been determined, the chart shows the approximate location, "in or near Chester County, SC," as suggested by available sources, also explained on the back.

Children #2, #3, #4, and #7 never married, as shown by the dashed lines. A blank space with no marking would indicate that the marriage information is not yet determined.

The blank birth dates for several of the children mean that the exact dates are not known. If they are ever found, they can be added. The years have been estimated from census records and family letters. Nothing is known about children #5 and #8 after they married; no death date can be guessed. Child #7 died as a young man, about 1886, judging from available sources. These sources can be explained on the back of the chart.

Because so many seventeenth-, eighteenth-, and nineteenth-century families were large, and other nineteenth- and twentieth-century families have been generally smaller, I have found it useful to have two sizes of family group sheets. One has lines for eighteen children and vital statistics, as in Figure 3. One has room for eight children with more space to write in where they were born, married, and buried. On both charts, with smaller families, I sometimes use the extra lines to record data on the children's spouses.

Begin your own family group sheets with your childhood family: your parents as *Husband* and *Wife*, you and your brothers and sisters as the *Children*. Fill in full names as they would appear on a birth certificate. Nicknames can go in parentheses, or you can underline the name a person goes by. For example, one little girl is called Bitsy, but her real name is Sarah Elizabeth. On the chart, she should be listed as Sarah Elizabeth (Bitsy). Cordelia Celeste was always called Delia. Her entry on the chart would be Cordelia Celeste.

Make a second family group sheet for your father's family, with his parents at the top and their children, your aunts and uncles, listed below. Fill in another for your mother's family, one for each grandparent in his or her childhood family, one for each great-grandparent as a child, etc. Because we research the cluster of friends, siblings, cousins, and neighbors among whom an ancestor lived and worked, we need to keep track of them as well. The family group sheets on the people in the cluster provide not only a place to record information systematically but a ready reference. By studying the charts of a group of brothers and sisters with their spouses and children, you may also find clues to former generations, residences, maiden names, and naming patterns. You may also discover discrepancies which then necessitate additional searching on your part. For example, tombstones may show birth dates for two brothers only six months apart. You would need to use other sources to determine the actual dates, for your own ancestor's birth date may have been engraved incorrectly. The family group sheets help you study such details more thoroughly, more completely, and thus, more accurately.

If you keep these charts handy, you can readily add information to them. I like to keep the appropriate family group sheet as the first page of each notebook section. In the case of the four Coleman brothers living in the same county, all four group sheets appear at the beginning of the Coleman-Tennessee notebook section. Other family group sheets, on families for whom I have no notebooks, I file alphabetically in a single notebook.

Copies of your five-generation charts and family group sheets can be sent to relatives when you are seeking information, along with a letter explaining your project, like the one below.

Dear Aunt Jane,

I am working on our family history and am trying to gather all the information I can on Grandma Smith's side of the family. I'm enclos-

FAMILY RECORD OF THE Elliott Glen Coleman FAMILY

Birth date 1824
Birth place Cumberland Co VA
Death date 3-17 Feb 1892
Burial place Kyle - Hays Co. Tx unmarked grave
Military service:

ELLIOTT GLEN COLEMAN II
Full name of husband

Birth date 25 Feb. 1828/29
Birth place SC in or near Chester Co.
Death date 19 June 1901
Burial place Zephyr, Brown Co. Tx

MARGARET CATHERINE PATTON
Full name of wife with maiden name

Other spouses
none

Marriage date 12 OCTOBER 1847
Place FAYETTE CO, TENN. moved to Hardeman Co - Bolivar.

#	Sex	CHILDREN Full Name all Coleman	Birth Day	Birth Mo	Birth Year	Death Day	Death Mo	Death Year	Marriage to	Date
1	F	MARY ELIZA CATHERINE "	23	Sept	1848	7 Whiteville	Mar	1908 Tenn	PITSER MILLER BLALOCK Bolivar Tenn.	30 Nov 1869
2	F	LUCY "			1850	before		1860	—	—
3	F	WILLIE "			1853-4	before		1860	—	—
4	M	FERDINAND GLEN "			1855	31	Aug	1928	—	—
5	M	THOMAS PATTON "		bu	1858				SALLIE M. JACKSON	14 JULY 1889
6	F	KATE EWING "	11	JUNE	1859	16	OCT	1942	HENRY MONTGOMERY	29 JAN 1890
7	M	ELLIOTT GLEN III "			1862		c	1886	—	—
8	M	EDWARD M "			1865				MATTIE PENNINGTON	21 JULY 1887
9	F	LOUISA JANE HARDY "	16	Feb	1868	24	MAR	1917	GEORGE WASHINGTON ADAMS	29 AUG 1889
10	F	LILLIE "	15	Dec	1870	14	MAY	1951	JAMES THOMAS FISHER	SEPT 1889
11	M	EZEKIEL McNEAL "	5	Aug	1872	19	Aug	1955	ELLA MAE MINOR ARNOLD	13 SEPT 1909
12	M	JAMES TURNER "	16	Oct	1875	24	Sept	1931	MARTHA ELLEN FISHER	5 APR 1899
13										
14										
15										
16										
17										
18										

Husband (notes) To Tenn - 1845. To Tx - 1872. CARPENTER - built Episcopal Church, Gonzales Tx + Methodist Church, Kyle Tx. FARMER Too. Presbyterian.

FERDINAND GLEN COLEMAN
Husband's Father

ELIZA PHILLIPS
Husband's Mother dau Peter Talbot Phillips and Elizabeth A. Allen.

Wife (notes) Presbyterian

THOMAS PATTON
Wife's Father

CATHERINE EWING McFADDEN
Wife's Mother dau of Isaac McFadden of Chester Co SC. + Elizabeth Steele

FIG. 3: COLEMAN FAMILY GROUP SHEET

ing a family group sheet with her children on it. I've filled in what I could; you see there is a lot I don't know. Would you please fill in whatever you can and return the chart to me? I'd appreciate any information that you can fill in. Thanks a million! I'll send you copies of whatever I can gather from other sources.

Love, Sarah

CHAPTER FOUR

How to Begin the Puzzle: The Outside Edges

The logical way to begin anything new is to start with what you know. In working a jigsaw puzzle, it is easy to begin with the outside edges because they are straight and easily identified. Similarly, in genealogy, begin with yourself and work backwards. The five-generation charts and family group sheets will show you how much you already know.

The best source to use in filling in the rest of the "straight-edged" pieces of your family puzzle is the people in your family: your parents, brothers and sisters, grandparents, great-grandparents, and aunts and uncles. With their answers written down and filed in your notebook, you have a springboard from which to gather other information. If you are lucky enough to have grandparents and older relatives living, you have a gold mine at your fingertips. They generally love to talk, especially when you are interested enough to listen carefully and ask questions. Some of their stories may seem totally unrelated, but record, either in writing or on tape, as much as you can. You never know when you may need this information.

Say you decide to talk with your grandmother. You are armed with your charts, paper, pencil, and a list of questions. A logical place to begin is "Where were you born?" If your grandmother is like mine, she will answer quickly, but it took me five years of asking to find out *when*. Who were her parents? Who were her brothers and sisters? When did she and Grandaddy get married? Where? What was his full name? When and where was he born? Who were his parents? When did he die?

You can move in any of several directions next. You may decide to inquire about your aunts and uncles. Does she remember any birth dates of her children (your aunts and uncles)? Even a year filled in is better than nothing. Encourage her by letting her know that you appreciate any piece of information, even if it is incomplete. Whom did each one of the aunts and uncles marry? Does she remember when they married? Together, can you list your cousins? Probably she has their addresses so that you can write to them directly to ask for any missing information.

Once Grandmother has shared her own life with you, ask her what she remembers of her parents, grandparents, or great-grandparents. Who were her brothers and sisters? When and where was each of them born? Whom did they marry? Are they still living? Get their addresses. Where and when did her parents marry? When and where were her parents born? When and where did her parents die? Where are they buried?

Did she know her own grandparents? What were their names? When and where were they born? When and where did they marry? When and where did they die? Who were their children? Who were their brothers and sisters? Who were their parents? Where did they live? Where are they buried?

If Grandmother cannot remember exact dates, use a general reference point to help both of you. Did he die before World War I? Was she born before you were? Did he get married when the family was still living in Palestine? Any piece of information may help you pinpoint the date you are seeking. For example, she may tell you about the house burning down. When was that? Well, she was about eight, so it was about 1908. Yes, Grandpa was still living with them then. So you conclude that her grandfather died after 1908. Cousin Mahala may remember that Grandpa died just before her wedding, which was in 1915. So you begin to narrow the gaps. Their grandpa died between 1908 and 1915.

Lists of brothers and sisters are not really vital statistics, but they are vital pieces of information to have. The only information we could ever get out of my grandfather was a partial list of his twelve brothers and sisters and his father's name. This was mighty little to go on, especially after we lost the slip of paper containing these names. But we remembered his father's name and one sister. When I got into the search, I found several men by his father's name but only one with a daughter named Theodocia. It was the sister's name that led us to the right family in our search.

Once you have picked your grandmother's brain, there are other people who can help you fill in the gaps. You can contact aunts and uncles, great-aunts and great-uncles, your parents' cousins, and older friends of the family. Ask them about the vital statistics of their own part of the family and about your direct ancestors to whom they too are related. Write down whatever they tell you, even if it is sketchy.

Sometimes you may find differences of opinion on names or dates. Two aunts give different death dates for Grandpa. Two cousins give different names for cousin Sarah's husband. Write both in your notes. At a later time, when you find out which name or date is correct, then mark out the incorrect answer. But in the meantime, you don't know which to keep and which to discard. Keep them both.

So far, you have been gathering pieces for your puzzle by talking and listening to the people around you. When you cannot talk with them in person, the next best method is to write to them. To increase their cooperation, make their job easy. In a letter, explain your project and ask for their help. Enclose a self-addressed, stamped envelope and a page of typed or neatly printed questions with space left for their answers. They can simply fill in the blanks and return the page to you. Title the page with a heading such as "Questions from Susan Metcalf to Mrs. Wilmer Medders, 19 June 1975—CAMPBELL family." When the page is returned, you know to file it under Campbell in your notebook. From the answers, add to your charts. I always reassure these correspondents that I appreciate any information they can give, however small, because it's more than I have now. After all, not everyone is a walking memory bank. It is better that they leave some blanks than make up something to fill in!

If you are seeking information on two different families, such as Campbell and White, send a separate question page on each family name. Each one will fit nicely into the notebook. Filing systematically can be just as important as gathering the information.

Regardless of any other information you seek, try first to gather this basic information *for each generation* as you work back in time:

1. Names of parents and their brothers and sisters.
2. Names of their parents and grandparents.
3. Names of spouse(s) and children for each person.
4. Vital statistics (birth, marriage, death dates and places) for each person.

CONDUCTING AND TAPE RECORDING AN INTERVIEW

As the interviewer, make a list of questions in advance, and give your informant either the questions or an idea of what you want to cover before you begin. Of course, you are not limited to these questions. Ask any others that occur to you as the interview progresses. Make your questions short and to the point, and ask one question at a time. The following attempt to be "formal" ended up being wordy, redundant, and confusing:

"Now, Aunt Ellie, I'd like to get a little background as to your birth and childhood, your full name at birth, when and where you were born, your parents' names, and something about your brothers and sisters, as to their names and whether they were older or younger than you if you can't remember their birth dates, some of your early education and childhood experiences, especially as they relate to what it was like to grow up on a farm."

A much better attempt is to begin simply: "Okay, Aunt Ellie, let's begin at the beginning. When and where were you born?" She may give you all the rest of the information you might have asked for, without your having to ask. If she leaves something out, or if you get confused or lost, ask for clarification. You may have to ask other questions to help her with an answer or to keep her on track. It may be helpful to summarize periodically to make a graceful transition into a new subject, to stimulate any further memories, to return to the subject you want to pursue, or to be certain that you understand what she is really saying.

Word your questions so that they encourage more than *yes* or *no* answers. Try to elicit facts as well as feelings, reactions, and descriptions. Remember, the facts you seek are more than names and dates. Although you often must begin with these, you also

(SAMPLE INTERVIEW LETTER)

Emily Croom to Emily Blalock, 9 July 1973:

Dear Aunt Emily,

Here are a few more questions...please...

1. When grandpa Pitser Blalock married Emma Bishop, she had 2 daughters. What were their names?

She had three daughters – Lucy Nell (who was married and living in Memphis when they married), Egene and Alberta.

2. I found Emma and Sim Bishop in the 1880 census with a 3-month-old son named Robert. Did he die young or move away? I had never heard of him before.

Robert died before Emma married Pitser. I do not remember his age when he died but I did hear her speak of him and I know he died before he reached adulthood.

3. Do you have any idea what Emma's maiden name was?

No, if I ever knew I have forgotten.

4. I found a county court order of 1867 binding 6 black children to Jesse Blalock. Do you have an idea of why this was done? It didn't say they were orphans.

No, I do not know. I have never heard this story.

5. When did Emma Bishop Blalock die?

I do not know the exact date of her death. I know that she was living when Lowe died in 1940. It seems to me that she died in the early or middle forties, though. However, we were not notified at the time of her death and heard it sometime later.

FIG. 4: SAMPLE INTERVIEW LETTER

want to find out *how, why* or *why not*, and *with what results or effects*.

Experienced genealogists will agree that in order to be a good genealogist, one must also be a good historian. In order to make the most of your session, you must have done enough advance preparation to know what questions to ask. You should be sure that your questions relate to the topic or period under consideration. Your interviewee may mention an event, person or tradition that is new to you or that you neglected to include in your outline of questions. Be alert and learn to catch such "jewels" when they are tossed your way; they may be more important in the long run than your prepared questions. Feel free to divert the conversation away from your list to expand and develop these new topics.

How do you handle sensitive or controversial subjects? Very carefully. If they must be brought up because of their importance to the overall picture, hold these questions until you and your interviewee are comfortable talking and sharing with each other. The session is not a forum for expressing your own opinions or winning a convert to your view. All you need is your interviewee's statements, even if you disagree.

Be alert to the reaction of your interviewee to your bringing up this kind of subject. If he or she is willing to talk, you may get valuable information. If it seems to be an emotionally upsetting topic, be prepared to drop it for the time being. Every family has "closets" they prefer not to open for airing. We need to be sensitive to their wishes, even when our curiosity is aroused.

While your interviewee is speaking, be an attentive listener, but think ahead at the same time. Eye contact, enthusiasm, appropriate facial expressions, and natural reactions encourage and reassure your informant. If the interviewee seems to be getting tired, confused, or involved too deeply in a topic that you consider completely off the subject, you may be able to initiate a short break.

You may want to tape record your interview even though you are taking notes. Here are a few suggestions for having a successful taping session:

1. Use the best quality tape recorder you have available and a good quality tape. Usually a 60-minute tape (30 minutes per side) is sufficient, although to be safe, bring an extra tape along. A battery-operated tape recorder may not be able to pull a longer tape with good results. Take extra batteries or use an AC/DC adapter and cord.

2. Assure your informant that it will be an informal visit. Both of you need to relax and be comfortable. Tell him that you will gladly stop the tape at any time if he wants to say something "off the record" or if he gets tired. Create an atmosphere conducive to thinking and taping by turning off televisions or other noisy appliances and by sending pets and children elsewhere.

3. Place the microphone (or tape recorder if the microphone is built in) an equal distance between you and your interviewee so that both voices can be heard equally well. If the speaking voices differ much in natural volume, place the recorder closer to the softer voice. Place the tape recorder on a stationary object such as a table rather than in a lap to minimize noises made when someone shifts positions or rattles paper.

4. Test your equipment and voices before you begin, and listen to the sample to affirm that all is working and voices are being heard and understood. Label both sides of the tape before you begin.

5. Identify on tape each person involved in the session and the date and place of the interview. If more than two are present, it might be helpful to have each person introduce himself or herself, to put a voice with the name for easier identification in the future. Include yourself in these introductions.

6. You will get a better recording if each person who speaks remembers:
   a. to speak slowly and loudly enough to be clearly understood.
   b. that dropping one's voice (trailing off) at the ends of phrases will mean losing what is said. The longer the interview, the more the voices tend to drop in volume and clarity toward the end.
   c. that more than one person speaking at a time means a garbled, confused section of tape in which no one is understood. When it is possible, it is advantageous to limit the session to you and one interviewee.

7. It is helpful to spell aloud any proper names mentioned, especially those which may be unusual or misunderstood on tape. Beginning and final con-

sonants are easy to lose on a tape. For example, is the name "Card" or "Carg"? "Paul" or "Carl"? "Bud" or "Pug" or "Pup"? This problem is complicated by people who speak with regional or "foreign language" accents, as well as those who speak rapidly or trail off on the ends of words and phrases.

8. It is helpful to leave the tape visible in the tape recorder so that you can tell when the tape is running out. If you can, finish one topic before the side of the tape is completed, and begin the new side with a new topic.

9. Don't let the tape control the interview. Pauses for thinking or reflecting are often valuable to the conversation; you do not have to fill every moment of tape time with sound.

10. Remember that many people, especially the elderly, are nervous around tape recorders and do not like to hear their own voices played back. Do what you can to allay these fears and, at the same time, to make yourself and the tape recorder less important than the interviewee and what he or she is saying.

11. Be sure that you and the interviewee have the same understanding about how the tape is to be used. If necessary, write out a "contract" for both to sign that explains the purpose and intended uses of the tape.

When the interview is completed, you will want to thank your interviewee, perhaps take pictures to commemorate the occasion, and leave the way open for another session at a later date.

If videotaping equipment is available to you, you may want to record family gatherings and group interviews. Both videotapes and audiotapes become valuable for their content and for the memories.

CHAPTER FIVE

What's in a Name?

Names present special challenges to the genealogist. For example, your family name may be spelled several different ways in public documents. The census taker recorded what he heard, or thought he heard. The copier wrote down what he thought he read. A variety of spellings is often found for the same name and same family:

Metcalf-Metcalfe-Midcalf-Midkiff-Medcalf
Robinson-Robertson-Robberson-Robison
Allen-Alan-Allyn-Allan-Alline-Alin
Neale-Neil-Neill Neal-Neele

In *Family Names: How Our Surnames Came to America* (New York: Macmillan, 1982, p. 324), J.N. Hook reports 17 different spellings of Robertson and 21 variations of Sullivan in the 1790 census.

Surnames may change over the years. A French immigrant named Pierre de la Chapelle may find his name Americanized to Peter Chapel. The German immigrant Johann Peter Muth became Peter Mood. Zimmerman may be translated to Carpenter; the French Le Blanc may become White.

Such changes can reflect the way the family pronounced their name or the attempt of a clerk to approximate what he heard and make it manageable for the English-speaking community. In this way, an Irishman named Sean Maurice could become John Morris; a Welshman named ap Howell might become Powell; and the German Koster has been altered to Custer.

Surnames, of course, do become given names. There are many examples, such as Allen, Keith, Glenn, Clyde, Davis, Lloyd, Elliott, Dudley, and Newton. Combining surnames has given some nineteenth-century Southerners really interesting names: Green Bird, Bright Bird, Green Cash, Ransom Cash, Green Hill, Green Moss, Wiley Crook, and Valentine Cash.

Given names (Christian or first names) may be spelled in varieties of ways and Americanized just as surnames are. However, given names present the additional challenge of nicknames and abbreviations.

Female nicknames, by which the individuals were known to their contemporaries, are often found in place of "real" names in documents. Many good dictionaries can help you determine the given name from a nickname. Here are some common first names with their usual nicknames:

Mary	Mamie, Molly, Mollie, May, Maisie, Polly, Minnie, Moll
Margaret	Maggie, Peg, Peggy, Meg, Midge, Madge, Daisy, Maisie, Meta, Greta
Martha	Marty, Martie, Mattie, Patty, Patsy
Elizabeth	Beth, Eliza, Liz, Liza, Lizzie, Lisa, Lise, Elsie, Betty, Betsy, Bitsy, Bess, Bessie, Libby
Eleanor	Ella, Ellie, Nell, Nellie, Nelly, Nora
Sarah	Sallie, Sal, Sadie
Frances	Fran, Frankie, Fannie
Ann(e)	Annie, Nan, Nannie, Nina, Nancy
Katherine	Kathy, Kate, Katie, Kat, Katy, Kay, Kitty, Kit
Henry	Hank, Harry, Hal, Hen
Richard	Dick, Rick, Ricky, Rich, Richy
Robert	Rob, Bob, Robby, Bobby, Dobbin, Robin, Robbie
John	Johnny, Johnnie, Jack, Jackie, Jock
James	Jamie, Jim, Jimmy, Jem

Theodore/Theodorick	Ted, Tad, Teddy, Theo, The, Dode, Dory

Sometimes records give us nicknames of previous centuries which are less common today:

Sukie, Suchy	Susan
Tillie	Matilda, Mathilda
Effie, Effy	Euphemia
Tempy	Temperance
Millie	Amelia, Mildred, Millicent
Lettie	Letitia
Hettie	Esther, Henrietta, Hester
Ollie	Olive, Olivia
Winnie	Winnefred
Hallie	probably Henrietta or Harriet

Of course, nicknames were, and are, used as complete given names. *Lucy* is often a "real name" instead of a nickname for Lucretia, Lucia, Lucille, or Lucinda. Stella was both a given name and a nickname for Costella and Estelle, just as Larry is often a given name rather than a shortened form of Lawrence today.

Some nicknames can substitute for more than one given name:

Patty	Patricia, Patience, Martha, Matilda
Lina, Lena	Eveline, Emeline, Carolina, Angelina, Selina, Selena, Helena, Paulina, Magdalena, and others
Bell(e)	Arabella, Anabelle, Isabel, Rosabel
Nora	Honora, Honoria, Leonora, Eleanor
Dora	Theodora, Eudora, Dorothy
Ed(die)	Edgar, Edmund, Edward, Edwin, Edwina
Nell	Ellen, Helen, Eleanor
Frankie	Frances, Francis, Franklin, Francine
Delia	Cordelia, Adelia, Ledelia, Adele
Sam(my)	Samuel, Samson, Samantha
Jenny	Jane, Virginia, Janet, Jeannette (Jennet), Jennifer
Allie	Alice, Aline, Alene, Aletha
Cindy	Lucinda, Cynthia

In documents copied by hand, male names are often abbreviated. These are some common examples:

Daniel	Danl
Samuel	Saml
Jonathan	Jno
Richard	Rich^{d}
Thomas	Thos
James	Jas
Nathaniel	Nat^{l}
Christopher	X^{r}
Alexander	Alex^{r}
Joseph	Jos

Naming practices vary from place to place and century to century, but certain consistencies have existed for nearly four centuries in the area we now call the United States. For example, children were, and still are, often named for grandparents and other relatives. Sometimes a middle or given name is a clue to the mother's maiden name or to a grandparent's name. For example, Benjamin Allen Phillips (1801) was named for his grandfather Benjamin Allen. Emily Cooper (1882) was named for her father's deceased first wife, Emily Blalock Cooper. Emily Cooper Blalock (1874) was named for the same deceased lady, in this case, her father's sister. On the other hand, Pitser Miller Blalock (1848) was named for a neighbor, not thought to be a relative.

In *In Search of Your British and Irish Roots* (Baltimore: Genealogical Publishing Company, 1991 reprint, p. 47), genealogist Angus Baxter suggested a pattern to naming practices of the eighteenth and early nineteenth centuries, especially in England and Wales, which may give clues for studying families of the American colonies and the United States.

Eldest son—often named for the father's father.
Second son—for the mother's father.
Third son—for the father.
Fourth son—for the father's eldest brother.
Eldest daughter—for the mother's mother.
Second daughter—for the father's mother.
Third daughter—for the mother.
Fourth daughter—for the mother's eldest sister.

In the United States, this pattern may be considered a clue but certainly not a rule. Some families did name eldest sons for paternal grandfathers, but the naming of children for relatives generally followed no particular pattern or order. Families also named eldest sons for relatives on both sides of the family or for no one in particular. Each child in these examples was an eldest son. Hunter Orgain Metcalfe (1887) was given his maternal grandmother's maiden name, Orgain. Samuel Black Brelsford (1829) was named for his maternal grandfather, Samuel Black. Edward Philpot Blalock (1837) was named after his father's foster brother, Edward Philpot. Thomas Blalock King (1972) was given one name from each grandfather.

Of course, a daughter was, and still is, sometimes given a feminine form of her father's name: Josephine/Joseph, Georgianna/George, Pauline/Paul, Philippa/Philip, Willie/William, Jessie/Jesse, Charlotte/Charles, and even Drusilla/Drew. Almanzon Huston even named one of his daughters Almazona.

Every culture and era seems to have names whose origins are obscure. They may be nicknames, "made-up" names, combinations of other names, names of characters in literature, or place names. Parents may have simply liked the sound of a name or wanted to choose something different. When we genealogists find these names in records, sometimes they are a result of phonetic spelling. Some may be corruptions of other names or attempts to keep names in a family within a particular pattern: names in alphabetical order, or names beginning with the same initials. These are some of the numerous such names found in this country from 1750 to the present: Benoba, Bivy, Callie, Devra, Dicy, Dovie, Floice, Fena, Hattie, Jincey, Kitsey, Lovie, Luvenia, Laney, Lottie, Levicy, Mittie, Nicey, Ora, Olan, Olean, Ottie, Ozora, Parilee, Parizade, Perlissa, Peariby (Pheribah, Pheriby, Fereby), Rebia, and Sinah.

In the United States, each era seems to have had its favorite names, in addition to the standard ones which have been used for centuries. The "period" names may be related to the attitudes, events, or personalities of the generation, even in subtle ways; or they may be simply "fads" which give way to new patterns after several decades.

Girls, and sometimes boys, of the latter seventeenth century and the eighteenth century, especially among New England Puritans, were named for virtues: Patience, Piety, Prudence, Amity, Obedience, Rejoice, Reason, Temperance, Truth, Grace, Charity, Civility, Mercy, Faith, Honour, Hope or Hopeful, Constant or Constance, and Pleasant. Another group of names perhaps suggested experiences of the parents: Desire, Sorrow, Mourning, Comfort, Anguish, and Seaborn. Some Southern men had the given names of Merit and Sterling, which could come from surnames as well as from valued traits.

In the late seventeenth century, Germans poured into Pennsylvania, bringing with them their custom of giving children two names. Some families even kept the first name the same for all the sons, for example, and varied only the middle name: Johann Peter, Johann Friedrich, Johann Sebastian, and Johann Georg. As these families and their descendants moved throughout the colonies, other ethnic groups picked up the double-naming custom. By the mid-nineteenth century, the practice was widespread. As we have seen, the idea allowed parents to name children after grandparents and to perpetuate a surname from previous generations at the same time. Patty *Field* Allen, Hiram *Hawkins* Brelsford, Elliott *Glen* Coleman, George *Rogers* Clark, and many others carried surnames as their middle names and give genealogists at least a clue to another set of roots.

Especially between 1650 and 1860, many children received Biblical names, some of which, of course, are "standard" names which have been favorites for centuries. Common female names included Sarah, Elizabeth, Rebecca, Susanna, Rachel, Martha, Mary, Priscilla, Ruth, Hannah (Anna, Anne), and Judith. Less well-known Biblical names were also used: Jerusha, Keturah, Dorcas, Ascenath, Jemina, Zilpah, Phebe (Phoebe), and Orpah. Favorite male names from the Old Testament included Isaac, Jacob, Joseph, Benjamin, Levi, Jesse, David, Samuel, Daniel, Joshua, Moses, Elijah, Seth, Jeremiah, and Ezekiel. New Testament names, of course, included Matthew, Mark, Luke, John, Simon, Peter, James, Thomas, and Rufus.

United States children were, and are, also named in honor of famous Americans or prominent local personalities. In the early years of the Republic, some families showed their patriotic feelings by naming daughters or sons Liberty, Justice, or America. Other families, caught up in the westward movement, named daughters for their new or former states: Virginia, Carolina, Tennessee, Missouri, Louisiana, and Georgia.

These given names from the eighteenth and nineteenth centuries were not titles but actual first names: Major Croom, Admiral Croom, Squire Blalock, Pharaoh Lee, Doctor Godwin, Lieutenant Campbell, and Patsy Empress Jones.

From the mid-eighteenth century to about the mid-nineteenth century, Europe, and therefore the United States, experienced a revival of classical architecture, language, and cultural influences, which seems to have carried over into naming practices. Of course, Latin and Greek had for centuries been part of the "classical" school curriculum. These are some of the Latin and Greek names and derivatives used during that classical revival period. Some are still used today and are considered quite usual. Others were used for boys and girls alike: Aurelius, Artemis, Artemesia, Caesar, Cassius, Cassia, Claudia, Clementine, Chloe, Fortunatus, Florian, Fabius, Fabian, Fabia, Guglielmo, Guglielmus, Horatio, Honoria, Hortense, Julius, Junius, Justin, Justina, Latinus, Lydia, Lucian, Lucius, Lucia, Marcellus, Marcus, Nonna, Ophelia, Octavius, Octavia, Pericles, Pompey, Primus, Parmenius, Phyllis, Philena, Portia, Penelope, Parmelia, Philadelphia, Quentin, Rhoda, Sylvanus, Sylvia, Stephanie, Sophia, Sibyl, Sophronica, Theophilus, Theodocia, Tessa, Urban(us), Valentine, Virginious, Virgil, Xene, Zeta, Zenobia, Zephyr.

Many nineteenth- and early-twentieth-century daughters, especially in the South, received the names of flowers and gems: Violet, Pansy, Rose, Daisy, Lily, Ruby, Jewel, Pearl, and Opal. Interesting combinations have come from these names: Lillie White, Rosey Brown, and Pansy Violet Flower.

In the late nineteenth and early twentieth centuries, more children than in recent or later generations seemed to be named Edna, Elvira, Ethel, Gladys, Gertrude, Gussie, Lillian, Lula, Malvina, Maude, Mildred, Nora, Thelma, Verna, Albert, Alvin, Claude, Elmer, Ernest, Grover, Herbert, Marvin, Maurice, Maynard, and Oscar. Likewise, the mid-twentieth century had a set of popular names that were not so common in earlier or later years: Barbara, Carol, Carolyn, Diane, Gay(e), Janet, Jill, Joan, Joyce, Karen, Linda, Marilyn, Sharon, Shirley, Carl, Dean, Dennis, Jerry, Kenneth, Larry, Ron(ny), and Terry.

Finding popularity from the 1970s forward have been names which have no ethnic, historical, or genealogical relationship to the family using them. Some are derived from surnames, and some are used for both boys and girls: Allison, Ashley, Barrett, Brian, Brittany, Cody, Dara, Darin, Derek, Eric, Erin, Hailey, Heather, Jason, Jennifer, Jordan, Justin, Kendall, Kendra, Kevin, Kimberley, Kristen, Kyle, Lauren, Lindsey, Megan, Meredith, Michelle, Nicole, Nicholas, Paige, Ryan, Scott, Shawn/Sean, Stacy, Taylor, Tiffany, Travis, Trevor, Trey, Tyler, and Whitney. In addition, the latter twentieth century has seen a renaissance of such Biblical names as Adam, Benjamin, Daniel, Jeremy, Matthew, Michael, and Zachary.

Through all these eras, certain "standard" names have continued in popularity: Anne, Catherine, David, Elizabeth, Emily, George, James, John, Margaret, Mary, Richard, Robert, Sarah, Susan, Thomas, and William.

Names can present special problems to the genealogist when several people of the same name appear in the same location at the same time. Their relationship, if any exists, cannot be assumed. Eighteenth-century records bearing the name Daniel Coleman, James Shaw or William Black can baffle the researcher quickly. It is difficult to separate these men to determine just how many Daniels, Jameses, or Williams there were, and which records belonged to which man. The genealogist must be careful. We cannot assume the man is automatically our ancestor because the name is the same.

Estate names or other descriptive appellations sometimes help to identify men in the records. Peter Bland "of Jordan's Point" would distinguish this Peter from others. One James Turley drew an eye after his name to separate himself from other James Turleys in the area. He is referred to now, as perhaps he was then, as James One Eye. Perhaps this designation tells us something about his physical appearance.

Sometimes men added "Jr." or "Sr." after their names to distinguish themselves from their father or son or other relative of the same name. For example, three men named Isaac Croom lived in Madison County, Tennessee, during the mid-nineteenth century. The senior Isaac was the uncle of the other two. Of these nephews, one carried his middle initial, *N.*, and the other occasionally added "Jr." to his name. Isaac, Jr., was separating himself from his uncle Isaac rather than his father, who was Charles.

Discrepancies and problems related to names and relationships cannot always be solved. However, you can form educated guesses. Use primary (firsthand) sources as often as possible and evaluate them thoroughly. Gather as much information as possible. Sort it and use only the most reliable. Support your guesses with facts.

CHAPTER SIX

Hand-Me-Downs: Family Traditions

Oral tradition is the stories which have been passed down from generation to generation by word of mouth. This tradition is stronger in some families than in others, but genealogists can use whatever they find. Family stories sometimes grow with the age and imagination of the teller, but there is often much truth in them. Some of the details may get lost or altered, but the basic truths remain.

Many of these traditions tell of the origin of the family: Four brothers came to Texas from Prussia to escape military service; three McFadden brothers came from Ireland. The stories of origin often blur with age: "Mama used to tell me about a couple who eloped and came from Scotland." Somewhere, sometime, this couple may be identified. In the meantime, preserve the story. One important task of the family historian is to preserve this oral tradition by recording it on tape or on paper.

Traditions also give vital statistics: Grandpa was one of six boys and had six sisters—twelve children altogether. That was the oral tradition, and yet no one could name all twelve kids. By interviewing descendants, we finally listed ten names which we could prove with census and Bible records. That left two girls' names missing. After finding a distant cousin with a trunk of old letters, the family found a reference to "sister Luta sleeping in the crib" and another mention of "little Willie" recovering from the measles. Then cousin Bea remembered that she heard about a little girl named Willie. Using the dates of the letters and the census records, we approximated the dates of the lives of these two little girls who died in early childhood. The oral tradition had proved true.

In some cases, these family traditions can be documented and proved correct. The missing details can sometimes be returned to the story through newspapers, letters, public records and interviews. They can become history as the facts are reestablished. However, much tradition must be accepted as just that when the records or people who know are not available. For example, the father of those twelve kids was one of fourteen children, eleven of whom have names in the records. Tradition says that three of the children were boys who died in infancy. Their names, if they were named, have not appeared in any records. The tradition is considered correct because several branches of the family have handed down the same story, but it probably cannot be proved.

Many families pass on stories of Civil War experiences: the slave who saved the family or the family home, the wife who ran the farm, the day church services were interrupted by the approach of the enemy, or the enemy who befriended the family. My Civil War ancestor Susan lived in Columbia, South Carolina, when General Sherman's army marched through and burned the city. Susan was among many who fled from their burning homes. She carried the baby and instructed her other two children, a toddler and a preschooler, to hold tight to her skirt. In her other arm, she hoped to carry a little bag of family silver, handmade by her father-in-law and his father who had been fine silversmiths. As her little troop struggled on foot toward the "insane asylum" to find refuge for the night, they were approached by a Yankee soldier, who asked if he could help her. She knew she had to give him either the baby or the silver because she could not manage both. She regretfully handed him the bag of silver and resigned herself to the loss of a valuable and meaningful family collection. However, some years later, miraculously, the enemy soldier or his family returned to her the bag of silver! Throughout the years of great sectional bitterness which followed the war, Susan continually reminded her family that there was at least *one* honest Yankee in the world.

In almost every family there is some disaster which the family survived and still relates: the Drought, the Storm, the Flood, the Epidemic, or the Fire. One such story is preserved in several unrelated families: the fire in which everything was lost except the piano! The move westward provided many experiences which were preserved in oral tradition: selling the family heirlooms because they could not be moved, trying to carry the piano in the wagon, Indian raids, or the loss of loved ones along the way. As told in one family, moving from South Carolina to Texas was a lengthy, tiring process for Susan and her children, as they came to meet Papa. On the last leg of the journey, they traveled by stagecoach. At the last stop before their destination, the driver got quite drunk at the local tavern and apparently forgot about his passengers. Leaving him in the tavern, Susan herself (or was it her little son?) held the reins and let the horses take the coach on to their new hometown. The coach pulled up before the only building with a light burning—the tavern—but Susan was spared having to venture inside. A man stepped up, introduced himself as Temple Houston (son of General Sam Houston), and said his family was expecting them but had become worried because the stage was so late arriving.

Black families have unique traditions which sometimes include slave biographies: Great-grandfather was a field hand and his wife was a house servant; they lived in Louisiana near Shreveport; he ran away once, was found the next day, and was whipped. On occasion, public records, such as newspapers, the census, and deeds, bear out the details of such traditions. This kind of story, though a sensitive issue in a number of families, can prove very important in establishing the family's ancestry another generation or two back in time. One would hope that the older generation, who may prefer to forget such stories, would nevertheless pass them down to younger family members.

In almost every family, somebody claims close kinship with somebody famous. "Great-grandmother was a first cousin of Robert E. Lee." "We are descendants of the Presidents Harrison." "Great-grandmother was a close relative of Sam Houston." In truth, Great-grandmother was born a North Carolina *Lea*, in no way related to the Virginia *Lees*. The fact that Great-grandpa's name was Harrison and he had relatives who lived near Washington, DC, when one of the Harrisons was President, certainly does not even suggest any kinship. Very often these tales are simply wishful thinking. Very seldom are they even useful.

In the case of the "close relative of Sam Houston," the tradition has come down through several branches of that family and persists in spite of attempts by the family's genealogist to disprove it. After hearing Aunt Sally's claim of kinship with Sam Houston, Charlotte intensified her search in that particular part of her family. She discovered that Grandma Cummings's maiden name was Huston, sometimes spelled Houston, but her father was Almanzon, not Sam. As she presented this at the next family reunion, she was joined by Aunt Sally, who did not contradict her findings, but added, as if to be helpful, that they were descendants of one of Sam Houston's sisters. However absurd that sounded to Charlotte, Aunt Sally was confident of its accuracy.

Doing what genealogists are usually cautioned not to do, because it is usually a waste of time, Charlotte found a biography and a genealogy of Sam Houston's family. In this case, she was not trying to work forward from his family to hers; she was simply comparing two families of the same generation. She found that Sam Houston had three sisters, all born between 1797 and 1800 in Tennessee. The last one, named Eliza Ann, married a Moore. Her own Elizabeth, born in 1805 in Pennsylvania, married a Huston but was born a Newton. Aunt Sally's story was simply not true.

At the next family reunion, Charlotte was armed with her facts in case the subject arose. However, this time Aunt Sally "remembered" that their Almanzon Huston was one of Sam Houston's brothers or father's brothers, and that was the gospel truth. Charlotte was ready: Sam Houston had no brother named Almanzon. Although the two men were born only six years apart, Sam was born in Tennessee and Almanzon, in New York. Sam's father had only one brother, whose name was John, not Almanzon. Even Sam's grandfather's four brothers are not possible links.

Aunt Sally remains undaunted in her belief of close kinship with the state's popular hero, and she is not alone. Other relatives of her generation agree with her, whatever her story is at the moment, and several old newspaper clippings carry the tradition that Sam and Almanzon were "cousins." In her search, Charlotte found that the two men did know each other. Almanzon had been Sam's Quartermaster General in the Texas War for Independence. Perhaps they called each other "cousin" because of having the same last name. Gradually the younger generation is ignoring Aunt Sally's repetition of her tradition each summer at the reunion and concentrating on learning more about their own Huston ancestor.

Another interpretation of the word *tradition* is a set of customs which are repeated year after year, sometimes into second and third generations. These traditions, too, are part of the family history and are fun to collect. In one family, each child receives a small gift when one has a birthday. In some families the birthday person has the honor of choosing the menu for the evening meal, or where the family will go to dine out. One family hands down an antique quilt to the Sarah in the next generation. It has the embroidered signatures of related Sarahs dating back some two hundred years.

Holidays, especially, are full of traditions. One of my grandfathers had what his family considered a very peculiar custom of having salt mackerel each year for Christmas breakfast. One of my grandmothers always served boiled custard as a holiday treat. The other grandmother always wanted charlotte russe for Christmas dessert.

Holidays, of course, are often a time for family reunions and gatherings where these traditions are shared and continued. For the genealogist, these occasions are golden opportunities to ask questions, share and gather information, write down or tape stories, take photographs, get autographs, and show what progress has been made on the family history.

CHAPTER SEVEN

Life History: Beginning to End

As you gather and put in place the middle of your puzzle, what information do you want? Vital statistics, yes, but there is much more to family history than lists of names and dates. For example, if you have a pet, it surely has a name. What did Dad call his dog when he was a boy? What did Great-grandma call her cow? What did Great-grandad call his mule?

Each answer may suggest new questions. If you are really listening, you begin to wonder, "Well, why did he do that?" or "How did they do that?" or "What did it look like?" Ask.

There are hundreds of questions you can ask about each generation. The farther back you go, the fewer answers you receive. But a few answers will give you some picture. The questions suggested here will stretch over many visits and letters. Each person may answer several, but no one could be expected to answer them all. Some of the questions will produce unexpected responses: "Heavens, child! How old do you think I am!" or "Good grief, yes!" or "For crying out loud! Do you think we lived like the Queen of England?" Okay, we live and learn. That is why we ask questions.

You can start with yourself and make notes on your own history. Ask your parents about their childhoods, schooling, teen years, and early married life. Ask grandparents and anyone else who can contribute to the middle of the puzzle. Notes on these questions will be easier to keep in their proper time periods if you indicate at the top the time period you are dealing with: notes from Grandma Metcalfe about her childhood; notes from Grandma Metcalfe about her mother's childhood; notes from Great-aunt Wilmer about Grandaddy's early life, 1895-1915; notes from Mahala Yancy on the 1930s.

It is helpful to keep in mind that these questions serve basically two purposes: to extend the information on your charts and to gather life history. Information which contributes to these goals is desirable. Some pieces of information are more important than others. Some are more interesting. Historians seek any pertinent information, but the family historian will want to be careful not to intrude into someone's private territory and not to pull out of the closet skeletons which might cause harm or embarrassment. Family histories must be truthful, but families may prefer to leave some chapters closed where it is unnecessary to mention the information at all. We must honor their wishes.

There are incidents which may have caused embarrassment at one time but which we can laugh about now. These stories add spice to the history. One example is the story of a little girl's mischief. Maggie was five at a time when it was strictly improper for a lady, whether five or fifty, to speak of the body and its parts. Maggie learned a limerick from her older brother and made the mistake of sharing it with her mother. Mama, being concerned about propriety and horrified at Maggie's indecency, washed the little girl's mouth out with soap. The limerick was

There was a young lady named Mable,
Who loved to dance on the table,
But she blushed very red
When the gentleman said,
"Oh, look at the legs on the table."

Another little girl in the same family was about seven when the bishop ate Sunday dinner with them. Imagine the disgrace she suffered when, at a lull in the conversation, she addressed the guest, "You wanta hear me drink like a horse?"

The following questions are suggestions for researching a person's life history.

CHILDHOOD

1. Gather letters or stories about yourself when you were an infant and a child: firsts, growth, funny inci-

dents, curiosity, likes and dislikes, vocabulary, habits, diseases, accidents.

2. Brothers and sisters: names, your relationship with them. What stands out about them in your memory of childhood?

3. What is your earliest memory of your house, your family, your town, events in the news?

4. Who were your playmates, pets? What games, toys, celebrations, and playmates were your favorites? How important were television, movies, radio, bicycles in your childhood?

5. Where was your house? If in a city, what address? What county? What state? Is the house still standing? What did it look like? How many rooms? Which ones? Describe the house and furnishings: one- or two-story? frame? brick? painted? porch? garage? yard? outbuildings? fireplaces? kind of floor, wall coverings?

6. How easily or often did you get into mischief? Why? What punishments did you incur? Were your parents strict? What rules did you have to follow?

7. What are your most vivid memories of childhood?

8. What relatives do you remember and what stands out in your mind about them? What trips did you take to visit relatives?

9. What chores were yours to do? Did you get an allowance? How did you get your spending money? What did you do with it? What was the financial condition of the family?

10. How did you celebrate birthdays, Christmas, Thanksgiving, July 4, or other holidays?

11. What were family customs for weekends? Sundays? summer days?

12. What unusual events do you recall (fires, storms, moving, etc.)?

13. How far was school from your house? How did you get to school? During what hours were you in school? When did school start in the fall and let out in the summer? What subjects did you like best? least? Were you able to attend school regularly? What do you remember about your teachers? Does any one teacher stand out in your mind as having a large influence on you? How good were your grades? Did you feel pressure to make good grades? How did you spend recess? What memories stand out in your mind about elementary school? junior high school?

14. What did you do in the summer or when you were not in school? trips? sports? scouting? camping? working?

15. Did you study music, art, dancing? What hobbies did you pursue?

16. What were your childhood favorites: foods, clothes, sport, story, movie, hero, people?

17. What part did church and religious activities play in your childhood, both at home and away from home?

18. What were your dreams or plans for the future? Which have become reality?

19. What experience did you have with death as a child? What funeral or burial customs were followed by the family or area?

20. What neighborhood gatherings, social or working, do you recall?

TEEN YEARS

1. What high school did you attend? Where? How long? Did you graduate? Did you go to college? Where? How did you choose your college? How did you finance your education? In high school (or college), what were your favorite or least favorite subjects? Is there someone from these years who had great influence on you? How large was the school? What clubs or sports did you participate in? Did you enter competitions or contests? (Explain.) What do you recall about teachers? classmates? What were some of the school rules? dress code? How did you get to school? How far was it from home? What did you do for lunch? What courses helped you the most?

2. What kinds of parties did you attend? Where did you go on dates? When did you start dating? What rules governed dating at your house? What did you enjoy most for recreation?

3. What clothes were in style when you were in high school?

4. What were your plans or desires at that time of your life? Have you done those things?

5. What chores were your responsibility at home? (Describe.)

6. Did you have pets? What kind? names?

7. What did you read?

8. What unusual or special events do you recall?

9. Where did you live? Was it the same house you lived in as a child? If not, please describe it.

10. Did you enjoy music? dancing? art? other hobbies? Did any of the family sing or play musical instruments? Did you make any of your own clothes? Were you in the school band?

11. Did you have a job? Doing what? How much

money did you earn? How did you use your earnings?

12. What did you do in the summer?

13. What rules governed your household? Were you allowed to play cards? date without a chaperone? stay out past dark? go to movies? dance? eat with the adults? wear slacks to school? Were you required to go to church on Wednesday nights as well as Sunday? stand when adults entered the room? What was considered "proper" Sunday or Sabbath conduct? What were considered "proper" manners? "proper" dress?

14. Did you attend religious services? Where? What other religious activities did you participate in?

15. Did you participate in any service projects? (Explain.)

16. What neighborhood gatherings do you recall?

17. What experience did you have with death as a teenager? What funeral or burial customs do you recall?

ADULTHOOD

1. When and where did you get married? Describe the wedding, clothes, attendants, parties, gifts, etc.

2. What can you tell me about your courtship and dating? How did you meet your husband (or wife)?

3. What jobs have you held? What jobs has your husband (wife) held? How have wages changed since you first worked?

4. What trips have you taken? Which have you enjoyed most?

5. What religious, civic, club, political, or service activities have you participated in?

6. What is your political affiliation?

7. What is your religious affiliation?

8. Do you enjoy participating in music, art, gardening, handicrafts, needlework (knitting, crochet, tatting, etc.), sewing, carpentry, etc.? Which members of the family do (did) which of these activities?

9. How does the family celebrate holidays such as Thanksgiving, July 4, Christmas or other religious holidays? What other traditions have you established in your family? What other holidays do you celebrate? How?

10. What kinds of cars have you had? When did you get your first car? How much have the cars cost?

11. What are your favorite recipes?

12. What do you consider your special talents or abilities? What do you do best?

13. What gives you the most pleasure?

14. What are your favorite family stories?

15. When and where were your children born? What stands out in your mind about each one as a small child? as a teenager?

16. Where have you lived? Tell me about each house.

17. Do you have grandchildren? Who?

18. What rules did you set for your children?

19. Do you enjoy entertaining? friends? relatives? business associates? What kind of entertaining do you do?

CHAPTER EIGHT

History as the Family Lived It

In filling in the middle of a family puzzle, the family historian seeks to fit the family into the history of the city, county, state, and nation. The general political, economic, and social history of these areas can be found in published books and newspapers, but only the family can share their own reactions to the public events. For whom did *they* vote? What prices did *they* pay? What jobs did *they* hold? When did *they* get electricity? a telephone? a car? a radio? a television? air-conditioning?

Many of the questions in this section deal with events discussed in history textbooks. Yet many people living during the period were unaware of or unaffected by these events, or did not consider them important. To keep history in perspective, we must balance textbook history with what ordinary people thought and experienced.

The following questions are divided roughly into decades. Some of the public events, well-known people, and customs are included in the appropriate time periods. The questions are aimed at finding out about the family in each period. Use your imagination and add other questions as you think of them. A sample interview sheet is shown in Figure 5.

1940s

1. Did you or members of the family participate in World War II? If so, who? In what capacity? Where? What rank(s) did you (they) hold? In which branch of service? Did you (they) fight? In more than one place? List. What stories can you share about these experiences? Did the family lose members in the war?

2. What did you think of President Franklin Roosevelt at the time? Did you support him at election time, especially the third and fourth times? How did you feel about his third and fourth elections? Have you changed your opinion since then? How effective was he as President in the 1940s?

3. What did you think of President Truman?

4. What did you think of Churchill, Stalin, Hitler, Eisenhower, Patton, MacArthur, or other political or military leaders?

5. How did the war affect your own plans or life? Did you have to leave school or change your way of life very much?

6. Who in your family had jobs in war industry? In what job did you (they) work? Where? How many hours a day or days a week did you (they) work? How did you get to work? Was it easy to find a job or change jobs?

7. How did you feel about rationing? Did you know people who cheated or otherwise did not cooperate? What items were the hardest to get? What items were not so scarce? Did you raise, can, or preserve any of your own food? What sacrifices did you make? What items did you miss the most?

8. How much was rent? How much was gasoline? How much were food prices? wages? How difficult was it to find housing?

9. Did you travel? for business or pleasure? How did you travel? Was it difficult to get tickets or space on public transportation? Did you have a car? Did you have difficulty getting gasoline, tires, or parts?

10. What part did radio, movies, or sports play in your life during the 1940s? Who were your favorite personalities and what were your favorite programs?

11. What pleasant or funny family stories can you share from the 1940s?

12. What did you think at the time when you heard about the dropping of the atomic bomb? How necessary was it? How necessary was the second bomb? Have you changed your opinion since then?

13. Do you have and can you share any letters or diaries from the period?

14. How did you stay cool in summer without air-conditioning? Do you have air-conditioning now? When did you get it?

DEPRESSION 1930's Interviewer *Emily Croom* Date *May 1970*

Name *Mrs. H. O. Metcalfe*

Age group during most of the 1930's (circle one) Child (Adult) Teenager

Family Size (family with which you were living in the 30's) *4*

Residence in the 1930's *Marfa, Texas* urban rural (small town)

Educational level in the 30's (circle the appropriate) high school student/(graduate)
other *husband - college graduate* college student/graduate

If you were a student during the 30's, how did the depression affect your education?
Were you able to continue? *** How did you finance your education (scholarships, jobs, parents, etc.)? Did you or your friends drop out temporarily? *No* permanently?
**daughter in college did continue - financed her education with scholarships, summer & school-year jobs, & help from parents.*

For each job you held, what were the wages and hours? Please list chronologically.

Job	Location	Days/week	Hours/day	Wages or Salary
1. *housewife*	*Marfa*			
2. *husband lawyer*	*"*	*as necessary - (self-employed)*		*varied*
3.				
4.				
5.				

He always said people fight more & get into disputes more in bad times than in good so lawyers did okay - were kept busy.

What jobs did other members of your family hold?
husband - lawyer & U.S. Commissioner

note: Many hobos came by & we fed them too. Everybody in town did.

Were you self-supporting? *the family was* Did you help support your family? ____
Did you have trouble finding a job when it was necessary to change? ____
How were you able to find another?

What did you do for recreation or entertainment?
little dinner parties, bridge parties, young people had ice cream parties & tennis & baseball & basketball.
also attended reviews, polo games, etc at the army post, frequently went down to "meet the train," followed the fire truck.
Mr. Raetzsch owned Palace movie theater & we went to movies some - about 10-15¢ admission. Didn't get good radio reception except out on road to stock yard - so we went there.

Did your family raise, (make), can, preserve any of its own food? *yes* If so, what?
bread, desserts Canned peaches & other fruit. Made preserves.

Which food items were most difficult to obtain? easiest to obtain?
Could get what we were accustomed to having before.

Which commodities (clothes, appliances, tools, toys, etc.) were most difficult to obtain? easiest to obtain? What luxury items did you have to sacrifice?
appliances - scarce did without luxuries anyway
money - scarce [note: *daughter says she was excellent manager*]

Was your family a "do-it-yourself" group to save money? *Yes* What did you make?
Sewing most of the clothes for the 2 girls & myself.

Did you or your family own a car? *yes* More than one? *no* What make? *c1925 Chevy*
Do you remember the price of gasoline, or of the car? *No but 5¢/gallon on the army post in town (about 15¢-20¢/gallon)*

Were you able to buy on credit? *yes - nearly everything - groceries, cleaning, gasoline, drug store. Paid on first of each month.*

Did you travel? *yes - summer* By what means? *car mostly*
Were the trips mostly for business or pleasure? (Comments are welcome.)
to visit relatives in San Antonio.

How have your experiences during the depression influenced your attitudes of the present? *Made us appreciate the value of money more.*

FIG. 5: INTERVIEW—DEPRESSION 1930s

15. What were you doing when you heard about the Pearl Harbor attack? What was your reaction? Do you think we would have entered the war without the Pearl Harbor attack? What was the effect of the news on your area?

16. What were you doing when you heard about Roosevelt's death? What was your reaction?

1930s

1. To what extent did the Depression change your habits, way of life, schooling, plans? Did you "feel" the Depression? Was there a difference in the way the Depression affected people living in cities and people living in the country or small towns?

2. Which family members had jobs? Doing what? What was your pay? Were you paid in cash, goods, or scrip? How much was rent? Was it difficult to find housing? to find jobs?

3. At the time, what did you think of Presidents Hoover and Roosevelt? Have you changed your opinions since then? For whom did you vote in 1928 (Hoover or Smith), 1932 (Hoover or Roosevelt), 1936 (Roosevelt or Landon)? Why?

4. Did any family member work for one of the New Deal agencies, such as the CCC (Civilian Conservation Corps), the WPA (Works Progress Administration), or the PWA (Public Works Administration)? If so, who? Which agency? Doing what? How long? Where?

5. Did the family raise or hunt, can, or preserve any of its own food? If so, what? What food items did you find scarce or plentiful? Did you live on a farm, in a small town, or in a city? Did you notice any difference in the availability of food in rural and urban areas?

6. What part did radio, movies, or sports play in your life? Who were your favorite stars? When did you see your first movie in color? When did you see your first sound film? What was your reaction to these new developments? How much were movie tickets?

7. What sacrifices did you make? Why?

8. Did you have a car? If so, what make or model? How much did it cost? How much did gasoline cost? Did you limit your driving? Did you have to give up your car during the Depression? If you did not have a car, what kind of transportation did you rely on?

9. Did you have any money in a bank before or during the Depression? If so, did you lose any of it? If not, why not and where did you keep any cash you had? Did you lose any stock in the stock market crash?

10. Did the family sew or do its own carpentry, building, etc.?

11. How have your experiences during the Depression affected your attitudes of the present?

12. What games, toys, pets, playmates, etc., did the children have?

13. To what extent were religious, school, and family gatherings part of your life? What religious and school activities were you involved in?

14. Do you have and can you share any letters or diaries from the period?

15. What recollections and stories can you share about your experiences?

16. Did you hear Orson Welles's *The War of the Worlds* on radio on 30 October 1938? What did you think of it at the time? Did you fall for it? Why or why not?

17. Did the family move during this decade? Why? How frequently? Where? What conveniences did you have or lack?

1920s

1. To what extent were you aware of the "Roaring" Twenties at the time? How aware were you of Al Capone and gangster activities? How aware were you of Prohibition? Did it change your own habits? Did you favor it at the time? To what extent do you feel it worked or did not work? Did you obey it? Why or why not?

2. What electrical appliances or conveniences did you acquire for the first time during the decade? What was the first electrical appliance you bought? Did you have a washing machine? indoor plumbing? hot and cold water? What kind of cook stove did you have? What kind of heating? Did you have a car? If so, what make and model? What color? Do you remember its price or the cost of gasoline? How did you buy groceries? Were groceries delivered to the house? Did you shop at different stores for different food items? To what extent did you feel yourself part of the general "prosperity" of the decade?

3. What games, toys, pets, and playmates did the children of the family have?

4. Where did the family live? City or farm? What city, county, state? Did you move during the decade? How frequently? Why?

5. What part did radio, movies, or sports play in the life of the family? Who were your favorite stars? When did you get your first radio? What was your reaction

the first time you heard a radio? Was there ever any family restriction on movie-going? Where were movies shown? How much was admission?

6. What did the older family members feel about the fashions and youth of the "new age"? Were they alarmed or did they adjust to the changes pretty well? What do you feel were the greatest changes of the decade? What invention or development do you feel caused the greatest change?

7. What kind of house(s) did the family have? Describe it (them). Outbuildings? Electricity? Furniture? How much was rent?

8. What part did religious, school, and family gatherings play in your life? What religious and school activities were you involved in?

9. To what extent were you aware of political scandals of the decade? Whom did you support for President in 1920 (Harding or Cox), 1924 (Coolidge or Davis), and 1928 (Smith or Hoover)?

10. How did the family celebrate holidays, weddings, birthdays?

11. What did the family do for recreation?

12. Do you have and can you share any letters or diaries from the period?

13. What provisions were made for the older family members?

14. Did you find it difficult to acquire new cars? Was it easier to get used cars? How available were they?

WORLD WAR I

1. Did any family member fight in the war? If so, who, where, what rank(s), how long?

2. To what extent were you aware of Wilson's efforts to get the United States into the League of Nations? What was your personal opinion of these efforts? Did you favor League membership?

3. To what extent were you aware of anti-German feelings and activities in the United States during the war? Did any take place where you lived? Were you affected by any of these?

4. How did the family participate in celebrations at the close of the war?

5. Did the family grow a "Liberty garden"? Did you observe "wheatless" and "meatless" days? What did you substitute for meat, wheat, and sugar? Did you have trouble getting these foods? Were any other foods scarce? Did you buy "Liberty bonds"?

6. To what extent did religious or school activities influence your attitudes toward the war or your participation?

7. Did your family or any friends receive any special government allowances which some state governments awarded to families of servicemen overseas?

8. Were you aware of any exemptions to the draft policies? Were you aware of any physically handicapped men being drafted?

9. The Spanish flu epidemic of 1918 hit most of the United States and Europe. Estimates have said that it took twice as many lives as the war did. Was your family affected by this flu epidemic? Were there any family deaths from it? (Explain.)

1900-1940s

1. Where did the family live? How did they earn a living? Did any women of the family work outside the home? In what job? Did the family move during the period? How frequently? Where?

2. If you lived on a farm, what crops and animals did you raise? Which ones were raised for sale? Garden? Orchard?

3. Can you describe your house? When did the family get indoor plumbing for the first time? running water? electricity? Did each house have these conveniences? What kind of stove, heating, and lighting did you have? Outbuildings?

4. When did you get your first car? What kind? New or used?

5. Were the children in school? What do you remember of school subjects, rules, activities, hours, sports, clothes, holidays, homework, pep squads, etc.?

6. What games, toys, pets, and playmates did the children have?

7. What part did religious, school, or family gatherings play in your life? What religious and school activities did you participate in?

8. If you lived in a town or city, did you have such improvements as paved streets, street lights, sidewalks, parks? Describe. When did your town add each one? What was it like without them?

9. How would you classify your economic status at the time? On what do you base this decision? Did your economic status change? How? Why? When?

10. To what extent were you aware of or sympathetic toward minority groups? Did the town or area practice segregation? How did you feel about immigrants? about restricting immigration?

11. To what extent were you aware of urban and

industrial problems of this period? To what extent were you aware of reformers, muckrakers, progressives, and their efforts? Did you hear of *The Jungle* or read it? To what extent did you support or know about these reform efforts? To what extent were you affected by them?

12. What were the rules, restrictions, and etiquette governing your household?

13. What did people wear? Did the family make any of its own clothes? Did the ladies wear their hair long? use cosmetics? wear jewelry? (Explain.)

14. What relatives did you visit? What stands out in your mind about these relatives, especially older ones? How did you travel?

15. What part did mail-order catalogs play in your life? Which catalogs did you use?

16. What recollections stand out vividly in your mind from this period?

17. How did the family celebrate holidays, weddings, birthdays?

18. What household chores were assigned to various members of the family?

19. Do you have letters, diaries, or stories to share about events during the period, such as fires, storms, disease, or special achievements?

20. When did the family get its first telephone? What was your reaction upon hearing a telephone for the first time?

21. How did you wash clothes before you had a washing machine? How did you stay cool in the summer? How did you get groceries?

22. Describe fashions of each period. What were the hair styles? Did the men wear beards and moustaches?

23. Were the children of the family or young people allowed to play cards? date without a chaperone? stay out past dark? go to movies? dance? eat with the adults? wear slacks to school? Whose job was it to iron? wash clothes? wash dishes? chop wood? Were you required to go to church on Wednesday nights as well as Sundays? stand when adults entered the room? Was it customary to bathe on Saturday night? in the kitchen or in a bathroom? What were the special rules or customs for Sundays, Sabbath, and/or holidays?

24. What did you think when you saw your first car? What funny or interesting experiences did you have with cars and roads during this period?

BEFORE 1900

1. Where did the family live? How did they earn a living? Did they move? How frequently? Where? Why? Did any women of the family work outside the home? Doing what? What was the family attitude toward women working? toward single women in the family?

2. What provisions were made for older family members?

3. What kind of house did you live in? Describe it.

4. Were you or other family members in school? If not, why not? If so, what do you remember of school subjects, rules, activities, hours, sports, clothes, holidays, homework?

5. What games, toys, pets, playmates did the children have?

6. What kind of clothes did the children wear? the adults?

7. What part did religious, school, and family gatherings play in your life? Describe these.

8. Did any member of the family fight in the Spanish-American War (1898)? What was the family's attitude toward this war?

9. Do you remember any special celebrations at New Year's when 1899 gave way to 1900 and a new century?

10. What were the hair styles? Did the ladies wear jewelry or cosmetics? What kind? Did the men have beards and moustaches?

11. Were the children or young people allowed to play cards? date without a chaperone? stay out past dark? go to movies? dance? eat with the adults? What did they wear to school? Whose job was it to iron? wash clothes? wash dishes? chop wood? Were you required to go to church on Wednesday nights as well as Sunday? Were you supposed to stand when adults entered the room? Was it customary to bathe on Saturday night? in the kitchen or in a bathroom? Describe.

12. Did the family have electricity, running water, indoor plumbing, telephone, or gas lights before 1900? If not, what did you use? What kind of transportation did you rely on?

13. What Civil War stories have been handed down in the family? Did any family member fight in the war? If so, who? Where? How did the war affect the family? Which side did the family support? Where did the family live during the war? Did they move soon after the war? Why? When? To where? Did any family members die in the war or because of the war?

14. What family traditions still exist from the period

before the Civil War? How did the family earn a living? Did the family own slaves? Was the family caught up in the "westward movement"? Can you identify the various places they lived at various times?

IMMIGRATION

1. Who was the immigrant ancestor, couple, or family of this particular branch of the family? Where did this person, couple, or family originate? When and why did they come to this country? Are there family stories or records about where they sailed from, what ship they came on? Are there family stories about their coming and their early experiences here?

2. Does anyone know the names or locations of relatives still in the old country? Are there family Bibles, letters, or other records which give genealogical or geographical information about the family left behind in the old country, or ancestral information from the old country?

3. What traditions does the family preserve from the old country? names? recipes? customs? costumes? What vestiges of the former language still exist in the family? What language did the family speak before coming to this country? Are there pictures or personal belongings still in the family from the immigrant generation, or things they brought with them to this country?

See chapter twelve and Appendix B for resources to help you in searching for your immigrant ancestors.

AFRICAN-AMERICAN FAMILIES

1. According to tradition, which family members were slaves? Where did they live as slaves? Who were the slave owners? Do you know the name of the plantation or farm or town where they lived, the county, or any landmarks near the residence? How did each one choose his or her last name? If you cannot recall the slave owner's name, would anyone recognize it if he or she heard it? Were family members at the same plantation or farm for more than one or two generations?

2. Did family members leave the slave owner's farm after the Civil War? (or perhaps during the Civil War?) Where did they go? Did they go very far away? How did they choose where to go? Was there a particular skill represented in the family which would help one or more find jobs? (For example, blacksmiths, coopers, seamstresses, tailors, carpenters, etc.)

3. After the Civil War, or emancipation, did family members keep the given names they had as slaves, or did they change their names? If they changed their names, do you know what the earlier names were? Do you know the names of slave mothers in the family? Is there any family tradition or record of emancipation prior to the Civil War? Are there family traditions or stories about various places where family members have lived at various times in the past? Can you name any of those places or the approximate time period when family members were in that location?

4. After the Civil War, or emancipation, where did family members live? work? Were any self-employed? Who were brothers and sisters of the former slaves? Did a group of relatives live together as an extended family after emancipation? Do you know where the family or individual family members were living in 1870, 1880, 1900? What family traditions or records are there about education, religious participation or membership, and professional or social organizations to which family members belonged between 1865 and 1920?

5. Is there family tradition of where any family members lived before coming to the United States? Or when they came here? Did any immigrate as free men and women? Did any immigrate to this country after 1865? From where? When? Are there family names which are traditional in several generations which might give clues to places of origin, either in this country or elsewhere?

6. Are there family traditions or records of intermarriage with white, Indian, or other racial or ethnic groups? Do you have names of any of these ancestors who were non-black? Do you know anything about any of them?

7. Who is the oldest living member of this side of the family? Interview him or her if at all possible.

8. According to tradition, which family members were free blacks before the Civil War? Is there any tradition of a freedman buying other family members who were slaves in order to free them? Where did these ancestors live? What crafts, trades, or professions were represented in this part of the family? How did they earn a living? Did they attend school?

9. Consult the questions on the previous pages for more recent family history.

The farther away from these events we are, the fewer answers we have within the family. However, any information or tradition you can gather from these and similar questions can help you, even if the information is limited. See chapter twelve and Appendix B for additional help with your search.

As black men and women became free, they chose their own family names. Some wanted to be called Freeman or Freedman. Others chose the names of great Americans such as Washington, Jefferson, or Jackson. Some used the name of their former master or of someone in the community who had befriended them. Occasionally, members of the same family took different surnames. Are there traditions in your family about the origin of your surnames? (Remember, with eight great-grandparents, you could have eight different surnames to start working on.)

Slave owners often named their slaves in deeds and wills, which frequently identified slave children with their mothers. Slaves were enumerated, though rarely by name, in the 1850 and 1860 census records in separate slave schedules that are available on microfilm at many research libraries. Of course, after the Civil War, freed men and women and their children are found in the regular population schedules of the 1870, 1880, and 1900-1920 censuses, all of which are available to the public.

Other federal government documents, such as military records and files of the Bureau of Refugees, Freedmen, and Abandoned Lands, as well as county and state records can be helpful in tracing black ancestors. Before the segregation of churches and before the Civil War, church registers sometimes included servants and slaves in birth, death, and baptism records. Newspapers carried notices of runaway slaves and apprentices, often including physical descriptions and names. Such documents may be very useful for black genealogists, especially if they can determine the name of a former slave owner or plantation, or the approximate location of the place where the slave ancestor lived. Refer to later chapters in this book and to *The Genealogist's Companion & Sourcebook*, by Emily Croom (Cincinnati: Betterway Books, 1994) for more thorough discussion of these and other sources.

CHAPTER NINE

What Were They Like?

One of the most interesting aspects of the family history puzzle is discovering some of the personality traits and physical features which made up the family. You can probably answer these questions yourself for the relatives you know. In an effort to know something about those who are no longer living, you can try some of these questions on the people who did know them.

PERSONAL APPEARANCE

1. Do you have a photograph of him/her?
2. Was he/she tall, average height, or short?
3. Was he/she thin, average size, stocky, heavy, fat?
4. Was his/her face stern, pleasant, wrinkled, sad, etc.?
5. Was he bald? Did he have a beard or moustache? How did she wear her hair?
6. Was he/she healthy? sickly? In what way?
7. Was he handsome? Was she pretty? What color skin, hair, and eyes did he/she have?
8. What feature of his/hers stands out in your mind?
9. Were there physical features that showed up in more than one member of the family, such as a "drooping left eyelid" or flat feet?

HABITS AND PERSONALITY

You can adapt the following questions to learn about present as well as previous generations, including the person you are interviewing.

You may save time by using a number scale in answering some of the questions: 0 for *never*, 1 for *rarely*, 2 for *sometimes*, 3 for *frequently*.

1. How often did he/she . . . smoke, chew tobacco, drink, curse; travel, read; enjoy housekeeping, enjoy cooking; play tennis, golf, or other sports; ride a bicycle; skate, ski, etc.; raise animals or pets; like or raise cats; like or raise dogs; sleep late, rise early, stay up late, or go to bed early?
2. How often did he/she . . . play cards (what games?), tell jokes, tease others, play practical jokes, create nice surprises for others, entertain, correspond, visit friends, manipulate people?
3. To what extent or how often did he/she . . . smile, frown, laugh, get mad, cry, complain, gossip, see the bright side, dwell on the past, experience failure or success, look to the future for happiness, enjoy today, have a one track mind, start projects and not finish them, get things accomplished, work long hours, stay busy, work hard, make mountains out of molehills, imagine crises which were not really crises, organize well, worry, have a sense of humor, have common sense?
4. Did he/she have a nickname? What?
5. If he/she had a few hours to pursue an activity for pleasure, what would the activity be?
6. What were his/her special talents? abilities?
7. To what extent was he/she . . . a worrier, a loner, a hypochondriac, the life of the party, a good conversationalist, a willing worker, a perfectionist, a spendthrift, a stern disciplinarian, a good storyteller, a leader, a follower, a manager?
8. To what extent was he/she . . . demanding of self, demanding of others, hard (easy) to please, hard (easy) to work with, neat (sloppy) in habit and dress, absentminded, scatterbrained, literal-minded, argumentative, clever, ingenious, logical, lazy, ambitious, industrious, energetic, diligent, consistent, flexible, responsible, efficient, artistic, musical, creative, dramatic?
9. To what extent was he/she . . . possessive, sharing, affectionate, generous, warmhearted, kind, stingy, miserly, critical, jealous, blunt, outspoken, softspoken, clever with words, silly, open-minded, narrow-minded, forthright, angered easily, talkative, outgoing, understanding, empathic, sympathetic, henpecked, bossy, hard (easy) to get along with, hard (easy) to talk to, shy, quiet, considerate, courteous,

radiant, concerned about others, concerned about what others thought, aloof, confident, intuitive?

10. To what extent was he/she . . . moody, even-tempered, grumpy, gruff, self-centered, eccentric (explain), lonely, finicky (explain), stubborn, suspicious, philosophical, religious, strong in faith, jolly, serious, light-hearted, cruel, nervous, relaxed, carefree, thrifty, hurried, stern, angry, happy, courageous, cheerful, egotistical, humble, honest, sensitive, temperate, temperamental, modest?

11. How did he/she feel about . . . pregnancy, working women, housekeeping, hobbies, yard work, gardening, travel, death, sewing, spending money, daughters going to college, daughters getting married, single women living alone, women staying single, provisions for older members of the family?

FAMILY MEDICAL HISTORY

As science learns more about genetic, hereditary, and environmental factors in health and disease, it becomes increasingly important for us to record family medical history. Study of the cluster of blood-related siblings and cousins in each generation is particularly pertinent in this effort, for patterns of health history or disease within a family may help determine your own level of risk. Certainly, not all physical, emotional, or mental illnesses are inherited or "run in families." Each person's cultural and physical environment, lifestyle, health, and personal habits, such as diet, smoking, or alcohol consumption, can influence the onset or prevention of many diseases, whether or not they are prevalent in the family history. Gathering family medical history involves recording such personal factors in addition to cause of death, chronic conditions, and major illnesses for each of these relatives. It is also important to learn at what age an individual developed a given disease or condition and how it affected that person. The following is a partial list of diseases and conditions which are known or thought to have hereditary factors, some to a greater degree than others. Can you identify any family members who have been affected by them?

allergies
Alzheimer's disease
arthritis
attention deficit disorder
blindness
cancer
cataracts
cystic fibrosis
deafness
diabetes
epilepsy
fragile X syndrome
glaucoma
heart disease
hemophilia
high blood pressure
Huntington's disease
learning disabilities
mental retardation
multiple sclerosis
muscular dystrophy
Parkinson's disease
physical disabilities
physical malformations
sickle-cell anemia
stroke

If one or more of these, or other conditions, exist within the family history, the relatives of the present and future generations may be able to learn their risk levels from medical professionals and take steps to prevent or make early detection and seek treatment of potential problems.

CHAPTER TEN

Checklist of Family Sources

Family sources vary greatly from family to family, but genealogists should continually seek them out. Gathering names, vital statistics, and any other information from these sources is a logical place to begin one's search. The results will depend on the people available to talk to and the records and papers that the family has saved.

The search for and of family sources never really ends, especially as you broaden your study to include all eight great-grandparent lines and earlier generations. It is also an ideal way to pursue the cluster of an ancestor's relatives, friends, and neighbors. Studying this cluster can lead to valuable clues and facts about the ancestor. For example, learning the name of a cousin who visited from Mississippi, or the school an ancestor attended, or an organization to which he or she belonged may seem relatively trivial in the overall scheme of the family's history. However, the genealogist who follows up on these clues may learn not only more about the ancestor but may discover a genealogical gold mine: birth and death dates, a Bible record long thought lost, maiden names, evidence of children who lived and died between censuses, or names of another generation back in time.

Use this chapter as a checklist of family sources.

Relatives you already know are the first and most obvious source of family history information: parents, grandparents, great-grandparents, cousins, aunts and uncles, great-aunts and great-uncles, brothers and sisters, nieces and nephews. Make an effort to contact these people to tell them of your project, to ask their help, and to share what you are learning. Often they can contribute valuable information, and sometimes they will want to participate in the search with you.

Long-time family friends and neighbors can occasionally add as much information as relatives can.

Family Bibles and prayer books containing a register of births, deaths, and marriages may be available in several parts of the family, so check around for more than one. The most reliable of these sources is the record made at the time of the event. Look at the publication date of the Bible to determine whether the family entries predate or postdate the publication date. If the family dates predate the Bible itself, it is clear that the family entries were made some time, perhaps years, after the events themselves. In the course of time, dates may be remembered incorrectly.

Family letters, diaries, memoirs, and autobiographical sketches are often excellent sources of births, marriages, deaths, migrations, illnesses, education, daily life, church membership, and observations on contemporary events. My Elliott Coleman even wrote in a letter to his sister the weight of all his children! After all, sister Lucy had never seen his family, and he was describing everyone to her, and to us! He also expressed his opinion that "the plow should never have been brought west of the Colorado [River]." Written in one of the drier years of the 1880s, the letter is evidence of the problems that farmers had in adjusting to the West Texas and Great Plains environment. Such letters also furnish us with signatures and handwriting samples that may tell us more about the writers themselves.

Scrapbooks often contain newspaper clippings, funeral cards, party or wedding invitations, letters and postcards, speeches and essays, birth announcements, certificates and awards, photographs, graduation announcements and programs, diplomas, recital programs, and other mementos of important events in the person's life and family. They may yield vital statistics, family relationships, and "spice" for your family history.

School and college yearbooks and other school publications usually contain photographs of students and faculty and give a good picture of school life, both academic and extracurricular. From these you may learn what Grandpa's senior debate topic was, or that

Grandmother was elected Most Beautiful Freshman. These books can often be found at the library of the institution itself if the family does not have copies.

Photographs often have identifying labels and clues. They may be labeled with names you have not heard of before, which may be those of relatives after all. Pictures may also show the photographer's address, which could be a clue to the residence of the family in the pictures. People who moved away from home and family, whether across country or across the ocean, sometimes exchanged photos with family members who remained at home. These pictures could help you identify the place from which an immigrant came or the place to which part of the family immigrated. Clothing styles, automobiles, buildings or signs in the photos could help date them.

Family papers can be a wide variety of items, including deeds, land grants, copies of wills, birth certificates, marriage licenses, oil and mineral leases, voter registration cards, records of naturalization, records from a family business, household accounts and budgets, school report cards, school transcripts, old driver's licenses, membership cards from social and professional organizations, inventories made for insurance purposes, insurance papers, and other documents. These papers probably will give you some vital statistics, signatures of various ancestors, and interesting socio-economic data on the family.

Living relatives whom you may not know when you begin your family history puzzle can be very valuable sources. With the help of parents, grandparents, and cousins, you can usually find second and third and even more distant cousins who want to share in the family history project. Second cousins share a common great-grandparent; third cousins have a common great-great-grandparent.

My dad's first cousin in Tennessee still lives in the same town where the family moved in 1845. She herself was not particularly interested in tracing family history, but she helped me in many ways: providing me a place to stay when I went searching, sharing her own memories with me, introducing me to other cousins in her area, and passing along a letter from a distant cousin we had never heard of before. A Mississippi lady had traced some of her great-grandmother's Coleman brothers to Katherine's town, using family letters and the photographer's address on old pictures in her great-grandmother's album. She wrote to the local historian trying to find someone who might know about these Colemans. He gave her letter to cousin Katherine to send to me, and we were "reunited" with our very own distant Coleman cousins. We were able to identify some of Elliott's children in the photos and were allowed to copy them. The trunk of century-old family letters in Mississippi proved invaluable in piecing together our common history. Likewise, my search had found some information that was new and helpful to her.

Our task now is to interest the younger generation in maintaining the ties which we have reestablished. One way families can do this is through **round-robin letters**. The first family sends a letter to another family of relatives; they add their letter and send both to a third family. The third family adds theirs and sends all three letters to a fourth, and so on, until all who have agreed to participate have received the packet. The last family returns the packet to the original family, who replaces their original letter with a new one and sends the packet around again. Each family in turn replaces their previous letter with a new one.

Another method of exchanging information and keeping up with each other is through a **family association**. Some family associations are highly organized, with officers who have specific duties. Others are less structured, with one or two people taking the lead. Some families have a **periodic reunion** or publish a **periodical newsletter**—bimonthly, quarterly, semi-annually, or yearly—as a means of sharing information among their own group and any others searching the same surname.

A Texas genealogist compiles an annual list of some six hundred family newsletters and periodicals published throughout the country. Her list also includes newspaper genealogy columns in Alabama, Arkansas, California, Florida, Georgia, Illinois, Indiana, Kansas, Louisiana, Maine, Maryland, Michigan, Mississippi, Missouri, Nebraska, New Jersey, North Carolina, Ohio, Oklahoma, Pennsylvania, South Carolina, Texas, Virginia, Washington and other states. *Family Periodicals* is available for a small fee from Merle Ganier, 2108 Grace Ave., Ft. Worth, Texas 76111-2816.

Family periodicals sometimes have a rather short life span, and they vary considerably in quality. However, if your surname has a periodical available, a subscription could put you in contact with people who can help you in your search. Many of the family newsletters do deal with the various spellings of their name. Figure 6 lists some of the family newsletters available.

Figure 6: Some Surnames in *Family Periodicals*

Alford	Eidson (sic)	Lipscomb	Purcell
Alton	Elliott	Littell	Ramey
Ames	Ellis	Locke	Rich
Austin	Estes	Love	Robertson
Ball	Faust	Madden	Robinson
Bartee	Foley	Martin	Russell
Beach	Fuqua	Matkins	Sears
Bell	Gann	Mauzey	Shannon
Bennett	Gebhart	McCrary	Shirley
Berry	Gibbs	McKinney	Simmons
Blair	Graves	McVay	Sparks
Boggess	Green	Mercer	Stephen(son)
Bunker	Gunn	Miller	Strong
Campbell	Hanks	Moore	Taft
Carroll	Harrington	Moriarty	Terry
Carson	Haskell	Neff	Thompson
Clark	Hawkins	Nelson	Towne
Cloud	Hicks	Nichols	Townsend
Collier	Hite	Nye	Turner
Courtney	Hogg	O'Dell	Upchurch
Crane	Horton	Odom	Usher
Creekmore	Jolly	Overholser	Valentine
Daniel	Keefer	Pace	Van Aken
Davis	Kelso	Packard	Vaughan
Dawes	Kirkpatrick	Peacock	Warner
Deweese	Knight	Perkins	Wells
Durkee	Knowles	Phillips	Williams
Eads	Lamb	Potter	Wolf
Edgar	Landry	Prescott	Worden
Edson	Lillard	Preston	Yarnell

CHECKLIST FOR FINDING DISTANT RELATIVES WITH WHOM TO EXCHANGE INFORMATION

1. Relatives you already know and family friends can often help you find second, third, or more distant cousins.

2. Family papers and letters may contain addresses, or at least town names, which may help you locate any of the family still in that area.

3. Family association newsletters.

4. Queries in newspaper genealogy columns in your research locale.

5. Ads in newspapers of your research locale.

6. Queries in genealogical periodicals. *The Genealogical Helper* (The Everton Publishers, Inc., Logan, UT 84321) and *Southern Queries* (P.O. Box 726, Durham, NC 27702-0726) are two periodicals which devote considerable space in each issue to genealogists wanting to exchange information on particular families. Regional genealogical society periodicals contain queries about families from that county, district, or region. Membership in a society in your research area is often money well spent.

7. Surname lists of genealogical societies. Genealogical societies often publish with their membership rosters the surnames that each member is searching. These lists are sometimes for sale from the society office. A useful book for locating a genealogical society in your research area is *A Directory of Historical Orga-*

nizations in the United States and Canada (Nashville: American Association for State and Local History, latest edition). Sometimes a letter to the local public library or other agency inquiring about a genealogical society in the area may help you find one.

8. Hereditary society membership rosters. If you have an ancestor who could qualify you for membership in an organization such as the Daughters of the American Revolution or the Daughters of 1812, you may be able to obtain membership records of other relatives who have also qualified by being descendants of that same patriot. With current membership rosters or the help of the chapter from which the relative joined the society, you may be able to get in touch with these distant cousins. To know whether anyone has joined from your particular ancestor's family, check the society's ancestor or patriot index.

DAR Patriot Index. Washington, DC: National Society of Daughters of the American Revolution, Vol. I, 1966; Vol. II, 1980; Vol. III, 1986.

1812 Ancestor Index. Eleanor Stevens Galvin, comp. Washington, DC: National Society of United States Daughters of 1812, 1970; II, 1992.

The Hereditary Register of the United States. Jerome Francis Beattie, ed. The Hereditary Register Publications, Inc., latest edition. Gives addresses for the many hereditary societies, a list of family associations and their publications, genealogical societies, and certified genealogists.

9. Published or privately printed family or county histories which pertain to your families may contain the address of the author or the publisher. Publishers will often forward a letter from you to the author. Because these histories vary greatly in quality and reliability, use them with great caution. If one contains little or no documentation of the sources of its information, use that information carefully as clues to further your search for proof. Most county histories do not have the space to include documentation for every family included, but they usually give the name of the submitter. Contact the editors to try to locate the submitter of your particular family's history. The widely advertised world-books-of-your-surname, family registries (of one surname), and histories-of-your-surname, which solicit your money through the mail, are not genealogies, usually do not tell you one iota of *your* specific family history, and usually are a waste of money, unless you want lists from telephone directories of people who bear your surname. Remember, however, that having the same name does not make two people related, and your relatives are not limited to only those with your surname.

10. Telephone directories, whether in your own area or that of your ancestors, can sometimes give you the names of people who have the same surname as the one you are researching. Contacting these people may or may not lead you to a relative, but I have met some very helpful people by using this technique.

11. Photographs labeled with the photographer's address or containing some other clue to the place where the photo was taken may in turn give a clue to the residence of the family, which can in turn give you a locale in which to search, using some of the techniques already listed.

12. Computer databases in the worldwide branch libraries of the Family History Library in Salt Lake City. Several databases of names are available for searching at these family history centers. Because the information they contain is not checked for accuracy, they must be used with great caution. They contain both correct and incorrect information. It is up to you as the genealogist to check out and seek to prove any piece of information you glean from such sources. You can learn from them, however, the name of the submitter, who may turn out to be a relative. Even finding people working on the same surname in the same research area can prove beneficial.

SPICE FROM FAMILY SOURCES

Your family history puzzle takes on depth and character in proportion to the amount of "spice" you add to it as you search. There are many extras you can add to the information you collect.

Some families are fortunate enough to inherit antique furniture as part of their heritage. Others receive smaller personal belongings, such as books, crocheted work, teaspoons, and jewelry. Each of these items takes on new meaning as you learn of its past and its former owners. If these items belong to other family members, you can photograph those you wish to include in your history.

Photography offers a wide range of extras for you, from furniture to houses, from tombstones to people still living. Some photographs are already taken and waiting to be claimed. These are often unidentified faces in albums, tintypes in an old trunk, or water-stained sketches hidden behind later pictures in a frame. With the help and permission of older family members or those who own the pictures, you can label the photographs and have copies made. They

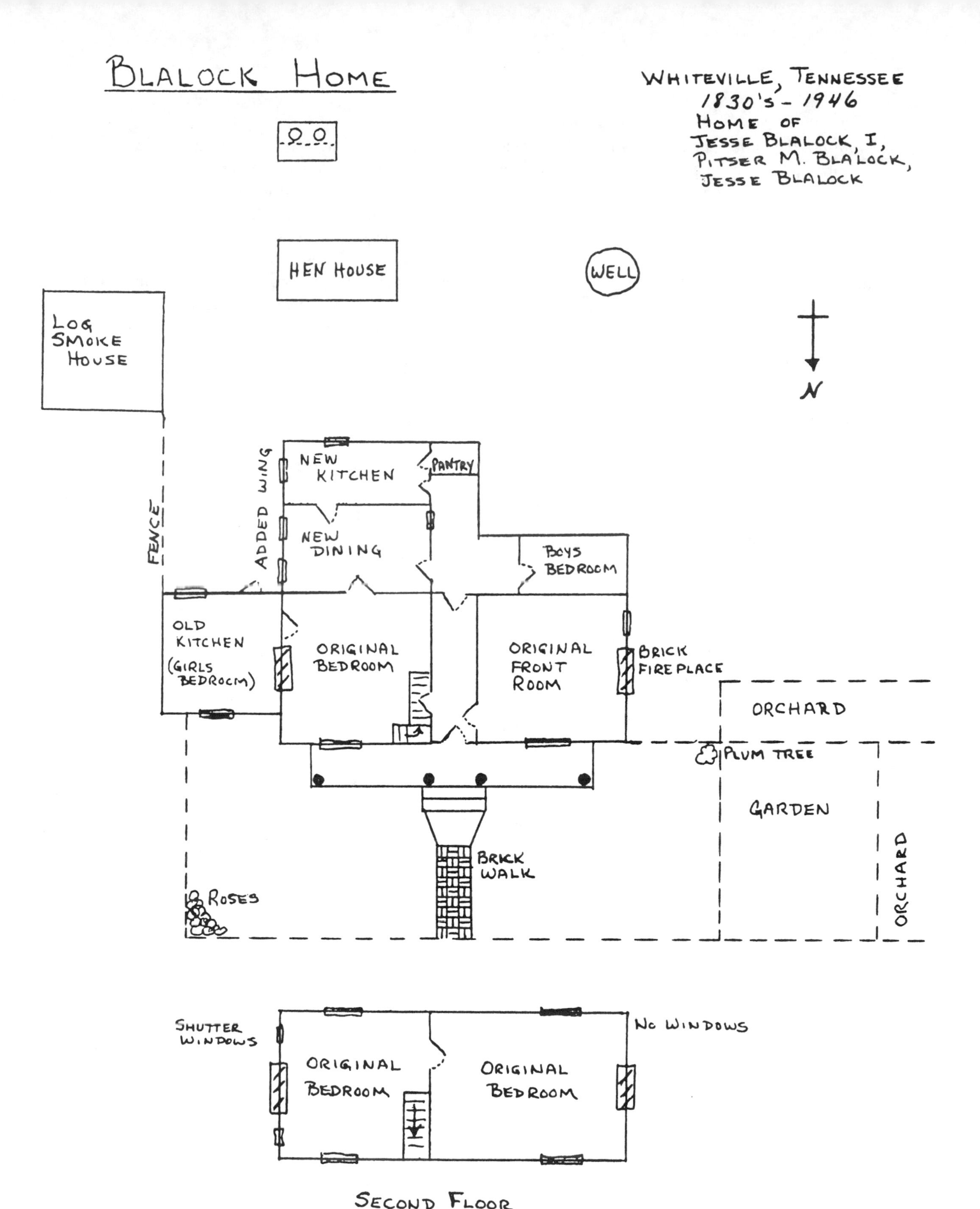

BLALOCK HOME
WHITEVILLE, TENNESSEE
1830's - 1946
HOME OF
JESSE BLALOCK, I,
PITSER M. BLALOCK,
JESSE BLALOCK
HEN HOUSE
WELL
LOG SMOKE HOUSE
N
FENCE
ADDED WING
NEW KITCHEN
PANTRY
NEW DINING
BOYS BEDROOM
OLD KITCHEN (GIRLS BEDROOM)
ORIGINAL BEDROOM
ORIGINAL FRONT ROOM
BRICK FIREPLACE
ORCHARD
PLUM TREE
GARDEN
ORCHARD
BRICK WALK
ROSES
SHUTTER WINDOWS
NO WINDOWS
ORIGINAL BEDROOM
ORIGINAL BEDROOM
SECOND FLOOR
EAC_
AS DESCRIBED BY
KATHERINE BROOKS

FIG. 7: THE BLALOCK HOME

make nice surprise gifts and preserve an important side of family history.

When photographs are not preserved, you can create your own pictures by sketching such things as houses or household items. Descriptions of houses, inside or outside, can come from those who lived in them. With their careful observations and your careful notations, together you can provide sketches or floor plans for future generations. An example is the floor plan of the Blalock house of Whiteville, Tennessee, which housed four generations of that family. The house is no longer standing, and there are few photographs of it. The sketch provides the descendants one view of their "ancestral home." (See Figure 7.)

More difficult to find but equally entertaining are handwriting samples from your ancestors. I enjoy collecting their signatures. These are most readily found in old letters, as were the two illustrations shown in Figure 8 (see page 42), written in 1855 and 1854, respectively. Handwriting may also be identified in a family Bible, on original copies of deeds, wills, or other documents, or on old report cards from school. Reverend Henry Metcalf made it easier for his descendants to find his signature by signing and returning to the county courthouse the marriage license for each couple whose wedding ceremony he performed.

Studying the old letters can tell you something about the people who wrote them. Did they consistently misspell the same words? Were they consistent in the way they formed their letters? Are they academic or free from rules in matters of punctuation, grammar, spelling, and choice of words? Are the lines of writing straight or slanted? Did they think faster than they wrote, as shown by words which they added when they proofread the letter? Is the letter neatly executed? Are the writers sentimental? Do they express their affections? Do they express their hopes and dreams? Do they reveal their faith or religious beliefs? Do they gossip? Do they give advice? Do they feel a duty rather than a desire to write? Do they mention any enjoyment or pleasure? Do they concentrate on health and greetings, or on business? Nineteenth-century letters can say less in more words than we can imagine. They mention receipt of letters, apologies for delays in answering, wishes for good health, inquiries into the health of each member of the family, and greetings to everyone in the family. If they have not run out of space by the end of the page, they may share a little of the "nuse" of the neighborhood: weddings, births, parties, and always illnesses and deaths.

Here is a letter written from Sommerville, Tennessee, 2 February 1848, to a brother in Buckingham County, Virginia.

Dear Brother,

Yours of date 15 of Jan reached us on the 31rst, you seem to be repenting that you had not writen to me before asking me to forgive you I will if you will not do so again I havent much nuse to communicate, but will answer you and make it an invariable rule to answer all the letters I get as soon as I possibly can and ask the same of all my correspondents You stated in your letter you were at Fathers a few days before you wrote and they were all well, except Sister Lucy I am sorry to hear her health is bad. I am afraid she grieves too much after our dear and affectionate mother. I hope she is better off, as it is useless to grieve after her but endeavour to follow her—You wrote Aunt Susan was to be married to Wm Miller sometime during this month. If she has her choice I haven't a word to say but wish her all the happiness this world can afford You spoke of coming to this country [sic] *I came in the summer I don't think it prudent for a person to leave their friends unless they can better themselves. If you will let me know what you are doing or in other words what wages you are getting and I can tell whether you can do better here than you can in Va Cotton is selling for a very low price from 5½ to 6 very little selling at present All that can are holding on until spring thinking it will be higher negroes are selling very low compared with the sales twelve months ago there is a trader in this place by the name of Brooks with a drove of negroes he cant get first cost for his negroes corn is selling from 1.75 to 2.00 dollars cash, pork from 4 to 4¼ dull at that I delivered your message to Catherine she requested me to send her love to you in return for yours says you must write to her and she will answer. This leaves us well present my best love to all enquiring friends and relations and accept the same yourself. I must conclude as I havent anything more to write adiue* [sic] *dear brother I remain your devoted brother*

E G Coleman

What can we learn from this letter?

Margaret Catherine Patton
m.
Elliott G. Coleman
parents of Mary Catherine Coleman Blalock

This leaves all well—hoping
this may find and all the
family in the enjoyment of
the same blessing. I must close
write soon—

Your Affectionate
Son—
E G Coleman

Sister write soon we feel so lonely and distressed tell
Sister Mary that I just received a letter from her and
will answer it soon give my love to all of the family
and except a portion your self no more
but remains ever the same
your affectionate Sister untill death
Catharin M. Coleman
Adieu Sister Adieu

FIG. 8: PHOTOS AND HANDWRITING SAMPLES

1. It took sixteen days in January for Archer's letter to reach Tennessee.

2. Elliott disciplined himself to answer correspondence. He wanted to hear from family.

3. Their mother had recently died. (A Bible record shows that she died on 24 December 1847, about five weeks before this letter was written.)

4. Elliott loved his mother and his family.

5. Elliott could face death around him without over-grieving.

6. He apparently thought Aunt Susan was making a mistake in her choice of a husband. Other records show that this aunt was his father's sister.

7. Aunt Susan planned to marry in February, 1848.

8. Elliott left home and moved to Tennessee in the summer (several years before the letter was written).

9. Elliott realizes and advises that moving away from home is a pretty permanent break and such a move should be well considered and investigated.

10. His wife, Catherine, was making an effort to know her in-laws, whom she had never met.

11. Elliott followed the standard patterns of expressing his love and concern for his family and their health.

12. Punctuation did not concern him.

Another interesting addition to your puzzle is a map showing the movement of your family within the United States. A dot can be used to locate each place the family lived. Highway maps or atlases can help you locate the cities or counties within each state. If you know when the family arrived at each location, you can write the year of arrival beside the dot.

After placing the dots on the map, connect them with a line. Begin with your own residence and work backward, in order, to the earliest known location. If you trace more than one family per map, use dotted or dashed lines to distinguish them clearly. You may wish to use a different color for each family. In a legend or key, explain your marks and identify each date with the name of the city or county.

The example shown in Figure 9 is of the Croom and Coleman families, which were united in 1900. As was the case with numerous families, whose descendants later married each other, these two families had lived in the same county in the eighteenth century, had gone separate ways, and had ended up in the same county again a century later.

The extras which can add spice to your history are numerous and depend on how much depth you want your history to show and how much effort and time you want to give to it. The results are always enlightening. These efforts, when shared within the family, help strengthen family ties, broaden understanding, and increase appreciation for each other and for your common heritage. Even my uncle who wants no part of the search or the results does his part by providing me a place to stay when I travel his direction to do research.

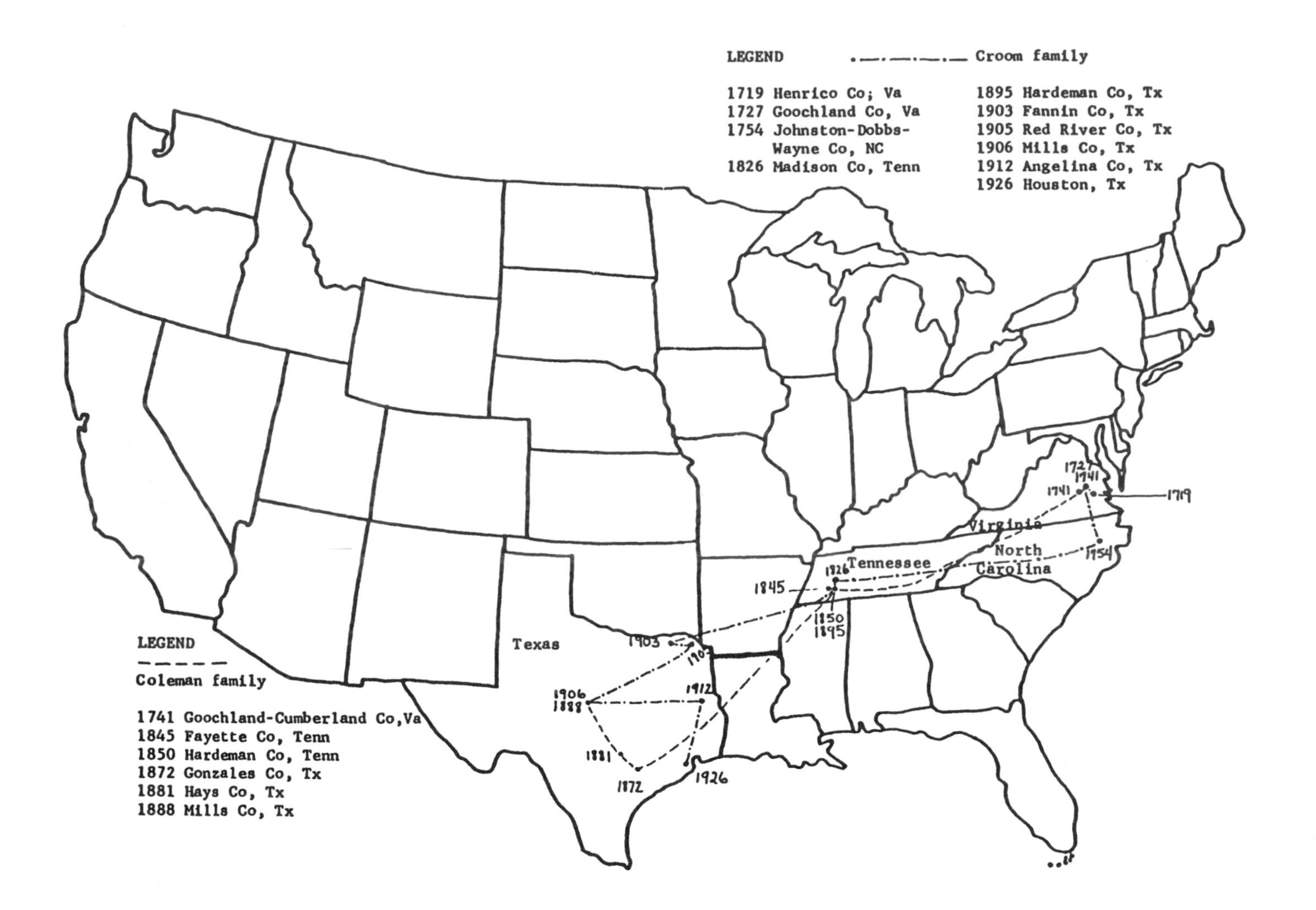

FIG. 9: MAP OF FAMILY MIGRATIONS

CHAPTER ELEVEN

Beyond the Family: Local Sources

After gathering basic information from family sources and filling in your charts at least back to the early twentieth century, you can see which pieces of the puzzle are missing. You are then ready to consult the many public sources available to genealogists because you have some facts to use in finding new answers. From this point on, you will use family sources and public sources together, for genealogists never really finish with either kind. Hopefully, you will discover new family sources as you learn of new public ones.

As our research branches out beyond immediate family sources, genealogists do well to remember these points.

1. We cannot believe everything we read in print, hear from relatives, or receive from other researchers. Ask yourself, "What documentation proves or supports what they say?" With documentation from original records, you are in a position to evaluate the facts and draw conclusions yourself. You are the detective in the case and surely don't want to contaminate the results of careful research with material of undetermined origin or accuracy. A friend of mine is working to clear up such a situation in her family. A cousin happily sent her a family group sheet announcing that she had found the long-sought-after parents and siblings for their common ancestor, George. The chart listed two incomplete, unverifiable references for its data. As my friend compared the chart with her own ongoing research, she realized there were few similarities between the two: the name George, the same surname, the name Samuel as a possible brother, a close (but not the same) birth year, and North Carolina as George's birthplace. The cousin apparently picked up the information from a published source or computer database and made a giant leap of faith. However, the results of *real research*, concentrating on the known ancestor, now suggest that these Georges are two individuals from entirely different families.

2. We must be ready to seek original documents to provide evidence for the best possible answers: the *right* people with the *right* cluster of friends and relatives in the *right* places at the *right* times. Many researchers have early successes, but sooner or later all run into seemingly impenetrable brick walls. You must decide for yourself how hard you want to work for answers and how much you are willing to travel or spend in the effort. For many of us, the challenge and exhilaration of finding solutions is what keeps us searching.

GOING BEYOND FAMILY SOURCES

You may decide first to pursue the line of your favorite grandparent, the only great-grandmother you ever knew, or the grandparent you know the least about. Whatever project you choose, there is a virtually endless supply of public sources to investigate.

Among these public sources are city, county, and state records, which include such documents as marriage records, wills and probate records, deeds, birth and death records, tax and court records. Local cemeteries, newspapers, and churches also provide important information for many searchers. Useful federal sources include the census, military service and pension records, immigration and naturalization papers, congressional documents, and public land records. Libraries and archives at all levels (city, county, state, university, and federal) often have research collections of great value for genealogists.

Where do you turn first? When I began my research, the 1900-1920 censuses were not yet open to the public, and I did not always know enough about the family I was investigating to begin with the 1880 census. When I did know where the family was in 1880, I began with that census and worked backward in census records before turning to county records. If I did not have enough information to begin with the 1880 census, I began with county records, cemeteries, and other local sources. Today, when I begin a new family and have reviewed available family sources, I like to (1) start with the 1900, 1910, or 1920 census, (2) do as much census research as possible with the information I have, (3) consult county and local sources, and (4) continue with these and whatever other records are needed to find the answers. Fortunately, today, federal censuses and many local records are available at research libraries and from various rental and lending libraries. (See the end of this chapter for more information.) However, if you can visit the local research area, you may find a more complete set of resources and have some of those special experiences that occur only "in the field."

This chapter concentrates on the primary sources available at the local and county levels. Chapter twelve will consider state and federal sources.

CEMETERIES

Tombstones are excellent sources of dates, birthplaces, husbands' and wives' names, maiden names, parents' names, evidence of children who died young, and even military service. I try to locate and photograph the tombstones for as many ancestors as I can. Family members were often buried in a family plot, so locating one ancestor's tombstone may give you access to many more with good information. Of course, not all family members were buried in the same plot or the same cemetery. The search may lead you over a wide area.

Larger cemeteries often have files or maps to help you find a particular stone. Without such aid, your alternative is to walk up and down the rows reading each stone, checking for the person's name. You may have to check both sides of the stones, for in older cemeteries, tombstones in the same row may face different directions.

When you are lucky enough to find the stone you are seeking, copy the information carefully. A photograph of it offers additional proof. If you are not sure of a letter or number, you may need to make a rubbing of it. (See Figure 10.) To do this, put a piece of paper over the stone and rub the paper with a crayon or pencil. Then study the rubbing. Be sure to title your page of notes with the name and location of the cemetery and the date you were there. If the cemetery is large or the stone is difficult to locate, you may need to sketch a map to show its location for future reference. When visiting cemeteries, follow the courtesies of not removing or damaging any stones.

If you know which cemetery to go to, take along an older relative who can take you directly to the family graves. If you do not know which cemetery to look in, consult older residents of the area, local funeral directors, published histories of the area which may contain cemetery listings, obituaries, and death certificates of the ancestors whose graves you are seeking. If none of these narrows the search, you may have to visit a number of cemeteries. Detailed county maps, such as those printed by the state highway departments, show most of the cemeteries. Ask local residents about any cemeteries not listed on these maps.

Our search for our great-great-grandfather Harrison's tombstone took us to many cemeteries and eventually gave us the dates of his life, but the search had two other very valuable and unexpected "payoffs." One concerned our Orgain ancestors, whom I had found unexpectedly in the 1850 census in a Tennessee county where we had relatives from the other side of the family. The Orgains had subsequently moved to Texas, but I did not know where. We had temporarily laid aside that search to concentrate on the Harrison line. In the county where the Harrisons had lived, we had searched all the cemeteries that we could find, without any luck, and had just completed a second search of the Hutto City Cemetery. As we stood debating what to do next, my brother-in-law, Fred, squinted ahead, thinking he saw tombstones on a little rise in the distance. I was sure he was seeing a mirage, the kind you see when you close your eyes and see nothing but weeds after you have been weeding the garden all day. But we decided to follow his hunch. A dirt road led us somehow to the gate of a tiny, very old and overgrown cemetery. We split up to speed the search. I did not recognize any name I saw and found no Harrison, but soon my sister, Judy, called out, "Hey, have you ever heard of a Reverend Sterling Orgain?" Shrieking with delight, I plunged through the tall weeds toward her voice and her treasure. There it was: a double stone for Reverend Sterling Orgain and Mary E. Orgain, his wife, complete with dates! We had caught up with them again, at last. When I calmed down, I had presence of mind enough

to copy and photograph the stone, and to copy other stones around it, which did turn out to be those of relatives too. I also remembered to map the little place so that I could take my eighty-year-old great-uncle to see what no one else in the family had known existed, in a place where we would never have thought to look.

We were still searching for the Harrison tombstone but felt better about visiting so many cemeteries. We returned to search a second time near the tiny town where the Harrisons had lived. The feed store was about the only business open that Saturday, so we stopped there and asked where we might find a local historian who could give us information about other cemeteries in the area. The man pointed to a house within view and said that the couple who lived there had been in town forever. We knocked on their door and explained our mission. Mrs. Richardson invited us in and began asking questions. Where are you from? Do you have relatives near here? Oh, one of you now lives in the county? Has your family ever lived here? Oh, your grandparents once lived in Georgetown? We used to live there too. Who are your grandparents? When we told them, there were looks of great astonishment on their faces. Mr. Richardson grinned: "I used to date your grandmother when your grandaddy was courting her sister." And Mrs. Richardson added, "And I was your grandmother's maid of honor in their wedding!" What a visit we had!

Before we could get back to the community to search again for the Harrison tombstone, that dear couple went to the city cemetery and found our stone. We had overlooked it because it was facing the opposite direction from all the others around it. The couple copied it and drew us a sketch of where to find it. From all this effort, we not only learned the birth and death dates and burial place of that Harrison ancestor, but we also found birth and death dates for the two Organ ancestors and met the lovely couple who shared with us so much about our grandparents.

Then I started looking for the parents of this Harrison ancestor. From the 1850 census, I learned their names and the fact that they were living in Victoria. I could hardly wait to go to Victoria. At the cemetery, on her tombstone there, I learned the mother's birthplace: Nottoway County, Virginia. That one piece of information led me to her marriage record, her maiden name,

FIG. 10: TOMBSTONE RUBBING

and nearly two centuries of Bland ancestors in Virginia.

These two early experiences made me a firm believer in the value of cemetery research. Of course, it is not always possible to find or visit ancestral cemeteries. In addition, not all graves received tombstones, not all tombstones have survived, and not all tombstone inscriptions remain legible. Furthermore, tombstones themselves may contain errors, made either by the engraver or the family member who gave him the information. See pages 90-91 for examples of tombstone research problems.

Fortunately for genealogists, many inscriptions have been copied, published, and placed in libraries, not only in the community where the cemetery is located but around the country. If you find a book or periodical that includes transcriptions of your ancestors' tombstones, remember that such resources may contain mistakes. If possible, get photographs of the stones to confirm the information. Another problem of relying exclusively on printed transcriptions is that many of them are published in alphabetical order, not in the order the tombstones appear in the cemetery. People are not buried in alphabetical order but in family plots or groups, including those with different surnames. When you do visit the cemeteries themselves, take advantage of the opportunity to identify and record the cluster of stones in the same plot with or in the vicinity of your ancestor.

LOCAL HISTORIANS AND ELDERS OF THE COMMUNITY

My cemetery research and travels introduced me to the value of local historians and the elders of any community. In a small Tennessee town where I have many relatives, whom I met through genealogy, I used to spend hours in the private library of a local historian. He had a sizeable collection of letters, diaries, and other papers from local families. He let me read and make notes from these, as they pertained to my family. I hope that, since his death, his family has given these to the local library or historical society. He himself was able to show me one house that had been in my family during the Civil War.

One day, in the same town, I was walking around to find various old buildings I had been reading about. I had just learned that my great-grandmother had been christened in the little Presbyterian church, where her mother had been a charter member. I was anxious to see and photograph the church. As I stood in front, the door opened and a very elderly lady emerged from the sanctuary where she had been "straightening up." I introduced myself and told her why I was interested in the church, and she invited me in. The most exciting part of the visit was her letting me play the little pipe organ that was 100 years old. She sat down at the piano, which was more or less in tune with the organ, and by ear and from memory played with me any hymn that I started. Not only was it enjoyable to play this antique instrument, but this was the same organ that my great-grandmother, whom I never met, had heard each Sunday. And this was the same sanctuary where she and her parents had worshipped together. This was a new experience for me. I am from a "newer" city where very few things that stood 100 years ago still exist, and I grew up knowing very few relatives and never seeing a family artifact more than 50 years old.

Experiences like these are not rare; there are "old-timers" everywhere who are happy to share their communities with those of us who are sincere in wanting to know about them. All it takes is asking and listening.

NEWSPAPERS

Some of the most entertaining historical and genealogical information comes from gossip columns, social news, advertisements, and editorials of local newspapers. That's where I learned that Elliott Coleman was "putting up the Episcopal Church," "a neat, substantial building," and that Mrs. M.E. Hodge offered room and board for $20 a month (Gonzales, Texas, *Inquirer*, 17 July 1880, 30 April 1881; Bolivar, Tennessee, *Bulletin*, 5 January 1867). From the editor of the Bolivar, Tennessee, *Bulletin*, we learned almost everything we know about Elliott's brother Alfred S. Coleman. "We notice that A.S. Coleman with a good force has been planting young shade trees in and around the public square this week. . . . We hope Alf will live long to enjoy the fruits of his labor and the thanks of fellow citizens" (Bolivar, Tennessee, *Bulletin*, 13 March 1874). From other such mentions, we learn that this young bachelor was a busy carpenter, a volunteer firefighter, a cook at all the barbecues, a volunteer on civic committees, an officer in the Odd Fellows Lodge, a member of the Presbyterian church and the Sons of Temperance, and a "sterling" Democrat. Then the editor announced in February, 1882, that "Alf Coleman has started for Texas with his celebrated Gate Hinge. Success and safety to him."

In addition to news of church, school, lodge, club, and civic activities and participants, the newspapers also gave local birth, marriage, and death announcements, although not with as wide or complete a coverage as we genealogists would like. The editors also seemed to feel a civic duty to express judgments and opinions about local issues. One of my favorites appeared in the Bolivar *Bulletin* on 13 June 1873, as the editor warned boys not to stand and smoke in front of the churches, either day or night. If this practice did not stop, he would print names!

The small-town weekly papers usually contained about four pages. Of course, at least one was advertisements; two were national and state news; and one, local news. By examining a few issues, you can tell where the local items are found. You can save time by turning directly to that section. The newspapers are usually not indexed, so you must read each issue.

When taking notes from these papers, record the name of the paper, the date of the issue, and where you can find the paper again should the need arise. If you are fortunate enough to read the originals, handle with care, as they become very brittle with age.

How do you find newspapers? I have occasionally found old issues, either originals or microfilm copies, at the newspaper office, the local public library, or the county courthouse. State archives or libraries, historical society libraries, and university libraries often have originals and/or microfilm copies. Contact such institutions in your research area for a list or catalog of their holdings. Some provide interlibrary loan of microfilm.

Another procedure for finding newspapers is to use union catalogs. Many libraries and state archives have such lists for their state. The following three standard references for finding newspapers are found in many large libraries. Listing newspapers by state and town, the first two guides give dates of issues known to exist and where researchers can find them.

1. *American Newspapers, 1821-1936: A Union List of Files Available in the United States and Canada.* Winifred Gregory, ed. New York: H.W. Wilson, 1937, reprint by Kraus Reprint Corporation, New York, 1967.

2. *Newspapers in Microform, United States, 1948-1983.* 2 Vols. Washington, DC: Library of Congress, 1984.

3. *A Checklist of American Eighteenth Century Newspapers in the Library of Congress.* John Van Ness Ingram, comp. Washington, DC: Government Printing Office, 1912.

COUNTY COURTHOUSES

Counties organize their materials differently, but you can generally start at the office of the county clerk or registrar. Explain that you are working on family history and want to see marriage records, wills and probate records, and deeds. The clerks are usually glad to show you around, but they cannot search for you. If you cannot visit the courthouse in person, try to get microfilm records on interlibrary loan through the American Genealogical Lending Library, the state archives or historical society, or the nearest branch of the LDS Family History Library. (See Interlibrary Loan, page 60.)

Before reading county records, familiarize yourself with their particular system of indexes. Some records are indexed at the beginning of each volume; some, in general indexes covering multiple volumes. Older indexes often group surnames under their initial letter in chronological order, as the documents came in for filing. (Sometimes, they were filed years after the original events took place.) Other indexes use a system that divides names into alphabetical groups: all names beginning with *Pa* indexed on one page, *Pe* on another, then *Ph*, *Pi*, and so forth. Records such as court minutes, births and deaths, or tax rolls may not be indexed at all. These index styles usually help you find entries with alternate spellings. If you are seeking records of W.T. Walter, and you see W.T. or William Waters in the index, look at the document. It may well be the right ancestor with simply a misspelled name.

Once you begin to read the record books, document each book, volume, and page number, as in *Presidio County, Texas, Deeds, Book A, page 24.* As part of your note-taking process, make note of whether the parties could sign their own names or signed with their marks. The handwriting in the record books is rarely that of your ancestors but usually that of the clerk, who indicates whether they signed or made marks. Some courthouses preserve the original marriage bonds and licenses, wills and related estate settlement documents. These normally show the signatures or marks of the parties involved.

Marriages

First, study the indexes that cover your research time frame and write down the references that seem pertinent to your search. Sometimes there are separate indexes for brides and for grooms. Some counties after the Civil War had separate marriage books for blacks and whites. Look up all entries pertaining to your surname(s), not just the records of direct ancestors. Write down all information: bride, groom, their ages and other personal data if given, date and place of marriage, the name of the person who performed the ceremony, any witnesses or bondsmen, any parental permission given for an underaged person, and of course the volume and page or certificate number of the entry. Get copies of at least those documents pertaining to your direct ancestors.

Caution! The marriage entry may give four different dates: the date of the license or bond, the date of the marriage ceremony, the date the minister returned the license to the clerk, and the date the license was recorded. Make note of all four and of what may be missing. If you do not find a marriage record that you had expected to find in a given county, make note of that fact as well; then look in surrounding counties. If you find only a record of the license being issued but no indication of the marriage date, you cannot assume that the ceremony did or did not take place. You need to look for other sources, such as the newspaper, which may answer the question.

Marriage records seldom spell out family relationships, but many witnesses, bondsmen, and even ministers were relatives of the bride or groom. Read page by page to see whether your ancestor acted as bondsman or witness for someone else. (Original indexes usually do not include participants other than bride and groom.) Men often served in such a capacity for a brother, cousin, son, son-in-law, or best friend. Thus, these records can be valuable clues for further research as you seek to reconstruct the cluster of an ancestor's relatives and friends.

Before the twentieth century, grooms, before getting married, were often required to sign a bond acknowledging that they would owe a stated sum of money to the colony or state if there was any lawful cause that would prevent the marriage from taking place. A relative or friend acted as surety on the bond.

If you find published transcriptions of marriage books, try to get a copy of the original record to confirm the published information. Human error does sometimes occur in transcribing. For a number of states, such as Mississippi, North Carolina, and Alabama, statewide sets of marriage transcriptions have been published in book form or on microform. Many more are now available on computer disk and CD-ROM.

Wills and Probate Records

Usually in the same clerk's office, you can look through will books and probate records. In early years, wills and deeds were sometimes recorded in the same books. Getting copies of wills and probate records, when possible, saves time and gives you valuable references for later study. If you abstract the information from the documents yourself, copy everything, especially all names, relationships, residences, dates (of the will, of probate, of inventory, of administrator reports, etc.), locations of property, conditions affecting distribution, witnesses, and the volume and page number(s) of each document. Witnesses and executors were often relatives or close friends of the deceased. Wills and other records relating to estate settlement often provide both evidence and clues in your search of cluster genealogy.

Be aware that you will seldom find a death date in old probate records and certainly not in wills. However, the information given in the will or estate settlement can be useful in narrowing down the death date possibilities. See pages 78-79 for examples of evaluating probate records for death date possibilities.

A will usually names the person's children and/or grandchildren. It is therefore proof of kinship. In the will, the testator distributes his property among his heirs and friends. You can learn such things as what property he owned, his religious beliefs, his wishes for burial, and his instructions on the division of his estate.

In characteristic style of the period, Isaac McFadden of South Carolina began his will in 1818:

> *I, Isaac McFadden, . . . feeling the firmities of old age and the wastes of disease making progressive advances upon my bodily frame, yet possessing a competent soundness of mind, do conceive it to be dutiful to make the annexed arrangement of my worldly concernments.* (Chester County, South Carolina, Wills, Book 2-G, p. 50)

In traditional order, Isaac continued in a style which shows his practicality as well as his faith. He commended his "soul to God (from whom it was received) resting on the efficacious mediation and merits of our glorious redeemer." He wished his "body to be committed to the dust in a decent and Christian manner, without parade or unnecessary expense in the hope of the resurrection from the dead, the reunion of Soul and body and the final admission of both into the abodes of bliss in the immediate presence and enjoyment of God" (*Ibid.*). After requesting the payment of debts, he divided his property among his wife and fourteen living children.

Because women's property rights, for the most part, were severely limited until the mid- to late-nineteenth century, widows often found themselves destitute and dependent on their children or the community for support. In keeping with common law and the applicable statutory law, many early wills set conditions on the wife's inheritance of her husband's estate. Some wills were more generous than the minimum "widow's third" or *dower* that the law usually provided. In 1818, Elliott Coleman incorporated one of the common limitations into his will, but the bequest of his personal estate to his widow would be considered advantageous for her and the minor children: "To my wife for whose affection and duty I owe every sence [*sic*] of gratitude and acknowledgment of a husband I give the tract of land wherein I now live and also all my personal estate *during widowhood* in order the better to enable her to support educate and advance our children . . ." (Cumberland County, Virginia, Will Bk. 7, p. 146, italics added). The provision *during widowhood* also implied *for the rest of her life, if she remained unmarried.* His personal estate included slaves, livestock, farming implements, furniture, and household goods, all of which allowed the widow to keep the farm operating and generating support for herself and her family.

A different provision is found in the will of Richard Phillips in 1793: "I lend to my beloved wife Lucy all my whole estate both real and personal excepted [*sic*] two feather beds and furniture which I shall hereafter dispose of [,] which estate I desire she may possess and enjoy *during her natural life* . . . my will and desire is that all my estate lent to my said wife be equally divided *at her death* amongst my eight children . . ." (Amelia County, Virginia, Will Bk. 5, P. 36, italics added). Since Phillips was about age 60 and his children seem to have been grown at the time of his will, he may have felt that his wife probably would not remarry and thus he felt no need to specify that the estate was hers during widowhood only.

Probate records are valuable sources of information that can give a picture of family relationships, activities, lifestyle, financial status, and even quarrels. After one's death, the estate was often inventoried. Each knife and fork, kettle and candlestick, sheep and horse, bed and chair, hoe and ax was counted and recorded. If the estate was sold, a report lists who bought each item and for how much. Other records appoint guardians for minor children and monitor their affairs.

Reports of executors or administrators often detail the income and expenses of the estate and the division of money, land, and personal property among the heirs. One example is a partial distribution from the estate of Peter T. Phillips in 1833 (Cumberland County, Virginia, Will Bk. 9, pp. 129-131). Eight male and female heirs with the name Phillips received property valued at $500 each. Because of this distribution in equal amounts, we know that they were sons and unmarried daughters of the deceased, who seems to have died intestate (without a will). No one else would have had a claim to an equal share, unless specified in a will. Others are named as "having received advancement during the life time" of the said Peter T. Phillips: Benjamin Phillips, Ferdinand G. Coleman and wife Eliza, and Newton Hazelgrove and Lucy Ann, his wife. Even without other supporting documents, you could surmise that Eliza and Lucy Ann were married daughters of Peter T. Phillips, as their husbands are named with them. If Coleman and Hazelgrove had been heirs in their own right, the wives would not have been listed. (In this case, that conclusion is supported by their marriage records, deeds, and their mother's will.) With the settlement record alone, you still would know that if they received their portion in advance, they were more than likely children, not grandchildren. In such a distribution, grandchildren would not be entitled to a share in the estate except to divide the portion due their deceased parent. In that case, their relationship is more likely to be spelled out.

See chapter thirteen for several case studies in evaluating information found in marriage, probate, and other courthouse records.

DEED AND PROPERTY RECORDS

Marriage and probate records can provide maiden names, event dates, names of children or parents, clues to relationships, and clues on age or death, from which birth or death dates can be suggested. Deeds may or may not be so specific in the information they provide, but they are extremely valuable resources and often reveal important clues. They may spell out relationships and events, as in a deed written 18 October 1810, through which Phoeby Garner, Frances Garner, Nathan Brelsford and Elizabeth Brelsford, his wife, of Kentucky, sold their interest in 244 acres in

Hampshire County, Virginia, to William Lockhart of that county (Christian County, Kentucky, Deed Bk. C, p. 133). The text stated that the three ladies, Phoeby, Frances, and Elizabeth, were daughters of Henry Garner, deceased, and each was selling her undivided seventh part of the property. From this statement, we learn that there were seven heirs and that Phoeby and Frances were probably not married, for no husband joined in the deed with either. A researcher would want to investigate the possibility that Lockhart was the husband of another sister, for heirs often sold their portions to another heir.

Another deed by the same four grantors, dated 11 October 1810, sold their interest in 384 acres in Frederick County, Virginia, to Peter Dick (Christian County, Kentucky, Deed Bk. C, p. 137). This deed adds the information that Henry Garner died intestate (without a will) and that he had bought this land originally on 6 September 1776 from Henry Garner and his wife, Jane. Was Dick the husband of another sister? Who were Henry and Jane Garner? Parents of Henry, the deceased? These deeds give both specific pieces of information and questions for further study.

These two records also contain a section customary to the period. Elizabeth, as a married woman, could not own, buy, or sell property on her own, nor could her husband sell her inheritance without her permission. The court of each Virginia county, thus, asked the court of Christian County to get from her an acknowledgment, obtained by examining her "privily and apart from her said husband whether she willingly signed and sealed the said indenture without the persuasion or threat of her said husband. . . ." The documents contained no such reference to Phoeby and Frances; the omission again suggests that they were not married at the time.

Most colonies and states, until the mid- or late-nineteenth century, adopted some form of an old English common law that a widow had the right to one-third of any land that her husband had owned during their marriage. In most cases, when a husband sold land, the buyer wanted assurance that the wife would not try to claim her third at some future date; thus, she had to relinquish this *dower right* as part of the transaction. Such documents, which may be the only evidence of a wife's name, tell us that she was alive at that date. When Abraham and Robert Whitesides of Chester County, South Carolina, sold land to Isaac McFadden in November, 1804, two ladies relinquished dower rights: Margaret Whitesides, mother of Abraham, and Janet Whitesides, wife of Abraham (Chester County Deed Bk. K, p. 266). The facts suggest to the researcher that Abraham may have inherited the land from his father since his mother was asked to relinquish her dower right to it. (The mother would not have had any such right to it if it had not belonged to her husband during their marriage.) The deed suggests that Robert was not Abraham's father since Margaret was identified as Abraham's mother, not as Robert's wife. Was Robert Abraham's brother? Was he not married since no wife was mentioned? Again, the deed gives some specific genealogical information and prompts questions for further study.

Deeds also contain potentially important information which may or may not lead to genealogical discoveries. For example, property laid out in the metes and bounds form of surveys was often described by its boundaries: *thence to a post oak at Henry Jones' southwest corner*, or *bounded on the south by Thomas Ferrel and Samuel Farris*. These men were neighbors who may have also been relatives or in-laws.

Deed books generally have two indexes: grantee index (buyers) and grantor index (sellers), sometimes called reverse and direct indexes. Use both, and look up your primary surname in that county, as well as other names known or thought to be related. Realize that indexes can contain errors and omissions. Watch for index entries which add *et al.* (and others) after a name; it often signals a group of heirs selling land they inherited. Write down (or get a copy of) all information given in the documents: date of the instrument, date of the filing, date that the seller's wife relinquished her dower rights, date that a wife was examined on her willingness to sell, buyer(s) and seller(s) and their residences, price and other considerations, size and location of the property, witnesses, signatures or marks, any other names mentioned, such as neighbors, and volume and page numbers for each document. Witnesses, like neighbors, often were relatives.

Deeds are written primarily to transfer ownership of land, buildings, or, before 1865, slaves. Warranty deeds, deeds of gift, and deeds of trust are probably the most common types of use to genealogists. The foregoing examples were warranty deeds, also called simply *deeds*, which transfer property with the assurance of a good title.

Deeds of gift frequently were made by a parent to a child, with the key words "for and in consideration of the Natural Love and Affection he hath and bears unto his son. . . ." Many parents distributed their property among their children in this manner, instead of or in addition to a will.

Deeds of trust were made by one paying off a mortgage or one in debt who was trying to pay off creditors. When Elliott G. Coleman of Hardeman County, Tennessee, executed a deed of trust to his brother and another man in 1867, he listed all his property of value, which was to be sold at auction if he could not pay his debts within one year. As the genealogist wanting to identify Elliott's parents, hardly knowing where to begin, and having no clues except that Elliott was born in Virginia, I was ecstatic when I read in that deed of trust "all interest I have in [the] real and personal estate of my late father Ferdinand G. Coleman, dec'd, late of Cumberland County, Virginia" (Hardeman County, Tennessee, Deed Bk. U, p. 56). An experience that turned into a nightmare for Elliott, because he was unable to pay the debts, became, for his descendants, a genealogical gold mine. The discovery reaffirmed for me these rules of genealogical research: to work from the known to the unknown, not to skip back in time too soon, but to gather clues from one generation's records before trying to move to the previous one.

Deed books in a county courthouse may include a number of legal instruments other than deeds, including bills of sale, prenuptial agreements, powers of attorney, contracts, affidavits, wills, and even voter and jury lists. Except for these lists, the documents usually were created because of the involvement of property between individuals.

Two helpful books for the study of property are these:

1. *Inheritance in America From Colonial Times to the Present*. Carole Shammas, Marylynn Salmon, and Michael Dahlin. New Brunswick, NJ: Rutgers University Press, 1987.

2. *Women and the Law of Property in Early America*. Marylynn Salmon. Chapel Hill, NC: The University of North Carolina Press, 1986.

The following is a rather typical warranty deed. Underlining is added to show what a researcher needs to abstract when taking notes.

(Christian County, Kentucky, Deed Bk. C, p. 191)

This Indenture made the 13th day of May 1811 between Nathan Brelsford and Elizabeth Brelsford his wife of the one part and Garvener Stuart of the other part all of the county of Christian and State of Kentucky witnesseth that the aforesaid Nathan Brelsford and Elizabeth his wife, for and in consideration of the sum of three hundred dollars to them in hand paid the receipt whereof is hereby acknowledged have granted bargained sold aliened and confirmed unto the aforesaid Garvener Stuart a certain tract or parcel of land containing one hundred and twenty five acres be the same more or less situated lying and being in the county and state aforesaid on the waters of the east fork of little river originally granted by the county court of Christian to Joseph Cravens in February 1802 by survey bearing date the 16th day of March 1803 and patented to the said Brelsford the 15th day of December 1810 and bounded as follows [copy the description] *to wit beginning at a post oak in Cravens line thence with it south sixty five west one hundred and twelve poles to two post oaks, thence south thirty west one hundred and twenty five poles to a black oak sappling thence south fifty east one hundred and fifty poles to a black oak on a . . .[?] thence north nine east two hundred and fifty poles to the beginning to have and to hold the aforesaid tract of land with all and singular the appurtenances thereunto immediately belonging or that may hereafter belong to the only proper use benefit and behoof of him the aforesaid Garvener Stuart his heirs and assigns forever from ourselves our heirs and assigns forever and the aforesaid Nathan Brelsford and Elizabeth his wife for themselves their heirs and assigns doth covenant and agree to and with the aforesaid Garvener Stuart his heirs and assigns that the aforesaid tract of land and bargained premises they will forever warrant and defend unto the said Garvener Stuart his heirs and assigns free from any claim or demand whatever from themselves their heirs and assigns and from all persons and manner of persons whatsoever claiming In witness whereof the said Nathan Brelsford and Elizabeth his wife have hereunto set their hands and seals the day and year first above written in presence of* [left blank—no witnesses given]

Nathan Brelsford [signature] *(seal)*
Elizabeth Brelsford [signature] *(seal)*
At Christian County Court, June 18th, 1811

/Wife Elizabeth voluntarily relinquishes her dower right at this time./

Researchers of United States land records need to know the difference between public land states and state land states. The original thirteen states plus Vermont, Maine, West Virginia, Kentucky, Tennessee, Hawaii, and Texas originally had ownership and control of their own land and the authority to transfer ownership to others. Records of such transfers are found in the state and county records. The remaining states are public land states because the federal government first acquired and owned the land. Thus, records of the initial transfer of ownership from the federal government to private hands are federal records, accessible through the land office tract books. (See page 70.) Subsequent sales of each piece of land were recorded in county deed books because those sales were no longer the jurisdiction of the federal government.

Other Courthouse Records

Courthouses have additional records which genealogists may find helpful, including birth and death registrations, property tax lists, various court records, divorce records, voter registrations, and others. Sometimes, courthouses become storage places for school records, school censuses, newspapers, manuscript county histories, and other gems. Most of these volumes, whether generated or stored at the courthouse, are not usually indexed, with the exception of birth, death and divorce records.

Each state has a somewhat different procedure for birth and death registration. Thus, the county clerk or other courthouse office may or may not have these records, and you may or may not have access to them. Most states have only scattered birth or death records until the late 1800s or early 1900s. Birth certificates may furnish such genealogical information as the child's name, race and sex, birth date and place, parents' names and birthplaces, and sometimes the mother's maiden name. It is useful to gather siblings' birth registrations because specifics on the parents sometimes differ from one entry to another. Ask also about the whereabouts of delayed birth certificates. These are exactly what the name says: registrations filed years later by those who were not registered at birth. Supporting documents for delayed certificates are usually returned to the registrant, not kept by the county or state.

Death records may provide the same facts as birth registrations, plus the cause, date, time and place of death, place and date of the burial, the name of the funeral home and doctor, the name of the informant (usually a relative), and the Social Security number for those who died after 1936 and who had registered with that administration. Remember that the birth information supplied on a death certificate may or may not be correct, depending on the memory or knowledge of the informant.

In large cities, these records are often kept by the city health or vital statistics office instead of by the county. Birth and death certificates and sometimes marriage records may also be obtained from the state vital statistics office in the capital city. Two very helpful source books for this kind of information are (1) *Where to Write for Vital Records: Births, Deaths, Marriages, and Divorces* (Hyattsville, MD: U.S. Department of Health and Human Services, Public Health Service, 1993 or latest edition), and (2) *International Vital Records Handbook*, Thomas J. Kemp, comp. (Baltimore: Genealogical Publishing Company, 1994 or later edition).

Some counties keep old property tax records; some keep them only twenty or thirty years. Often the older records are stored in basements, attics, warehouse space, or an old jail. If you can find these tax records, you may learn what part of the county the family lived in, possibly who their neighbors were, and what taxable property each family owned, such as land, horses, cattle, carriages, clocks, or, before 1865, slaves. Appearance on the tax lists can give you clues to when a man became 21 (and began owing taxes) or died (and ceased to appear on the list), or when the family moved into or out of the county. If, for example, census records suggest they moved away between 1870 and 1880 and you find them last in 1875 in the tax records, you can guess they moved in 1875 or 1876.

Court records, including dockets, minute books, and case files, give information on civil and criminal justice cases. Ask in your courthouse for the court clerk's office with divorce records, as each state has its own system. The minute books may also contain estate divisions; jury lists and pay records; evidence of local residents hired to do contract work for the county; evidence of naturalization of new citizens; licensing fees paid by local taverns, ferries, lawyers, and medical professionals; registration of livestock marks and brands; and grand jury bills charging local citizens with law violations. In some counties, these items of county court business were noted in the minute book but the records themselves were written in separate volumes marked *Juror Records, Divorces, Naturalizations, Marks and Brands*, etc. Court records, like tax records, may be hard to find and time-consuming to use, but they sometimes prove not only very interesting but also valuable in solving genealogical problems.

County clerks' offices and storage shelves sometimes contain miscellaneous volumes and papers of historical interest and potential genealogical value. These may be business ledgers which later became county record books and, thus, contain entries from both uses. They may be papers of an early judge. They may be original documents salvaged from a courthouse fire. In one Kentucky courthouse, I found a group of very old, neat little bundles, tied with string. They were actual polling lists of which men voted for which candidates in congressional and presidential elections dating back to the 1820s! (Remember, they had no secret ballot as we know it.)

County courthouse offices sometimes answer queries by mail and sometimes do not. If you choose to try to get information by mail, make your request short, easy to read, concise, to the point, and accompanied by a self-addressed, stamped envelope. Limit your request to something that can be handled quickly: "In working on family history, I am looking for a marriage record about 1797-1803 for Samuel Black and Keturah Shaw. Do you have such a record? If so, what is the cost of obtaining a copy?"

Louisiana is organized into parishes rather than counties and, due to its Spanish and French roots, operates under civil law rather than the English common law tradition of the other states. One unique aspect of the civil law system is the office of notary in each parish. Since the early eighteenth century, notaries have drawn up, witnessed and preserved a multitude of documents that form an important resource for genealogists. Centralized and housed since 1867 in the New Orleans Notarial Archives (421 Loyola Avenue), these documents are items of legal and personal business, including wills, marriage contracts, business agreements, estate inventories, partitions and sales of estates and businesses, mortgages, slave sales and emancipations, and records of family meetings. (In Louisiana, family meetings are held on behalf of minor heirs before a sale of estate property or to protect the interests of the minors before the remarriage of the surviving parent.) The Notarial Archives do not contain litigation or adversarial court proceedings; the purpose of the documents is contractual. The records involve primarily Louisiana residents but also some from other states. A genealogist planning to research in the Archives needs to do preliminary work in the family's parish of residence to try to determine the name of the notary or notaries the family may have used, as there is no general index.

LOCAL PUBLIC LIBRARIES

Public libraries are generally centers for more secondary research sources than primary sources. That is, they do not contain many original records, but copies or abstracts of them. It is best to use the primary sources whenever possible, but they are not always accessible. So, most genealogists use a combination of the primary and secondary sources.

Some public libraries have set aside an entire wing or room for their genealogy collection. Smaller libraries may have one section of shelves for these materials. Some maintain a "vertical file" in which local families or their descendants can place their Bible records, family papers, and family history charts for other searchers to use. Occasionally the public library is the depository for back issues of the local newspapers and local archives. Of course, there are public libraries with large and extensive genealogy collections. Some of these are included in Appendix C for your convenience.

Most public libraries cannot handle genealogical research by correspondence. In many libraries, the staff is not trained to do genealogical searching, and in most libraries, the staff simply cannot take the time to answer all the requests they would receive if they offered such a service. However, you may want to inquire whether they have genealogical records and periodicals, family papers, back issues of local newspapers, and local or county history, including cemetery inscriptions, census transcriptions, or church records. This information can help you plan a visit to the area.

Another way to find out about libraries in your research area is to consult the *American Library Directory* in your own public library. They are fascinating volumes which describe each library, state by state. They can tell you if your chosen public or college library has a special genealogy or local history section or collects church archives or local newspapers. The directory could also inform you of a genealogical or historical society library which could be helpful in your search.

When you visit your ancestral hometowns, include a stop at the local public library. You may be pleasantly surprised at what you can accomplish there, and you may be able to contribute to their holdings. To make the most efficient use of your research time in the library or county courthouse, make a list of the sources you want to use and the information you hope to find.

If the historical and genealogical material in the library is extensive, the library catalog can tell you what sources they have on your research area. The genealogical materials are often cross-referenced: (1) under the *subject*, i.e., cemeteries, census, deeds, genealogy, history, indexes, inventory of church archives, inventory of county records, archives, manuscripts, immigration, microfilm holdings, militia, tax lists, naturalization, passenger lists, wills, newspapers, etc.; and (2) under the *name* of the city, county, state, family, or country to which they pertain.

LOCAL SCHOOLS AND COLLEGES

If you know or can learn which school or college a particular ancestor attended, you have a variety of additional sources, often in the institution's library or archives, from which to learn about his or her life: the school yearbook, newspaper, or literary magazine; school catalogs and information bulletins; a school history or scrapbook of clippings; graduation programs; departmental records; faculty and/or student lists; and transcripts.

The federal privacy law of 1974 has restricted our access to transcripts. For the most part, only the student himself can now request copies of his transcript. If your older relatives are agreeable and if you are interested in transcripts as a part of the family history, it might be wise to request them while these former students are living. The handling of records of deceased students, especially one's ancestors, is not clear in the law. Some schools will not release records of deceased students without a court order, which is expensive. One college sent me a copy of my great-grandmother's transcript without delay. Another university refused to send my deceased grandfather's record without his signature! They finally released the transcript when my grandmother, as executor of his estate, although no longer able to sign her own name, made her very feeble mark on a request as witnessed by a third relative who had power of attorney over her affairs. You should contact the school in which you are interested to learn what its policy is.

Sources of Education Information About an Ancestor:

- Local newspaper stories about schools, teachers, sports, graduation, contests, school-sponsored programs and activities.
- History of city, county, school or college; student or alumni lists.
- Family letters, diaries, scrapbooks.
- Interviews with older relatives and family friends.
- 1850 and later censuses asked which children attended school during the year and whether each adult could read and write.
- 1890 and later censuses recorded whether each individual could speak English.
- Wills or estate settlements or guardian accounts, which sometimes mention tuition and schooling for the children.
- Wills, deeds and other documents which show whether each party could sign his own name or had to sign with his "mark." (Of course, if a person signed his name to some documents and signed his will or later deeds with his mark, the change would suggest blindness or other infirmity rather than a lack of schooling.)

LOCAL CHURCHES

Occasionally local institutions maintain records old enough to be of use to genealogists. When you find records from an ancestor's church, you may find dates for baptisms, confirmations, marriages, deaths, removals, transfers in or out; names of parents or children; and perhaps minutes of the governing body.

Local church records are not always easy to find. If you know which church your ancestral family attended, then ask the pastor, secretary, a lay leader, or officer in the church whether there are records from the period you are interested in and where you might find them. A few state-level or regional church offices maintain archives. A diocese office sometimes stores older Catholic or Episcopalian records; a conference office may have Methodist archives. In some cases, the individual church simply stores or discards their records as they choose, or as the pastor chooses. In one Texas Methodist church, the preacher's wife got tired of storing "that old junk" at the parsonage and burned it all, including my mother's baptism record, which she had hoped to use in proving her existence in order to get a delayed birth certificate.

Other congregations have their own ex-officio historian who keeps the old record books. Some store their files in the church office or in a bank vault. A number of libraries, especially at church-affiliated colleges and universities, have church history or archives collections, which may contain records from individual congregations. If you find no church records in the town where your ancestors lived, you might try the closest denomination college or office.

Small rural Methodist, Baptist, and Presbyterian congregations who had circuit rider preachers may have had no records in the first place beyond the preacher's own register, which his family or descendants may or may not have saved.

A number of church records have been published, including many Episcopalian, or Anglican, church vestry books and parish registers from the colonial and early national periods, and many Quaker records. Gravestone inscriptions from individual churchyards and records of early congregations appear occasionally in genealogical periodicals. Check the index or contents of such periodicals from your research locale.

The Religious Society of Friends began about 1644, and hundreds of its members, called Quakers, came to the British colonies during the seventeenth and eighteenth centuries. The majority arrived at Philadelphia and spread southward through the Shenandoah Valley and eventually into the Northwest Territories. Thanks to the founder, George Fox, who required each local "meeting" to keep detailed records, genealogists today have a wealth of records to search for vital statistics and migrations of Quaker ancestors. The best source of such information is the records of the monthly meetings, which list births, marriages, deaths, transfers, committee reports, infractions of the rules, and members "disowned" for marrying a non-Quaker (marrying "out of unity") or being married "contrary to discipline" (being married by a civil servant or minister of another denomination).

Because the Quakers did not believe in rituals, their "weddings" were not ceremonies; nor did they have baptisms or funerals or tombstones. They did not enter military service or leave personal and financial records. Yet, it is possible to find them in census records and sometimes in tax, land, probate, and court records in county courthouses.

In order to use the Quaker records, you must know where your Quaker ancestors lived and to which monthly meeting they belonged. Civil records may help you locate your ancestors in a county and town so that you can identify their monthly meetings.

Some records of monthly meetings in North Carolina, Pennsylvania, Virginia, and Ohio have been published: *Encyclopedia of American Quaker Genealogy*, 6 volumes, by William Wade Hinshaw, 1950, originally distributed by Friends Book and Supply House, Richmond, Indiana. These volumes are available at many genealogical libraries. The Friends Historical Library at Swarthmore College, Swarthmore, Pennsylvania, has the largest collection of Quaker records. See Appendix C for other Quaker collections. For a thorough discussion of searching for Quaker ancestors, see *Our Quaker Ancestors: Finding Them in Quaker Records* by Ellen T. and David A. Berry (Baltimore: Genealogical Publishing Company, 1987).

The most unusual aspect of Quaker meeting records is their notation of dates. Until 1752, Britain and the American colonies, and therefore the Quakers, officially used the old Julian calendar, under which each new year began on March 25. (See pages 88-89 for a more complete discussion of the calendars.) Under the "old style" calendar, March was the first month; April, the second, and so forth. The Latin names of the months called September, October, November, and December correspond to their places in the year as the seventh, eighth, ninth, and tenth months. Because the names of the other months were derived from pagan origins, the Quakers chose to substitute numbers for the names of the months in their records. They usually listed the day, then the month, then the year, as much of the world still does, but in their own style: *12da 5mo*, or 12th day of the 5th month, which was July under the Julian calendar but May under the "new style" Gregorian calendar. The chart on page 58 compares the Julian and Gregorian dates, using the Quaker style of writing them.

Here are some other sources for church records:

1. State historical society collections, state archives, state libraries. Ask in your research area.

2. Catalogs of the American Genealogical Lending Library and the Family History Library, Salt Lake City. (See Interlibrary Loan page 60.)

3. *Directory of Archives and Manuscript Repositor-*

Date as written in a record book	*Date under "old style" Julian calendar*	*Date under "new style" Gregorian calendar*
12da 5mo*	12 July	12 May
1da 10mo	1 December	1 October
29da 1mo 1703	29 March 1703	29 January 1703
7da Feby 1728/29**	7 February 1728	7 February 1729
1da 11mo 1750 O.S.	1 January 1750	(O.S. applies only to the Julian calendar.)

*When only the number of the month is given, you cannot know which name it stands for until you know which calendar was in use.

**The dual dating of the year applies only to January, February, and March. After March 25, the year was the same under both calendars.

To find out which church or denomination . . .

- Interview older relatives, family friends.
- Read family letters, diaries, scrapbooks, funeral cards, wedding announcements or invitations. Funerals and weddings often, but not always, took place at the family's church, as did special anniversary celebrations.
- Check the family Bibles, especially the register page, a gift inscription, bookplate, or identification information.
- Read the local columns of contemporary newspapers, where you may learn who attended the Presbyterian ice cream social or who organized the Catholic bazaar, or where you may find a family wedding or anniversary story or obituary which identifies their church.
- Read marriage records, estate settlements, deeds. These can mention where events took place, which ministers performed their ceremonies and services, gifts they made to churches, church officers conducting church business.
- Check county and church histories for lists of members, officers, families.
- Search church records of your research area whenever you find them.

ies in the United States. 2nd ed. Phoenix, AZ: Oryx Press, 1988.

4. *The Genealogist's Companion & Sourcebook.* Emily Croom. Cincinnati: Betterway Books, 1994. Chapter 6.

5. *Guide to Archives and Manuscripts in the United States.* Philip M. Hamer, ed. New Haven, CT: Yale University Press, 1961.

6. *National Union Catalog of Manuscript Collections.* Washington, DC: Library of Congress, 1990. P. xl under *Religion* lists reporting repositories 1975-1990.

7. *Preliminary Guide to Church Records Repositories.* August R. Suelflow. St. Louis [now Chicago]: Society of American Archivists, 1969.

8. *A Survey of American Church Records.* 4th ed. E. Kay Kirkham. Logan, UT: Everton Publishers, Inc., 1978.

9. *The Vital Record Compendium.* John D. Stemmons and E. Diane Stemmons, comp. Logan, UT: Everton Publishers, Inc., 1979.

10. *Yearbook of American and Canadian Churches.* Nashville: Abingdon Press, latest edition.

11. Works Progress Administration inventories of church records or other such inventories, found in libraries and archives. In research libraries, consult library catalog under *state name—church records.* Ask reference librarian for assistance if necessary.

CHECKLIST OF LOCAL SOURCES

In searching for your family history, you are the judge of what you want to accomplish and how extensive your search will be. You may decide simply to fill in your charts with basic vital statistics on most lines while you study only one at a time in depth.

Of the many local sources available to genealogists, perhaps only a few will give you information on a particular ancestor. You may find newspapers that enlighten you on two ancestral families, church records for three others, and school records for only one. It would be unrealistic to expect to find information in all these sources for all your ancestors. Of course, some searchers gather only vital statistics for each ancestor (date and place of birth, marriage, and death, and spouse's name); they don't really collect family history. Consequently, they may never try many of the available sources, and they miss out on a lot of fun. Likewise, some searchers, by preference or necessity, do not visit the local hometowns where so much information is often found. They too miss a lot of fun and satisfaction, as well as information, for much of the local data is not available elsewhere.

The checklist presented here does not cover all possible sources but is intended as a guide to the most commonly available local sources in the community or county where the ancestor lived.

1. Cemeteries (tombstones).
2. Funeral home files.
3. Elders in the community: for their stories; memories; directions to and descriptions of houses, buildings, and cemeteries.
4. Newspaper files or microfilm copies in local, state, historical society or university libraries; archives in local or regional area.
5. County courthouse, especially county court clerk, circuit court clerk, or registrar's office:
   a. Marriage records
   b. Birth records, death records
   c. Wills, inventories, estate settlements, estate sales records, guardianship records, orphans' court and other probate court records
   d. Deeds, mortgages
   e. Tax lists
   f. Various court minute books, case files
   g. Polling lists, license and professional fee books, registration of livestock brands, etc.
6. City vital statistics registry at health department or registrar's office; duplicates at the state level.
7. Church registers, vestry books, and other religious archives.
8. Papers of families or businesses of ancestor's community on deposit in local, state, historical society, university libraries or archives.
9. Local school records, college records and publications.
10. Local historians or local historical society.
11. Local genealogical library or public library with genealogy and/or local history collection.
12. Local genealogists or genealogical society.
13. Published county or city history, especially one with biographical sketches. Goodspeed Bros. of Chicago and Nashville published a number of these as state histories with county by county biographies, mostly in the 1880s. Many of the county history and biography sections have been reprinted in recent years or microfilmed.
14. City archives: tax rolls, law enforcement records, city censuses, etc.

As you prepare to visit libraries, archives, or courthouses, you may find it helpful to use a Quick Reference Chart, as shown in Figure 11, page 61. Not only can this chart serve as an index to your five-generation and family group charts, but it can also be a guide to each state, county, or region in which you are searching. As shown in Figure 11, page 61, a search in South Carolina records can be more efficient and more thorough with a Quick Reference Chart of your various South Carolina families. The example also lists ancestors from North Carolina counties who had South Carolina spouses or who have shown up in South Carolina records because they lived close to the border.

As you search for the ancestors of your primary interest, you may find other names which "ring a bell." Rather than copy a lot of information simply because it pertains to someone of the same surname as one of yours, refer to your chart. If your William Richardson lived in South Carolina in the mid-1700s, there's little reason to copy information about a William Richardson born in South Carolina in 1873. Especially for those families, such as Richardsons, Pattons, McFaddens, Bufords, Culps, and Gastons, who are numerous in South Carolina records, it is valuable to have at your fingertips the information on your specific ancestor so that you don't spend time unnecessarily "barking up the wrong tree."

It may prove advantageous to write down all the

information you find about contemporaries of your ancestor who had the same surname if it is rather unusual. They may or may not be related to you in the long run, but it's generally easier to get the information the first time than to keep rereading your sources.

It is wise to write down all information you find about people of the same name and time period and place as one of your ancestors. Certainly, not all the early eighteenth-century eastern Virginia deeds bearing the name Daniel Coleman belonged to the same man, but studying all available information may help the family historian sort them out. In the late eighteenth century, numerous families were named Black and Shaw. In looking for Blacks or Shaws, somewhere in North Carolina, you may run across many Black or Shaw families scattered over many counties. You may need to gather information about several of the families who lived at the same time in an effort to narrow down the search for your particular group.

INTERLIBRARY LOAN

You may be able to obtain considerable information on your research area by renting books or microfilm on interlibrary loan. Many public libraries offer this service to their local patrons at a nominal fee. If you provide accurate title, author, and publication information, including page numbers if applicable, your reference librarian can do the rest. If you do not know what is available from your research area, consult one of the lending libraries listed below or contact the state library, historical society, or university library in your research area for a listing of their interlibrary loan materials. Some state archives, state libraries, or historical societies make microfilm copies of county records, censuses, or newspapers available to researchers in their own state; some lend microfilm to out-of-state genealogists.

The following are some of the institutions which lend or rent genealogical materials:

1. American Genealogical Lending Library (AGLL), P.O. Box 244, Bountiful, UT 84011. An annual membership fee allows rental privileges from a large catalog of microform materials and discounts on purchases. The catalog includes much National Archives microfilm, county records, local histories, cemetery records, and some periodicals.

2. Family History Library, 35 North West Temple St., Salt Lake City, UT 84150. Rental from this vast collection is handled through hundreds of family history centers. Look in your telephone directory under Church of Jesus Christ of Latter-day Saints for a center in your area. The catalog includes censuses, county histories and records, church and cemetery records, family histories, and much more.

3. Genealogical Center Library, P.O. Box 71343, Marietta, GA 30007-1343. An annual membership fee gives you access to their sizeable collection of books only, with the largest concentration being for states east of the Mississippi River.

4. National Archives Microfilm Rental Program, P.O. Box 30, Annapolis Junction, MD 20701-0030. This private company rents federal population census schedules and selected American Revolutionary War records.

5. National Genealogical Society, 4527 17th Street North, Arlington, VA 22207-2363. Members may borrow selected books from the society library. Inquire for current catalog price.

6. New England Historic Genealogical Society, 101 Newbury, Boston, MA 02116. Members may borrow selected materials from their large library, which is especially strong on New England materials.

7. Mid-Continent Public Library, Spring and Highway 24, Independence, MO 64050. Catalog available.

8. Hoenstine Rental Library, P.O. Box 208, Hollidaysburg, PA 16648.

WHEN YOU TRAVEL

When you travel to ancestors' counties for research, you might want to contact a Texas-based guest room exchange network called Visiting Friends, Inc., P.O. Box 231, Lake Jackson, TX 77566. Begun by genealogists, the network has members, most of whom are genealogists themselves, in more than 100 locations in the United States and several in Canada and England. For a small lifetime membership fee and a nominal fee for each guest-visit, members have the privilege of staying in private homes when they travel and of being hosts to other genealogists or sightseers in return.

The purpose of the organization is "to introduce people of similar interests, to enable them to meet new friends in other places who will offer a safe private home for them to visit while they research or sightsee." To protect the privacy of members, no directory of names and addresses is published. Visits and exchanges are arranged through the office, considering the preferences and needs of both guests and hosts.

QUICK REFERENCE—ALPHABETICAL ANCESTORS

Surname or Maiden Name	Given Name	Birth Year	Death Year	Primary Residence	Location on 5-Gen. Chart	Family Group
North & South Carolina						
Blalock	Millington	1741	1827	Granville Co NC ?	5	
"	William	1764/69		m 1795 NC ? Granville Co	5	
Buford	William	1747	1810-11	c 1765 Williamsburg Dist	3	Richard son
Garner					McKennon	
Hitchcock	Hester			b SC m Daniel Jaggers	4	"
Jaggers	Daniel		1808	b SC d Hardin Co KY	4	"
"	Mary (Polly)			m John McBride	4	"
Judah	Daniel?	1790-1800		b SC Dale Co Ala	Metcalf	
"	Henry/John			b SC Dale Co Ala		"
Lea	Rosanna's father			1812- Johnston Co NC	5 Blalock	
Lee	John			Jones Co NC	28 McFadden	
"	Fanny			m James Steele	28	
Metcalf				Rutherford Co NC		C.W.M.
McBride	John	1791	1857	NC? Maury Co Tenn	4	
McFadden	Isaac	1753/4	1820	Chester Co SC	28	
"	Candor?	c1727			28	
MacFarlane	Alexander	Manchester Eng		Via Nova Scotia Charleston 1798	2	
McKennon	William	17__	17__	SC	4	
"	John	1745	1801	1801 Chester Co SC	4	
"	Elizabeth	1750	1845	1801 Chester Co SC	4	
Patton	Thomas	1794	1852	Chester/York SC Fayette Co Tenn	28	
Richardson	William	1743 Va	1786	m 1768 Charleston d Clarendon Co SC	2	Mood
Steele	Alexander		1752	wife-Mary Onslow Co NC	28	
"	Peter		1792	wife-Martha Jones Co NC	28	

FIG. 11: QUICK REFERENCE CHART

CHAPTER TWELVE

Beyond the Family: State and Federal Sources

Examining family and local sources often gives genealogists much of the information they seek. However, records of individuals are created at each level of government. Thus, genealogists have significant sources available at the state and federal levels as well. These differ from county and local records and from each other because they were created for different purposes.

CHECKLIST OF STATE SOURCES

Just as local sources will not always be available or practical to search, so state sources may be limited. You will not be able to use all these sources in all states or for all your ancestors, but they could help you determine a period or place of residence, a place or date of birth, or other significant information.

Some of these sources may be available at county courthouses or within the appropriate state agency, but older records will probably be in a state library, state archives collection, university library or state historical society library. If the records have been microfilmed or published, you may find them at university, public or genealogy libraries. (See Appendix C for a listing of libraries and archives.)

A number of state and university archives depositories have published guides to their holdings and update them periodically. The guide can be an extremely useful tool to own if your research is concentrated in a particular state. Here are some sources to check:

1. Colonial, territorial, or state census records. Many of the states have had one or more state-prescribed censuses. Many of these name only heads of households and group family members by ages or sex; others give everyone's name, age, occupation, birthplace, etc. (See Appendix E for more about these records.)

2. State land records (primarily in the state-land states), including Revolutionary War or other bounty land warrants issued by the states. State-land states include the original thirteen and Kentucky, Tennessee, West Virginia, Hawaii, Maine, Vermont and Texas. In these states, land was originally held by the royal, colonial or other parent government. (Original land records of the public-land states are at the Bureau of Land Management [see page 70], the National Archives, and sometimes at a state land office.)

3. Correspondence of colonial, territorial, or state officials which sometimes deals with individuals, such as your ancestors, and their problems or achievements.

4. Indian records, especially in Oklahoma, pertaining to the Five Civilized Tribes. Contact the Oklahoma Historical Society or the University of Oklahoma Western History Collection for their holdings, which include copies of National Archives records. See pages 71-72 for more information on Indian records.

5. Tax rolls, from county or from state assessments.

6. State pension records. (Revolutionary War pension applications which were denied may be in the county court minutes.) State pensions granted to Revolutionary War veterans and widows as well as claims against the state for losses incurred during the Revolutionary War. Confederate veteran and widow pensions from the Civil War (former Confederate states only). It was possible for a Confederate veteran to apply for a pension from the southern state in which he lived after the war. If he moved to another southern state, he could apply again in his new residence. Of course, not all who were qualified for pensions applied for them.

7. State militia rolls and records.

8. Pay warrants issued by the state.

9. Vehicle registrations and drivers' licenses.

10. Voter registrations, poll tax records.

11. Cattle brand registers (sometimes in county courthouses).

12. Records of state law enforcement, public safety, residential or correctional institutions.

13. In the South, Confederate records, both civil and military. Many of these records were copied by the federal government in their attempt to identify all those who were guilty of treason against the U.S. by their participation in and support of the Confederate cause, 1861-65. The National Archives has on microfilm the *Unfiled Papers of Civil War Soldiers* and a master index, *Consolidated Index to Compiled Service Records of Confederate Soldiers.*

14. Vital statistics registry, primarily birth and death records at the state level. (Marriage, birth, and death records are often available in the counties.) Birth and death certificates are usually available at the Department of Public Health or Bureau of Vital Statistics. To locate these records, consult (1) *Where to Write for Vital Records: Births, Deaths, Marriages, and Divorces* (Hyattsville, MD: U.S. Department of Health & Human Services, 1993 or latest edition), available from Superintendent of Documents, U.S. Government Printing Office, Washington, DC 20402, or from a U.S. Government Bookstore in large cities, or (2) *International Vital Records Handbook*, Thomas Kemp, comp. (Baltimore: Genealogical Publishing Company, 1994 or later edition).

15. Other state agencies, such as state hospitals, departments of education, state courts.

16. County records which may have been transferred to or copied by the state archives.

17. Family and business papers which may be housed at state or university archives. Ask about an index or guide to the manuscript holdings. An index might show your ancestor's name. A guide might show papers or records from his hometown, school, church, employer, or an organization to which he belonged.

18. Colonial government and Revolutionary War records, many of which were copied by the federal government to replace and reconstruct records destroyed in an 1805 fire in the War Department and in the 1814 burning of the Capitol and looting of War and Treasury Departments, which held the Revolutionary War records, by the British.

19. Miscellaneous records: memorials and petitions to the state legislature, election records, charters granted by the state, interments in the state cemetery, notary public files, bonds and oaths of office. For the former Confederate States (except Tennessee), amnesty applications and oaths, and 1867 voter lists.

FEDERAL SOURCES

The National Archives and Records Administration is the home of millions of records of individuals and their dealings with the United States government. These include such items as military service and pension records, naturalization papers, ships' passenger lists, passports, land-entry case files, homestead and bounty land warrant records, Indian annual census rolls, and census schedules.

Two pamphlets which are helpful in learning about the archives' holdings and services are free upon request from the National Archives, Washington, DC 20408:

1. *Using Records in the National Archives for Genealogical Research.* General Information Leaflet #5.
2. *Military Service Records in the National Archives.* General Information Leaflet #7.

A much more comprehensive survey of the records in the National Archives is the book *Guide to Genealogical Research in the National Archives* (Washington, DC: National Archives Trust Fund Board, 1985). Another useful resource is *National Archives Microfilm Resources for Research: A Comprehensive Catalog* (Washington, DC: National Archives Trust Fund Board, 1990).

Scattered throughout the country are branches of the National Archives which hold regional records and microfilm copies of some records stored in Washington. Write to the one in your research locale to learn what they have that may help you in your search. (See Appendix D for their addresses.)

Federal Census Records

Perhaps the most valuable of the federal records for the greatest number of genealogists is the federal census. Whenever I learn the names of "new" ancestors, I like to find them in a census record as soon as possible, as if this record makes them real people. The census is a good place to begin your use of public records.

The United States census is a list of families and individuals living in each county of each state. It has been compiled every ten years since 1790, mainly for the purpose of determining population in order to apportion representation in Congress. One day in each census year has been designated census day. The enumeration began that day, and its report was to be correct as of that day. Each household was to include all persons living at the house on that day, regardless of when the census taker actually visited. Persons who died after census day but before the census taker came were to be listed as if they were still alive. Babies born after census day were to be omitted!

Census Day 1790-1940

1790, 1800, 1810	Apparently the first Monday in August
1820	First Monday in August (August 7)
1830, 1840, 1850, 1860, 1870, 1880, 1890, 1900	June 1
1880—Indian Schedule	October 1
1910	April 15
1920	January 1
1930, 1940	April 1

Through 1840, only the head of each household was named, and the other members, both slave and free, were grouped by age, sex, and race. Beginning in 1850, each individual was named, or listed by initials, with age, sex, race, occupation, birthplace, ability to read or write, schooling during the year, and infirmities, such as blindness or deafness.

The slave census schedules for 1850 and 1860 are separate from the general population schedules. Many libraries have microfilm copies of these schedules, and they can be purchased from the National Archives. The records contain the slave owner's name and the age and sex of each slave. The slaves were listed by number rather than by name in almost all cases.

The 1890 census was almost completely destroyed by fire. However, some fragments exist for families in Alabama, Georgia, Illinois, Minnesota, New Jersey, New York, North Carolina, Ohio, South Dakota, Texas, and the District of Columbia. [See *The Genealogists's Companion & Sourcebook*, by Emily Croom (Cincinnati: Betterway Books, 1994) for a more comprehensive list.] Between 1880 and 1900, some states took their own censuses, which form useful substitutes for the missing 1890 census. Optional federal censuses were made in 1885 in Colorado, Florida, Nebraska, New Mexico Territory, and Dakota Territory. In addition, part of an 1890 special census of Union Army veterans and widows exists, mostly for states alphabetically from Louisiana through Wyoming, Oklahoma and Indian Territory, and for naval stations and vessels. Fragments remain for California, Connecticut, Delaware, Florida, Idaho, Illinois, Indiana, Kansas, Kentucky, New York, and the District of Columbia.

The 1900 census is the only one to include each person's month and year of birth. The 1900 and 1910 censuses asked the number of children born to the mother, the number of her children still living, and how long each couple had been married. All censuses through 1920 are open to the public.

Between 1850 and 1880, supplemental census schedules were made. I call these the AIMS schedules: agriculture, industry, mortality, and social statistics. The agriculture schedules report farmers' answers to questions on acreage, crops, livestock, and products. The manufacturing and industrial schedules report on products, raw materials, employees and their wages, means of production, and income. These two censuses do not contain basic genealogical information but reveal interesting history. The social statistics, likewise, are not genealogical but historical, on such institutions as libraries, schools, newspapers, and churches in each community and information such as wages for different classes of workers.

The mortality schedules, however, are genealogical in nature. They report the name and age of persons who died within the year prior to the regular census, the month of death within that year, and cause of death. Because these schedules include only those persons whose families reported their deaths to the census takers, there are omissions. The supplemental schedules are available in a variety of places, predominantly major research libraries and the state library, archives, or historical society in each state. Some can be borrowed on microfilm from the American Genealogical Lending Library and the LDS Family History Centers. A comprehensive listing is found in *The Genealogist's Companion & Sourcebook*, by Emily Croom (Cincinnati: Betterway Books, 1994).

Soundex

The 1880, 1900, 1920, and much of the 1910 census records are indexed by state using a code that is based on the sounds in the last name. This indexing system is called Soundex. It is most often available as a microfilm of the cards on which the information is written. Soundex is especially useful when you do not know where the family was living in the census year. It will show you what county and what community they lived in and where you can find them on the census. When you find the family in the Soundex, write down *all* the information given, especially the enumeration district number, the supervisor's district number, the precinct, page, and line numbers, as you will need these references when looking for the family in the census itself. One drawback of the 1880 Soundex is that it includes only families with children under ten years of age. If Grandpa's children were already over ten or were grown by 1880, you will not find Grandpa in the Soundex, unless he lived with a family which had small children.

The Soundex coding system groups letters by the way they sound. Similar letters are given the same code to account for spelling variations. In this way, Medcalf, Midcalf, Metcalf, Metcalfe, and even Mitchell all have the same code number and are grouped together in the Soundex. The code begins with the first letter of the surname; that letter is not coded with a number. Only subsequent consonants are used as key letters to make the code; you may cross out all vowels (*a, e, i, o, u*) and *y, w,* and *h*. Double letters that come together are coded as only one digit. If you run out of key letters before you have a three-digit code, you simply add zeros. Practice coding your own family names. (See examples on page 66.)

Code Number	*Key Letters*
1	b, p, f, v
2	c, s, k, g, j, q, x, z
3	d, t
4	l
5	m, n
6	r

There are entries in the census and other records in which the surname was written incorrectly, spelled with a *C* instead of *K*, or minus a final syllable, or spelled phonetically instead of correctly, or misunderstood for another name. My great-grandmother's marriage license gives her name as Ann Maria *Robertson*. Her mother's second marriage record gave her name as Mrs. Elizabeth *Robinson*. Ann's brother was listed in the 1860 census as T.J. *Robberson*. To this day, we do not know which name is correct. This dilemma is, of course, part of the challenge of genealogy.

If your name can have several spellings, especially with a different initial letter, or could be spelled phonetically in several ways, or could be mistaken for another name, it would be wise to look under all the variations when reading the Soundex or any index. Soundex codes which are almost the same, such as 450 and 452, are often grouped together. Sometimes prefixes such as *von, van, de, de la,* and *le* are omitted in coding.

In the library, when you want to read a particular roll of Soundex microfilm, you can ask the librarian for it in this way: "I'd like to read the 1900 Soundex for Texas for the code H452." "I'd like to see the 1880 Kansas Soundex for K620."

Census records from 1790 through 1920 are available on microfilm at many libraries. Some have been published or indexed. Use the indexes whenever possible to save time, especially when reading the 1880 or later censuses, but do not stop with the index. Read the real document.

In order to look for your particular family, you must know which census year you want to read and which state and county the family lived in. You would look for or tell the librarian you want to read, for example, the 1850 census for Williamson County, Texas, or the 1870 census for Montgomery County, Ohio. The roll of microfilm often has several counties on it. You must scan until you find the beginning of your county, usually marked with a divider card naming the county.

If you do not have access to an index, your alternative is to read the entire county, family by family. The process is long but sometimes rewarding. That's how I found Sterling Orgain in Madison County, Tennessee, quite by accident, while looking for someone else. I usually prefer to read the whole county for censuses of 1860 and earlier, or for counties where I know there were many related families of different surnames. Besides, the census can be as entertaining as an encyclopedia or dictionary. You will find people with very interesting names, such as two of my favorites, the two men in Dale County, Alabama, named Green Bird and Bright Bird. You will probably find people with the same names as people you know today. You will learn who was in jail and who the doctors and teachers

Examples of Soundex Coding

CAMPBELL C 5 1 4	C514. Double L and PB are each coded as one digit. Other names with same code: Cambell, Champlin, Chamblin, Campellona, Canfield, Chamblee, Chambless.
CARPENTER C 61 5 - -	C615. Disregard the last three letters since you already have a three-digit code. Other names with same code: Corbin, Craven(s), Crippen, Carbone, Cherrybone, Carabine, Cherubini, Charbonneau.
MATTHEWS M 3 20	M320. Add zero to complete code. Double T counts as one letter. Other names with same code: Mathis, Mathews, Mattes, Mutz, Muths, Metts, Metz.
RAY R 000	R000. Add three zeros since there are no key letters. Other names with same code: Rhea, Rea, Roe, Roehe, Rowe, Roy, Rue, Rye, Rey, Riewe.
SHOEMAKER S 5 2 6	S526. Names beginning with *Sc*, such as Schumacher—S526, are treated the same way they would be if the double letter appeared in the middle of the name. Other names with same code: Smucker, Smyser, Singer, Shinker, Sanker, Schanzer, Schen(c)ker, Schwinger, Schwenneker, Sangree, Sanacora.

Examples of Soundex Problems

Names that are similar, with different initial letters:

Ostien	O235	Garner	G656	Croom	C650
Austin	A235	Carner	C656	Groom	G650
Otwell	O340	Riggins	R252	Ebert	E163
Atwell	A340	Wiggins	W252	Hebert	H163

Names which may be confused with each other:

Garner	G656	Larson	L625	Saddler	S346
Gardner	G635	Lawson	L250	Sandler	S534
Rich/Richey	R200	Robinson	R152	Carson	C625
Ridge/Ritchie	R320	Robison	R125	Carlson	C642
Ridgeley	R324	Robertson	R163	Kallsen	K425
Waters	W362	Oren	O650	Finch	F520
Walters	W436	Owen	O500	French	F652

were. You will get a "feel" for the county: where most of the residents were born, where they came from most recently, which foreign countries were represented, which given names were most popular, and which occupations were prevalent.

Census reading poses its own special challenges. One that you meet quickly is handwriting. Some people write English as if it were Arabic. Nineteenth-century writers adhered to a standard style more often than contemporary writers do, but they had a few quirks that trip us up if we are not careful. For example, the old style double *s* looked like an *fs*. Capital *J*'s and *I*'s are sometimes indistinguishable. Names such as Lemuel and Samuel may be difficult to differentiate, or Daniel and David, if the script is angular and disjointed. However, with caution and common sense, you can generally decide the writer's intentions. (See chapter sixteen.)

A census check form is useful in capsuling the information gained from each census record for each family. When the chart in Figure 12 was made, the ancestor had not been found in the 1830-1850 censuses. The notes from other censuses show that Mississippi and Tennessee were reported as birthplaces for him. Preliminary searches of both states identified no Holmes family in 1850 that matched what we knew of his. After learning that he had come to Texas from Mississippi and had been visited once by his *brother Stephen*, we made an extensive search of the 1850 Mississippi census and finally located him in Tishomingo County, with parents and siblings. The census taker had recorded their surname as *Haynes* instead of *Holmes*. Keeping track of your census searches on such a chart can help you see at a glance where you have found the family, where you could search next, and new clues you have discovered. It may also save you from that irritating mistake of spending several hours reading a lengthy census, only to discover, afterwards, that you had already read it!

CENSUS CHECK ON William Francis Marion Holmes FAMILY

Born 3/4 Feb 1829 Where ______ First Census 1830

Father's Name ______ Holmes Age in First Census 1 year

Married 2nd - 1861 Spouse Matilda Y. Browne Died 7 May 1903

CENSUS YEAR	COUNTIES SEARCHED/ NOTES	COUNTY WHERE FOUND/ NOTES	PAGE
1830		age under 5	
1840		age 10-15	
1850	Mississippi index + all Holmes shown in index. All Texas Holmes shown in index. Try Tenn or Ark.	age 21	
1860	Gonzales Co Tx	Gonzales Co Tx in household of A.S. Miller, employed as overseer, single, age 31, says he was born in Miss.	Pr. Pg 117 written Pg 95
1870	Gonzales Co Tx	Gonzales Co Tx with Matilda 30, William 7, Sam H 5, Mary E. 3, Alvie 9 months. WFM age 42, says he was born in Tenn.	Pr. Pg 478 written Pg 6
1880	Gonzales Co Tx	Gonzales Co Tx with children. Says he was born in Tenn, father in Va, mother in Ga. WFM-age 51	Pr Pg 476
1900	need to read Gonzales Co Tx		

FIG. 12: CENSUS CHECK FORM

Military Records

Numerous military records are in the National Archives. They cover regular Army, Navy, and Marine Corps personnel service records, service records of volunteers, pension applications and records, bounty land records from lands offered to Revolutionary War veterans, and the special 1890 census of Union Army veterans and widows. The service records pertain to the Revolutionary War, soldiers under the United States Command from 1784 to 1811, the War of 1812-15, the Mexican War (1846-48), the Indian wars, the Civil War (1861-65), and the Spanish-American War (1898). Coast Guard records date from 1791 to 1919. Civil War files include many service records and pardon petitions of Confederate soldiers.

A first step in searching these military records is to read the indexes to compiled service records. These indexes and large collections of service records are available on microfilm at the National Archives, at many research libraries, and from the American Genealogical Lending Library. Arranged alphabetically, they are available for the Revolution, the period 1784-1811, the War of 1812, the Indian wars (1815-1858), the Mexican War, the Civil War (separate indexes for Union and Confederate servicemen), and the Spanish-American War.

The military service records contain information on when and where the person joined the military, served, and was discharged as well as engagements, capture, rank, promotions, etc. Copies of the records that relate to service that ended at least 75 years ago can be requested by submitting Form NATF 80, Order for Copies—Veterans Records. The forms are free on request from the National Archives, Washington, DC 20408. In order to have a search made for these military records, you must supply identifying information, such as the serviceman's name, the war in which he served, the state from which he entered service, and if possible, file numbers or pension application numbers.

Persons applying for military pensions had to prove their service; a widow had to prove her husband's service. Thus, the records can contain valuable genealogical information in addition to service history: vital statistics, family relationships, parents' names, wife's maiden name, or children's names. Microfilmed pension files, arranged alphabetically, are available for veterans from the Revolutionary War, Mexican War, Indian wars, and Civil War (Union). (Confederate pension files are in the records of each former Confederate state.) This microfilm may be rented from the American Genealogical Lending Library and is available in many research libraries. Published sources of use in looking for pensioners include these:

1. *Index to Revolutionary War Pension Applications in the National Archives.* (Washington, DC: National Genealogical Society, 1976.) [The society is now in Arlington, Virginia.]

2. *Report from the Secretary of War in Relation to the Pension Establishment of the United States.* Senate Document 514 (23rd Cong., 1st Sess.) Serial 249-251. (Baltimore: Genealogical Publishing Company, reprint, 1968.) Short title: *Pension Roll of 1835*, 3 vols.

3. *List of Pensioners on the Roll January 1, 1883.* Senate Executive Document 84 (47th Cong., 2nd Sess.) Serial 2078-2082. (The Serial Set is a standard reference collection in libraries that are government documents depositories.)

Records relating to more recent service, generally for those personnel who were discharged ("separated") after 1917 (Army officers), 1912 (Army enlisted personnel), 1947 (Air Force personnel), 1902 (Navy officers), 1885 (Navy enlisted personnel), 1895 (Marine Corps officers), 1928 (Coast Guard officers), 1914 (Coast Guard enlisted personnel), and for civilian employees of the Coast Guard's predecessor services (1864-1919), are housed in the National Personnel Records Center (NPRC), General Services Administration, 9700 Page Ave., St. Louis, MO 63132. Inquiries for information from these records may be submitted on Standard Form 180, Request Pertaining to Military Personnel Records. The files are not available for public use and are restricted to members of the veteran's immediate family or the veterans themselves. If the veterans are still living, their written consent is necessary.

The Atlanta (East Point), Georgia branch of the National Archives houses the file of World War I draft cards. A search for an individual name can be made for a $6 mailing fee, if you can supply the person's full name, town and county of residence at that time, and date of birth. Microfilming of these records is scheduled for completion about 1995.

For more detailed information on researching military records, consult *U.S. Military Records: A Guide to Federal and State Sources, Colonial America to the Present*, by James C. Neagles (Salt Lake City: Ancestry, 1994).

Federal Land Records

Land records in the National Archives pertain mostly to the thirty public land states created from the *public domain,* land acquired through purchase or in treaties following wars: all states west of the Mississippi River except Texas and Hawaii, states created from the old Northwest Territory, and the old Spanish and Indian lands which became Florida, Alabama, and Mississippi. The land records, mostly 1800-1974, include entries from several types of grants. The ones containing the most genealogical information are usually bounty land warrant applications and homestead applications.

Bounty land warrant applications in the National Archives are based on a man's wartime military service between 1775 and 1855. As an inducement to enlistment, first in the Revolutionary War, some of the thirteen colonies and the Continental Congress promised free land to those who served until the end of the war or to the widows and heirs of soldiers killed. Bounty land grants were also authorized after the Revolutionary War, the War of 1812, the Indian wars, and the Mexican War (1845-48). Warrants for such land grants were issued under laws passed between 1796 and 1855. Qualifications varied from time to time, and some people made more than one application. In order to apply for the warrant, the veteran or his heirs had to document his service. This documentation process is the source of most of the genealogical information in these files. Microfilm of these documents is available at many research libraries.

Some of the thirteen colonies issued warrants for grants on their own unsettled lands and western lands which they claimed. In this way, North Carolina granted land in Tennessee, and Virginia made land grants in Kentucky. Virginia also issued warrants for grants in south central Ohio, in an area known as the Virginia Military District. Central Ohio became the location of bounty lands for soldiers who had served in the Continental Army, under the authority of Congress rather than individual states.

Applications for Virginia warrants for land in the Virginia Military District of Ohio and the Register of Military Certificates located in Ohio and Kentucky are in the Virginia State Library. The federal Bureau of Land Management, Eastern States Office, has record copies of the Virginia Military District patents. See "Virginia Warrants used to patent Kentucky land, 1782-1793" in *Old Kentucky Entries and Deeds,* by Willard Rouse Jillson (Baltimore: Genealogical Publishing Company, 1987, reprint of 1926 edition, pp. 313-392).

The American Library Association has published indexes to certain land records in the *Federal Land Series: A Calendar of Archival Materials on the Land Patents Issued by the U.S. Government with Subject, Tract, and Name Indexes,* in four volumes, by Clifford Neal Smith (Chicago: American Library Association, 1972-1986). Volumes I and III deal with land patents between 1788 and 1814 and contain subject, tract, and name indexes. Volume II is an index to federal bounty land warrants of the American Revolution, 1799-1835. Volume IV indexes grants in the Virginia Military District of Ohio.

Individual claims are also found in the early land records. Many of the people making these claims had land grants or purchases from foreign sovereigns (French, Spanish, Mexican, British mostly) and settled the land before the United States acquired it. The United States had to decide who owned each tract and had clear title to it. Many records of these claims are published and indexed: *American State Papers: Public Land Series: Records relating to individual claims presented to federal authorities, 1790-1837. . . .* Walter Lowrie and Matthew St. Claire Clarke, eds. (Washington, DC: Gales and Seaton, 1832-61). Federal authorities who handled these claims included district land offices, district courts, U.S. Court of Claims, the General Land Office, the Supreme Court, and the Court of Private Claims (for Mexican lands).

The *American State Papers* are often found in research libraries and, because they are also part of the United States Serial Set, in many libraries that are government documents depositories. An index to the public land series is *Grassroots of America: A Computerized Index to the American State Papers Land Grants and Claims (1789-1837),* Philip W. McMullin, ed. (Salt Lake City: Gendex Corporation, 1972). Additional documents relating to grants and claims are reproduced in *The New American State Papers, 1789-1860,* 8 vols. on public lands, Thomas C. Cochran, ed. (Wilmington, DE: Scholarly Resources, 1972-1981). This set is not indexed.

Donation land entries. In Florida, Oregon, and Washington before the Civil War, the government began giving land to people who would settle in order to strengthen the United States claim to the area when ownership was disputed with another country. Because this land was given or donated to the settlers, the records of the grants are called donation land entries. The files in the Archives contain records for Florida, 1842-1850, and for Oregon and Washington, 1851-1903.

Homestead entry papers are a fourth kind of land record in the Archives. The Homestead Act of 1862 allowed settlers on public domain lands to obtain a free homestead farm of 160 acres for a small fee. In order to obtain title to the land, the homesteader had to live on the property for five years. In applying for this grant, a man gave certain information which the genealogist may find useful: name of the applicant and his wife, size of the family, residence, age or date of birth, the location of the land, and the date acquired. If he was of foreign birth, he gave evidence of his naturalization or his intention to become a citizen. His entry papers would include this application, his certificate of intent to make a claim, the testimony of two witnesses, the claimant's own testimony, the final certificate authorizing him to obtain a patent, and his naturalization papers or a Union Army discharge certificate.

Land Grants. The handling of land grants and the sale of former Indian lands was done at land offices. These offices in the early years were sometimes quite distant from the lands they sold. The index to the Public Land Series, *Grassroots of America*, identifies the land offices to 1840. The National Archives has a 4-volume index which lists the land offices responsible for a given region at a given time.

Title to public domain land was transferred from the government to new owners through deeds or patents, which were recorded in tract books in the land offices. The land offices east of the Mississippi River eventually transferred their tract books to the General Land Office, now the Bureau of Land Management in the U.S. Department of the Interior. The tract books for the thirteen public land states east of the Mississippi River and the first tier of states west of the river are kept at the Bureau's Eastern States Office, 7450 Boston Blvd., Springfield, VA 22153. Researchers may use microfilm copies of the tract books. However, by the end of 1996, the pre-1908 land title records for the thirteen states in its jurisdiction should be accessible on the GLO Automated Records System (in-house or by remote access) as well as on CD-ROM (from the Superintendent of Documents, P.O. Box 371954, Pittsburgh, PA 15250-7954). The office can supply a list of current BLM fees and services.

Some of the western tract books are kept in the Bureau of Land Management regional offices in Phoenix, Anchorage, Sacramento, Denver (Lakewood), Boise, Billings, Reno, Santa Fe, Portland, Salt Lake City, and Cheyenne. Other tract books are in the National Archives or its branches, state and local historical societies, or state archives or land offices.

The National Archives and the Bureau of Land Management both have records of land patents from about 1800 to 1908, although not identical files. The BLM generally has tract books, survey plats, and other land title documents. The Archives holds the case files of individual patentees as well as post-1908 entries.

From 1800 to 1820, public lands were sold on credit. The National Archives contains the Credit Entry files, 1800-1820, and the Credit Entry Final Certificates, 1800-1835. The Archives also has the Cash Entry files for 1820-1908 with a master card index for Alabama, Alaska, Arizona, Florida, Louisiana, Nevada and Utah. These land entry case files can be obtained from the National Archives by mail for a small fee. You need to furnish such information as the name of the patentee (person who bought the land), legal description of the property, land office, and entry number. If you have the name and legal description, you can find the other data in the appropriate tract book or contact the Bureau of Land Management regional offices or Eastern States Office at the address above.

Materials for African-American Genealogists

Basic genealogical sources, such as family papers, courthouse records, state and federal censuses, state archives, and newspapers, are useful for any genealogist, regardless of ethnic interest. However, the National Archives has extensive records pertaining to African-American genealogy.

One important group of sources is military records. In addition to service and pension records and their indexes, the Archives has the disallowed military claims of Colored Troops (1864-1893), index and compiled service records of volunteer Union soldiers who served with the U.S. Colored Troops in the Civil War, records of Colored Troops in the Adjutant General's Office, and The Negro in the Military Service of the United States, 1639-1886. These collections are available on microfilm and can be found at some research libraries around the country. The following are two helpful military references published by the National Archives:

1. *Data Relating to Negro Military Personnel in the Nineteenth Century*. Reference Information Paper 63.

Aloha South. Washington, DC: National Archives and Records Service, 1973.

2. *List of Black Service Men Compiled From the War Department Records.* Special List 36. Debra L. Newman, comp. Washington, DC: National Archives and Records Service, 1974.

A comprehensive reference to civilian materials at the Archives is *Black History: A Guide to Civilian Records in the National Archives,* Debra L. Newman, comp. (Washington, DC: National Archives Trust Fund Board, 1984). Among these are files of the U.S. District Court for the District of Columbia relating to slaves, 1851-1863; District of Columbia slave manumission papers, 1857-1863; and records of the Board of Commissioners for the Emancipation of Slaves in the District of Columbia, 1862-1863.

A variety of records, also available on microfilm, comes from two post-Civil War agencies, the Freedmen's Savings and Trust Company, 1865-1874, and the Bureau of Refugees, Freedmen, and Abandoned Lands, 1865-1872, commonly called the Freedmen's Bureau. The most genealogical of these records are the registers of signatures of depositors in the branches of the Freedmen's Savings and Trust Company, which operated in a number of major Southern cities, as well as Philadelphia, New York, St. Louis, Baltimore, and Washington, DC. These registers often include personal history and vital statistics, family members, maiden names, and former residences. Freedmen's Bureau records include some marriage records, mostly for Arkansas, Kentucky, Louisiana, and Mississippi, and apprenticeship records. The microfilm is available in some research libraries and can be rented from the American Genealogical Lending Library.

Additional resources for African-American genealogy, in and out of the National Archives, include these books:

1. *Black Genealogy.* Charles L. Blockson with Ron Fry. Englewood Cliffs, NJ: Prentice-Hall, 1977.

2. *Black Genesis.* James Rose and Alice Eichholz. Detroit: Gale Research Co., 1978.

3. *Black History: A Guide to Civilian Records in the National Archives.* Debra L. Newman, comp. Washington, DC: National Archives Trust Fund Board, 1984.

4. *The Genealogist's Companion & Sourcebook.* Emily Croom. Cincinnati: Betterway Books, 1994. Especially chapter nine.

5. *Slave Genealogy: A Research Guide With Case Studies.* David H. Streets. Bowie, MD: Heritage Books, 1986.

Native American Records

Native American ancestors basically fall into two research categories: those who remained identified with an organized tribe or band, many of whom became residents on reservations, and those who blended into non-Indian society. Regardless of which group an ancestor falls into, tracing the Indian line is a real challenge due to a scarcity of written records prior to about the mid-nineteenth century. Certainly, explorers, scholars, military record keepers, and observers have written about Indians since the first European contact, but these writers, for the most part, did not record genealogical data.

Nontribal Indians are sometimes identified in federal census records, court records, and public land tract books but are less frequently found in deed, marriage, and probate records in the counties. Indian naming and name-changing customs also can complicate one's search in the existing records. In many cases, family records or tradition may be the only indication of an Indian ancestral line. Proving the relationship and the specific identities is the difficulty.

Records of tribal Indians exist in basically two categories: the Five Civilized Tribes of the southeastern United States, most of whom were resettled in Oklahoma, and the tribes who were made wards of the government, living on reservations. Documents relating to the Five Civilized Tribes (Cherokee, Choctaw, Chickasaw, Creek and Seminole) can be found at the National Archives, its branch in Fort Worth, Texas, the Oklahoma Historical Society, the Western History Collection at the University of Oklahoma, and, to a smaller degree, the Atlanta (East Point), Georgia, branch of the National Archives. These include tribal census rolls, enrollment cards, allotment and payroll records, some trading house papers, tribal citizenship applications, service records of those who served in the military, especially for the Confederacy during the Civil War, and miscellaneous records.

A number of the National Archives regional branches as well as state historical societies have collections relating to reservation Indians. These files include the very important census rolls (1884-1940), records of the federal Indian agencies and superintendencies, and correspondence of the Office of Indian Affairs. In addition, there are registers of military service of Indian scouts and Civil War Indian home guards (both on microfilm), some marriage cards and registers, heirship records, Eastern Cherokee claim files (1902-1910), and Indian school records.

Some Native Americans served with the regular army during the Revolutionary War. Their service records and resulting bounty land warrant applications are also on file, as is a special 1880 census of Indians in Washington, Oregon, California, and Dakota Territory. The regional Archives branches in the western states have field office reports from the Bureau of Indian Affairs. For more detailed information on Indian records in the National Archives, consult such sources as these:

1. "American Indian Records in the National Archives," *World Conference on Records and Genealogical Seminar.* Edward E. Hill. Salt Lake City: The Genealogical Society of the Church of Jesus Christ of Latter-day Saints, Inc., 1969.

2. *American Indians: A Select Catalog of National Archives Microfilm Publications.* Washington, DC: National Archives, 1984.

3. *Guide to Records in the National Archives of the United States Relating to American Indians.* Edward E. Hill, comp. Washington, DC: 1984.

4. *Records of the Bureau of Indian Affairs.* Preliminary Inventory No. 163. 2 vols. Edward E. Hill. Washington, DC: 1982, reprint of 1965 edition.

Below is a sampling of additional sources, listed by title. In addition, consult your library catalog and *Books in Print* under the tribal name, geographical location, *Indians,* or *Native Americans.*

Black Indian Genealogy Research: African-American Ancestors Among the Five Civilized Tribes. Angela Y. Walton-Raji. Bowie, MD: Heritage Books, 1993.

Cherokee Advocate Newspaper Extracts. 7 vols. as of 1994. Dorothy Tincup Mauldin. Tulsa, OK: Oklahoma Yesterday Publications, current. Corresponds to microfilm rolls at Oklahoma Historical Society, 1844-1906.

Cherokee Roots. 2 vols. Bob Blankenship. Bowie, MD: Heritage Books, 1992 reprint. Covers Eastern (1817-1924) and Western (1851-1909) Cherokee rolls.

Dictionary Catalog of the Edward E. Ayer Collection of Americana and American Indians in the Newberry Library. 16 vols. The Newberry Library. Boston: G.K. Hall, 1961.

Ethnic Genealogy: A Research Guide. Jessie Carney Smith, ed. Westport, CT: Greenwood Press, 1983. Chapter 7, "American Indian Records and Research," by Jimmy B. Parker, deals mostly with reservation Indians.

Guide to American Indian Documents in the Congressional Serial Set, 1817-1899. Steven L. Johnson. New York: Clearwater Publishing Company, 1977.

Introductory Guide to Indian-Related Records (to 1876) in the North Carolina State Archives. Donna Spindel. Raleigh: North Carolina Division of Archives and History, 1977.

Native American Periodicals and Newspapers, 1828-1982. James P. Danky, ed. Westport, CT: Greenwood Press, 1984.

Our Native Americans and Their Records of Genealogical Value. 2 vols. E. Kay Kirkham. Logan, UT: Everton Publishers, 1980.

Immigration and Naturalization

Records of immigrant arrivals are often found in ships' passenger lists. Ship captains had to file a report of their passengers who had embarked in a foreign port and were disembarking at a United States port. After 1820, captains reported this information to the customs office in the port of entry. Few of these records still exist; those which have been found are published in a number of different books and periodicals. Lists of passengers arriving after the 1880s were filed with the Bureau of Immigration. Those which still exist can usually be found in the National Archives and its branches, as well as in research libraries and published sources.

In the National Archives, in the records of the U.S. Customs Service, are post-1820 passenger lists and some indexes from vessels arriving at Baltimore, Boston, Detroit, Galveston, New Orleans, New York, Philadelphia, San Francisco, Seattle, and other Gulf and Atlantic ports. Records of the Immigration and Naturalization Service contain passenger and crew lists, with indexes by ports, for the late nineteenth century and the first half of the twentieth century.

A major resource for immigration research is P. William Filby's *Passenger and Immigration Lists Index: A Guide to Published Arrival Records of About 500,000 Passengers Who Came to the United States and Canada in the Seventeenth, Eighteenth, and Nineteenth Centuries* [PILI], 3 vols. (Detroit: Gale Research, 1981). Annual supplements continue to increase the coverage, and well over two million names have been indexed. This massive work indexes published passenger, naturalization, and other immigration records. Its companion *Passenger and Immigration Lists Bibliog-*

raphy 1538-1900 by the same author and publisher (1988, second edition) catalogs over 2,500 of the published lists as a cross-reference.

A valuable reference in the search for immigrant ancestors is Michael Tepper's *American Passenger Arrival Records: A Guide to the Records of Immigrants Arriving at American Ports by Sail and Steam* (Baltimore: Genealogical Publishing Company, 1982).

A bibliography of immigration resources appears on pages 85-86.

In order to find naturalization papers for your ancestors, you need to know when they arrived in this country. Passenger lists, census records, land records, family papers, and county tax lists are some of the sources that can help you establish the arrival date. Ancestors arriving in this country before the American Revolution generally did not go through a naturalization process; in fact, many were already British citizens who were simply changing their residence within the British empire. Before the first naturalization law in 1790, the states handled the process on their own.

The first step toward becoming a naturalized citizen was to file a Declaration of Intention. Before 1906, an immigrant could file his "first papers" at any federal, state, or local court. Many did this in their port of entry soon after their arrival in this country. After 1906, the Declaration usually was filed in a federal court, sometimes in a state or county court.

The second step was to file "final papers," which included a Petition for Citizenship, an Oath of Allegiance, and papers proving residency for the required number of years. The residency requirement varied from time to time but generally was five years. The final papers did not have to be filed in the same court as the Declaration of Intention. The process was complete when the court issued the Certificate of Naturalization.

Naturalization records sometimes contain valuable genealogical data, such as the subject's birth date and place, the spouse's name and origin, children's names and birth information, former and current residence, and immigration data. Other information may include occupation and physical description. Records from the late nineteenth and twentieth centuries generally contain much more detail than earlier records.

Records of naturalizations before 1906 are scattered among state and federal archives, historical societies, libraries, and courthouses. Indexes and guides to each collection may help you locate the records you need. Papers filed after 1906 are usually kept with the records of the court which handled them. If you do not know which court your ancestor went to, inquire at an office of the Immigration and Naturalization Service for the proper form and procedure for having a search made.

Some naturalization records are available from the National Archives and its branches. Taken from federal court files and available on microfilm are indexes and/or records of naturalizations from Alaska, northern California, Colorado, Maryland, Montana, New England, Oregon, Pennsylvania, South Carolina, and Washington. For specific availability, consult the National Archives publication *National Archives Microfilm Resources for Research: A Comprehensive Catalog.*

Naturalized citizens who received land under the Homestead Act sometimes filed their citizenship papers with their applications for land. Therefore, the land entry case files in the National Archives are also sources to consult when you are looking for naturalization papers.

An excellent source to consult on immigration and naturalization is James and Lila Lee Neagles's *Locating Your Immigrant Ancestor* (Logan, UT: The Everton Publishers, Inc., 1975), which suggests sources in the United States and in the country of origin for your search.

Other Archives Sources

The Archives maintains records of the Continental Congress and Confederation Congress from the years prior to the writing of the present Constitution, as well as the papers from the Constitutional Convention. Several sets of territorial papers are available on microfilm. These papers are Congressional documents and records pertaining to the states which were once organized territories of the federal government, as most of the public land states were. A large collection of such papers has been published with indexes, by territory: *The Territorial Papers of the United States*, 28 vols. Clarence E. Carter, ed. (New York: AMS Press, reprints of 1934-1975 edition). Valuable as genealogical sources because they include thousands of individuals, the microfilm and printed volumes are available in many public and university libraries.

In the records of the Internal Revenue Service, you can read on microfilm the assessment lists for 1862-1866, by state. Within the records of the U.S. General Accounting Office are the Civil War Direct Tax Assessment rolls for Tennessee. The supplemental census schedules for a number of states, 1850-1880, are available in the records of the Bureau of the Census (see page 64).

The holdings of the National Archives are enormous, and many of the records are available on microfilm. The Archives publishes and sells catalogs of its microfilm records. One roll of interest to genealogists is #T325, *Examples of Records in the National Archives Frequently Used in Genealogical Research.*

Other Federal Sources

Records of civil service employees are somewhat restricted, but inquiries about service which ended after 1909 may be made to National Personnel Records Center (CPR), 111 Winebago St., St. Louis, MO 63118. The few existing records pertaining to employees before 1909 can be found in the National Archives. Inquiries should contain the employee's full name, the name and address of the federal agency where he or she worked, and the approximate dates of that employment.

Passport applications filed between 1791 and 1926 may be found in the National Archives. Limited searches can be made for age and citizenship information in the records which are at least seventy-five years old. Such searches require the applicant's name and the place and approximate date of his application. Inquiries for information from passport applications less than seventy-five years old should be made to the Passport Office, Department of State, Washington, DC 20520.

The Library of Congress in Washington, DC, houses an extensive collection of manuscript, published, and microform works of value to genealogists, including early state records, newspapers, maps, and family and county histories. Many bibliographies and finding aids describe the holdings and their use. An excellent reference, especially for those planning to visit the library, is James C. Neagles's *The Library of Congress: A Guide to Historical and Genealogical Research* (Salt Lake City: Ancestry, 1990).

Microfilm From the National Archives

Microfilm is no longer available on loan from the National Archives, but it can be purchased. Submit orders on Form 36-Microfilm Orders or institutional purchase orders. Orders must include the microfilm publication number, roll number, and price. Send check or money order payable to Cashier, National Archives Trust Fund Board, Washington, DC 20408. Orders may be charged to Visa or Mastercard. National Archives microfilm can also be purchased from Scholarly Resources, 104 Greenhill Ave., Wilmington, DE 19805.

Through a privately-owned company called National Archives Microfilm Rental Program (P.O. Box 30, Annapolis Junction, MD 20701-0030) and for nominal fees, you can rent censuses (1790-1920), including slave schedules and Soundex (1880, 1900-1920), and Revolutionary War service records and index, pension applications, and bounty land warrant applications. Your local library's interlibrary loan department can tell you which library nearest you participates in this program, or you can contact the company at the above address or at (301) 604-3305 for the library nearest you which participates.

National Archives microfilm and much more may be rented from two major lending libraries: American Genealogical Lending Library (AGLL), P.O. Box 244, Bountiful, UT 84011, and the Family History Library, 35 North West Temple St., Salt Lake City, UT 84150 (through their many branch libraries worldwide).

CHAPTER THIRTEEN

Where Do I Look for That?

As you fill in the middle of your puzzle for each generation and each ancestor, you will obviously find some pieces more quickly than others. The harder-to-find pieces will require more concentrated effort, but many of them can be found. As you look for this information, give each source a reliability test. Is the document contemporary with the event? Who probably gave the information? Did the subject furnish the facts? If not the subject, was the informant in a position to know correct names, dates, or places? Does more than one reliable source give the same data? Does other evidence support the information your find?

BIRTH DATE AND/OR BIRTHPLACE

Family sources for birth dates and places can include Bible records, especially ones made at the time of the event; interviews with older relatives and family friends; family letters, diaries, clippings, and scrapbooks; birth announcements, certificates, and baby books; autobiographical sketches, and family papers, which may include such items as transcripts, military discharge papers, passports, driver's licenses, voter registrations, or naturalization papers. Ask distant cousins about sources in their part of the family. Some family papers have been given to libraries or archives in the area where the family lived. Inquire at these institutions, or consult the *National Union Catalog of Manuscript Collections* (NUCMC, pronounced *nuck-muck*) and its corresponding *Index to Personal Names in the National Union Catalog of Manuscript Collections, 1959-1984*, 2 vols. (Alexandria, VA: Chadwyck-Healey, 1988). A reference librarian can show you how to use these books, or you can consult *The Genealogist's Companion & Sourcebook*, by Emily Croom (Cincinnati: Betterway Books, 1994) for instructions.

Public sources which may give birth dates and/or places include published Bible records in books or periodicals; church registers of births, baptisms, confirmations, or marriages (published or in a church or archives); courthouse marriage records that may show age; birth certificates (contemporary or delayed), hospital birth records or newspaper birth notices; school or college records; military service or pension files, World War I draft registrations, or military discharge papers (sometimes filed at county courthouses); Social Security applications (after 1936); organization or lodge membership applications or records; homestead applications; declarations of intention to become a citizen, naturalization papers, ships' passenger lists (sometimes give ages of passengers); and state or federal censuses which show age on a given date. Death certificates, tombstones, and obituaries may give birth information, but that information should be verified with other sources when possible. Some business sources may furnish birth information: insurance and funeral home files, employment records, and professional organizations. Published family and county histories may give numerous names and dates, but these often contain mistakes and should be verified with other sources.

An aid in the search for birth and death records is the *International Vital Records Handbook*, 3rd ed., Thomas J. Kemp, comp. (Baltimore: Genealogical Publishing Company, 1994). Two helpful government publications are (1) *Where to Write for Vital Records: Births, Deaths, Marriages, and Divorces* (Hyattsville, MD: U.S. Department of Health and Human Services, Public Health Service, 1993 or latest edition), and (2) *Age Search Information*, JoAnn Shepherd (Washington, DC: Department of Commerce, Bureau of the Census, 1990 or latest edition). Both are available at government bookstores or from the U.S. Government Printing Office in Washington, DC 20402.

For age information, censuses can be very helpful but are not always accurate, as you will see later in this chapter. The 1790 federal census is of only general help in determining age; it shows that free heads of household were alive and over age 16 (usually) as of the first Monday in August, 1790. It gives the number of free males (not specified as sons, or even as relatives) in the household over 16 or under 16. Females and slaves were not grouped by age at all.

The 1800, 1810, and 1820 censuses divided everyone into age groups: up to 10, 10-16, 16-26, 26-45, and over 45. Only the head of household was named, but he or she was not always the oldest person in the family. The 1820 census had a column for males between 16 and 18. The next column was for males between 16 and 26. The males in the 16-18 age group are listed under *both* columns and are not to be counted twice. Census records for 1830 and 1840 again name only the heads of household and group everyone in these age brackets: under 5, 5-10, 10-15, 15-20, 20-30, 30-40, 40-50, 50-60, 60-70, 70-80, 80-90, 90-100, and over 100. If your Jeremiah Johnson had only three sons and his 1830 census return shows three males aged 10-15 and none in the other columns, you can be relatively sure (not positively certain) that those three males are his sons. You would know then that they were all born between 1815 and 1820, if their ages were accurately reported and recorded. At least you have something to work with as you look for proof of their birth dates.

Beginning in 1850, each free person was named, and the age reported on the census was supposed to be correct as of June 1 of that year. This census is your earliest opportunity to find specific individuals with age information in the federal census. Of course, ages were not always reported accurately, and sometimes a person was left off the list altogether. The law did say to omit any child born after 1 June 1850 and to include everyone living on June 1. This meant the census would include anyone who died after June 1. Any baby less than one year old as of June 1 was to be reported by age in months, or a fraction of a year: $\frac{2}{12}$ for two months old, $\frac{7}{12}$ for seven months old, or $\frac{0}{12}$ for less than one month old. When these ages are accurate, they can help you estimate the birth date more closely.

These same procedures were followed for the censuses of 1860 through 1900. After 1900, and through at least 1940, the cut-off date changed from June 1 to a variety of others. (See page 64.) The 1870 and 1880 censuses did ask for the month of birth to be specified for babies born within the census year, that is between 1 June 1869 and 1 June 1870 or between 1 June 1879 and 1 June 1880. The 1900 census is the most helpful, specifying month and year of birth for all persons, though not always accurately. The 1910 census reverts to almost the same process used in 1850, asking only for age, but this time giving the fraction of a year for babies under two.

Censuses from 1850 forward asked for each person's birthplace: the state or the country. Beginning in 1880, they also asked for the birthplace of each person's parents. This information helps you narrow the search for the preceding generation.

Here is one way you can use the census records in finding someone's birth year. You will notice that there are obvious discrepancies in the ages of Johnson Godwin in the following chart. In 1850, he reported that he was 50 years old; ten years later he was only 8 years older. Why? Different people could have given the information to the two census takers; the census taker could have written the age incorrectly; many people rounded off their ages to the nearest 5 or 0. From census figures, therefore, we can determine only approximate birth dates. Subtracting the age from the census year in each illustration gives you a possible birth date.

Using the Census to Find an Approximate Birth Year

Census Year	*Age Given*	*You figure the suggested birth year*
1830	30-40	1790-1800
1840	30-40	1800-1810
1850	50	1800
1860	58	1802
1870	67	1803
1880	74	1806

According to the figures, his birth occurred between 1790 and 1806. Since 1800 appears three times in the chart and 1802 and 1803 are also suggested, it is likely that he was born between 1800 and 1803. Unless we find more information to go on, we have to give his birth date as "about 1800-1803."

When actual birth records and census data are not available, you can sometimes gather birth information from deeds, wills, tax rolls, marriage records, and other public documents.

When Robert Hester of Louisa County, Virginia, wrote his will in November, 1769, he provided useful information on his children and clues for further research (Will Bk. 2, pp. 71-72). To his son Abraham, he gave the 300 acres of land where Abraham was then living and named him executor of the estate in the event that his widow remarried. These provisions suggest that Abraham was the eldest son, if not the eldest of the thirteen children, and more than likely was well over 21 years of age. Daughter Sarah was already married to a Smith and had three children, Robert, Barbara, and Sarah Smith. There is no indication of how old these grandchildren were, but we know they were born by 1769, the date of the will. Their mother, married with children, was probably no less than 20 years of age and perhaps no more than 30. These estimates would suggest that she was born between 1739 and 1749. Hester also named his daughter Agness Walton and her two children Barbara and Anne Hester Walton, information which would place Agness in approximately the same birth range as her sister, possibly 1739-1750. Another daughter, Barbara Walton, was married, but no children were mentioned in the will. It is possible, though not certain from this document alone, that she was the youngest of these three daughters. The other Hester daughters, Anne, Ann [Are these entries for the same person or two different daughters?], Susan, Mary, and Elizabeth, were to receive their inheritance upon reaching the age of 18. We know, then, that they were all born after 1751. Sons James and Nathan were given land and were named in a provision with Abraham and their married sisters Sarah, Agness, and Barbara. The father stated that if any child died without heirs, that share of the remaining estate was to be divided equally between the then-surviving children *except* these six. This provision suggests that these were the six eldest children and had been given their inheritance to the limit desired by their father. Rounding out the list of children were three younger sons. Francis and Samuel were to receive a sum of money when they reached 21. This information tells us that they were born after 1748 and by 1769. The remaining son, Charles, was to receive the 431 acres where the parents then lived, with the provision that the widow, Barbara, was to have "free and Indisputable authority upon the same during her widowhood." The implication here seems to be that Charles was still living at home, may have been the youngest son, but without experience running a sizeable farm; thus, the father wanted his wife, not the son, to be in charge. If the father followed a practice that many others have, over the years, of naming his children in his will in birth order, then his sons, in order, were Abraham, James, Nathan, Francis, Samuel and Charles; his daughters, Sarah, Agness, Barbara, Anne (Ann), Susan, Mary, and Elizabeth. Other sources, such as marriage bonds, deeds, other family wills, estate settlement papers, tax rolls, census records from 1790 forward, Bible records, or tombstones, may give more birth information on these children and grandchildren, but the will alone provides good clues.

On 19 November 1763, Daniel Coleman of Cumberland County, Virginia, gave his consent for his daughter Elizabeth Coleman to marry Phillip Allen. His consent is an indication that Elizabeth was not yet 21. Virginia law at that time required a person under 21 to have the permission of father or guardian in order to marry.

A person's age may also be suggested in the county tax rolls. Depending on legal taxable age at that time and in that place, his presence on the roll as a poll (a head to be taxed) would indicate that he was of age, whether 16, 18, or 21.

CHRISTENING OR BAPTISM

A Bible record, church register of baptisms or confirmations, or certificate issued by the church at the time of the event may provide a date and place for a christening or baptism. Old letters, diaries, scrapbooks, clippings from church or local newspapers, or, less frequently, an obituary may include baptism information.

MARRIAGE DATE AND/OR PLACE

The most obvious source for marriage information is the marriage records of the county or town where the marriage took place. Other common sources are Bible records, church registers, contemporary newspaper announcements of the event, original marriage licenses, interviews with older relatives and friends, old letters, and diaries. Occasionally an obituary, a tombstone or a pension application shows a marriage date. The couple may have married in a different county from the one where they made their home, so check surrounding counties.

If no other records give a wedding date, you can sometimes suggest a marriage year by using the census records, but these records are not proof of the date. The 1850 and 1860 censuses have a blank to check if the couple married within the census year. The 1870 and 1880 censuses asked for the month of marriage if the couple married within the census year. The 1900 census asked for the number of years married, and the 1910 census asked for number of years of the present marriage.

For example, one set of great-grandparents is listed in the 1880 census, ages 32 and 30, with children ages 8, 6, 5, 3, and 2/12 (2 months). Their eight-year-old was born about 1872. Great-grandmother would have been born about 1850 and could have married as early as age 16 or about 1866. If no miscarriage occurred before the birth of the eight-year-old, and no older child had died, the marriage could have taken place in 1870 or 1871. An easy way to narrow the possibilities is to find them in the 1870 and 1900 censuses.

If they are listed in the 1870 census as a couple with no children, it is possible that they had been married less than two years. Of course, look for a mark in the column headed *Married within year*, which would indicate a wedding between 1 June 1869 and 1 June 1870. If you find these two ancestors living in the households of their individual parents, of course, they had not yet married by 1 June 1870. If they lived until census time in 1900, you may find another piece of helpful information, in the column headed *number of years married.* Pooling these puzzle pieces, you can determine fairly closely the year of their marriage.

Example:

1880—great-grandmother age 30, born about 1850, could have married as early as 1866 (age 16), oldest child age 8—born about 1872. Marriage between 1866 and 1871.

1870—great-grandparents shown as a couple, with a baby born in April of that year, no other children. The child must have died before 1880, but its presence in 1870 suggests the couple married in 1869 or before. Narrows down the possibilities to 1866-69.

1900—both still living, married for 32 years. Subtract 32 from 1900; marriage year of about 1868, which could mean the latter half of 1867.

Other records such as deeds, wills, and estate settlements may help you narrow down a marriage date. William Harrison sold a lot in Petersburg, Virginia, in November 1784, and his wife Lucy was "privately examined as the law directs" and freely acknowledged the sale (Petersburg, Virginia, Deed Bk. 1, p. 30). We know, then, that William and Lucy were married before this date. Several documents may be necessary to approximate the marriage date itself, but each additional record will help you make a more educated guess.

Occasionally, the county records give us a marriage agreement, such as the one signed by both William Harrison and Nancy Vaughan on 26 March 1789, acknowledging their "promise to marry each other." As part of the agreement, William gave Nancy his "mansion house" and other property. We know by this document that the couple married probably in 1789. Because William was giving his new wife the house called Porter Hill "where Harrison now resides," and the couple continued to make their home there, we may guess that they probably married in Petersburg where Nancy's family and Harrison both lived (Petersburg, Virginia, Deed Bk. 1, p. 492).

In Amelia County, Virginia, Richard Phillips wrote his will on 14 March 1793, naming among his family and heirs his daughters Elizabeth Tolbert Allen and Tabitha Phillips (Will Bk. 5, p. 36). This document tells us that Tabitha was not married at the time the will was written but that her sister Elizabeth Tolbert Phillips had married a man named Allen before this date.

DEATH DATE AND/OR PLACE

Many of the same sources that help us with birth information can also give us death information: newspaper obituaries, tombstones, death certificates, interviews with older relatives or friends, funeral home files, funeral programs or notices, Bible records, church registers, old letters and diaries, insurance documents, lodge or organization membership files, employment files, family and county histories, and federal mortality schedules for people who died in a census year. More recent deaths sometimes appear on the Social Security death index available on CD-ROM at many research libraries and the LDS family history centers. Death or moving may be implied by the omission of a person from census or tax records. City directories, published about every other year, often name widows. By comparing entries for the family, you may be able to narrow the possibilities for a husband's death date.

County probate files, wills, and deeds can give clues and facts on many aspects of genealogy. In the case of Elliott Coleman, the county probate file contained items which placed his death date within a two-week period:

Accounting of money paid in behalf of Mr. Coleman, deceased, including cost of medical services, coffin, digging the grave, and clothes for burial, dated 17 Feb 1892.

Bill from the doctor dated 18 Feb 1892 for visits to Mr. Coleman between 16 Dec 1891 and 3 Feb 1892.

(Hays County, Texas, Probate File #354)

These two items alone narrow down his death date to some time between February 3 and 17. If the burial had already taken place by February 17, it is likely that death occurred on the sixteenth or before.

A more common example is the case of Thomas Ballard Smith of Louisa County, Virginia (Will Bk. 2, pp. 309-313). He wrote his will on 13 August 1776 and added a codicil (addition) to it on 6 October 1777. The will was probated in court on 12 January 1778. The record indicates that his death occurred between 6 October 1777 and the following January, which was most likely the first time the court had met after his death. You could guess that he died, therefore, in October, November, or December 1777.

Wills, deeds, and estate settlements can also be used in determining information about other family members. When Richard Phillips wrote his will in March 1793, he named two grandchildren, John and Lucy Holt, "allowing them to be equal to one of my said children" in the division of his estate, to receive their "deceased mother's" portion (Amelia County, Virginia, Will Bk. 5, p. 36). We learn here of a daughter, unfortunately not named, who had married, had two children, and died before March 1793. This kind of discovery can help in establishing not only the death date of the person who wrote the will, but also birth, death, and marriage information for his family members, married names for older daughters, and maiden names, in this case, for John and Lucy Holt's mother.

William Harrison's wife Lucy freely acknowledged her husband's sale of land on 11 February 1786 at her home because she was "about to leave this State and cannot conveniently attend court" (Petersburg, Virginia, Deed Bk. 1, p. 257). Then on 26 March 1789, William signed a marriage agreement and deed of gift to Nancy Vaughan, a young neighbor girl. We cannot tell what had happened to Lucy, his former wife, in just these two sources, but we can realize that divorce was rare, especially for a clergyman, as William was. Besides, William and Nancy named their second daughter Lucy a few years later, and Nancy had no sister named Lucy to honor with such a namesake. It seems more likely that Lucy died during the three years between the documents.

NAMES OF A PERSON'S CHILDREN OR PARENTS

Look for old letters and diaries, funeral notices, Bible records, newspaper obituaries and wedding stories, birth certificates and announcements, interviews with older relatives and family friends, church registers, deeds, court records, parental permission for an underaged child in marriage records, wills and probate files, guardianship records, military pension and bounty land warrant applications, homestead or naturalization case files, and, of course, censuses. In addition, tombstones may identify children who died young, such as *Alma Cummings, daughter of MH and CE Cummings,* who lived and died between the 1870 and 1880 censuses. Birth and death certificates give the parents' names, although many death certificates give them incorrectly. Getting birth and death certificates for several children of the same family may give a consensus for the parents' names. Sometimes, children's names suggest the names of grandparents. Isaac McFadden Patton, Thomas Patton Coleman, and Pitser Blalock Croom were all named for their maternal grandfathers, Isaac McFadden, Thomas Patton, and Pitser Blalock. Of course, other records are necessary to prove these relationships.

Cluster genealogy is often the key to discovering names of children or parents. One Texas family that I researched had lost three infant children and buried them in three different cemeteries in the same county. Had I not been working on the cluster of brothers and sisters of the husband and thus visiting multiple cemeteries in the county, I probably would have missed those three tombstones. After all, how can one know to look for tombstones for people whose existence was not suggested in any other records found in the search? When applicable to your search, the 1900 and 1910 censuses can help by telling you how many children a mother had and how many were still living.

Working on the cluster can pay off in other ways as well. For example, a bachelor brother dies and names in his will his widowed mother and his brothers and sisters, including married names. If probate records for the parents do not exist or do not name their children, this may be the only evidence of these relationships. If you do not read the document because he is not your direct ancestor, you miss the information. If you neglect census records of brothers and sisters, you may miss an elderly parent or another relative living with one of the siblings. If you ignore families living around your own in the census, you may miss the parents, a married sister, a married daughter, or relatives of the wife living only a few houses away. The census will not tell you these relationships, but the clues of age, birthplace, parents' birthplaces, naming patterns, or occupation can wave a red flag at you to investigate the similarities for possible connections.

The 1880-1920 federal censuses provide each person's relationship to the head of the household, as do many state censuses from the same period. Federal censuses of prior years, 1850-1870, do not specify relationships but certainly suggest a list of children for each couple: those listed in descending age order immediately after the parents. Usually, other relatives, children by a previous marriage with a different surname, in-laws, or others living in the house are listed after the nuclear family.

Lest we jump to conclusions about the mother's identity, we must remember that the wife shown in the census, especially 1850-1870 where relationship was not given, was not automatically the mother of all the children listed. Especially if children by a different surname appear after the basic family, the researcher needs to identify these. Were they the mother's children by a previous marriage? Were they nieces, nephews, or grandchildren? Were they foster children? If there is a gap of more than three or four years between children in the family, the searcher must ask whether (1) a child (or more) had died, (2) the older group may have been children of the father by a previous wife, (3) the youngest ones might be grandchildren by the same surname, or (4) any of the children actually were the wife's by a previous marriage but were listed under the husband's surname. By the same token, a young woman listed just below an older man could be a new wife, an unmarried daughter, a widowed daughter-in-law, or a younger sister. Further study into other records will be necessary to sort out such relationships.

If you use compiled family or county histories for names and dates of parents and children, try to verify the information with your own research, as these sources vary greatly in their reliability.

MOTHER'S MAIDEN NAME

Sometimes finding a maiden name is as easy as finding a Bible record, marriage record, newspaper article on her marriage or death, or tombstone that gives her maiden name. A tombstone reading *Lottie Haynes, wife of H.G. Barnett* indicates Haynes as her maiden name. Sometimes tombstones use the French *nee*, meaning *born*, to indicate a wife's maiden name: *Denisha Jane Brelsford nee Turley* (born a Turley). However, one such stone that reads *Elizabeth Austin nee Huston* actually reports her name by her first husband, not her maiden name.

At other times, the name may come from interviews with older relatives and family friends, family letters and diaries, a will or probate record of her parent which names her with her husband, a deed of gift from the parent to the married daughter and her husband, or a deed whereby the daughter and her husband were selling property inherited from her parent. Birth or death certificates of the woman's children or her own death certificate may give her maiden name, but these often contain mistakes. Of these three certificates, probably the most reliable would be the birth certificates of her children.

Sometimes you can get a clue from the names of her children or grandchildren: Peter *Talbot* Phillips, William *Darby* Orgain, Sarah *Warren* Orgain, Catherine *Ewing* McFadden, and William Lucius *Heath* Harrison. In all these cases, the names are still clues, for no answers have been found to explain the presence of these particular middle names. One Virginia boy, *Archer Allen* Coleman, seems to bear the maiden names of his maternal grandmother and great-grandmother.

A wife's maiden name is sometimes suggested in a census record by the presence of a person with a different surname living next door to or with the family. Johnson Godwin, living with George and Effie Keahey in 1870, turned out to be Effie's father. Elizabeth Brelsford, living with Gracey and Young Colvin in 1860, was Gracey's mother. Young people listed after the immediate family in a census may be younger brothers, sisters, or other relatives of the wife. Similarly, tombstones within a family group, with different surnames, are sometimes members of the same family. A tombstone of an earlier generation may be the wife's mother.

In our effort to find the maiden name and parents of Charlotte's great-grandmother Cordelia Cummings, wife of Moses Cummings, we looked in the county marriage records and discovered Moses Cummings marrying Mrs. Cordelia Everett in 1865. With this evidence that Cordelia had been married before, we looked in the same county for a Cordelia somebody marrying an Everett and found nothing. From the 1880 census we learned that Cordelia was born about 1830 and concluded that she could have been married by 1850. Perhaps we could find her in the 1850 census. Since we knew that she had lived in Texas at least since the early 1860s, we began reading Everett entries in the 1850 census there. After reading entries in several counties, we found Cordelia Everett, age 17, born in Pennsylvania, married to William Everett, a carriage maker. They were living in San Augustine County, two counties away from where she lived after 1865. Reading other families on the same page, we found one family in which the mother and older son also reported Pennsylvania as a birthplace. What a coincidence that this family was named Huston, and Aunt Sally had been telling Charlotte that she was related to General Sam Houston. We noted the fact that Cordelia's age could place her between two of the Huston children still living at home.

Next, we tried the marriage records of the new county and found Cordelia Huston marrying William Everett in 1847. The Huston couple in the 1850 San Augustine census were named Almanzon and Elizabeth. We hoped that county probate records would link Cordelia to this family, but they gave us nothing. Almanzon Huston was a party to many deeds but none with a Cummings or Everett, and we decided to hold an extensive deed search for later.

Two census records provided the most convincing evidence. The 1860 census of San Augustine County listed A. and Elizabeth Huston, Cordelia (age 26) listed as Huston, four Huston teenagers, a young woman (who turned out to be a married daughter) and her child, a boarder, and Elizabeth and Almanzon Everett (ages 7 and 5). The 1834 census of San Augustine then revealed Almanzon and Elizabeth Huston with six children, including Cordelia (age 3) (*The First Census of Texas, 1829-1836*, Marion Day Mullins, comp. [Washington, DC: National Genealogical Society, 1959], p. 2).

Back in the little town of Alto where Cordelia lived after 1865, we found at the city cemetery a double marker indicating that the two people had died the same day: Alma, the eight-year-old daughter of M.H. and C.E. Cummings, and Elizabeth Austin nee Huston, age 73. The name Austin sent us back to the courthouse where the probate records, this time, yielded results. Among the heirs of Elizabeth Austin, formerly Huston, was Cordelia Cummings, two other married sisters, three brothers, and the children of deceased siblings (Cherokee County, Texas, Probate Minutes Bk. A, p. 288; Bk. B, p. 89). The next question was whether Elizabeth was really born a Huston (*nee* Huston, from the tombstone) as well as married to one.

A trip to the Alto public library unexpectedly provided the answer. It came from a vertical file of folders of family history, including a copy of the Huston Bible record. It showed Cordelia, born 11 February 1830, the fifth child of Almanzon Huston and Elizabeth *Newton* (born 29 March 1805), who married 6 April 1819 in Erie County, Pennsylvania. The search for one maiden name gave us two and explained why one son was named Newton Huston. Oh happy day!

ANCESTORS ON THE MOVE

Searching for ancestors or their clusters of relatives means that we often have to look for people who have moved. Frequently, this scenario occurs as we work backward in time, for few families stayed in one place for several hundred years. For example, we find a Texas family in the 1880 census and discover that the parents were born in Tennessee and their parents, in North Carolina. Perhaps an elderly grandparent living in the household, born in North Carolina, reports parents born in Virginia. We suddenly have four states in which to search as we reach back to those generations. At other times, we want to study the siblings of an ancestor to complete the cluster and try to learn more about the parents, and we discover that several brothers and/or sisters moved away from the family's home county. In these cases, we must work forward from where we last found evidence of these relatives.

Depending on the time period of the people you are seeking, a variety of sources may help you identify the place to which or from which ancestors moved: interviews with relatives and family friends, letters, diaries, scrapbooks, newspapers, Bible records, tombstones, church registers that may show transfers, county records, federal military or public land records, statewide census Soundex for 1880-1920, individual birth or death certificates, index to statewide birth or death records, membership records of national organizations, membership papers for one of the hereditary organizations (DAR, SAR, etc.), college alumni lists, city directories, county histories, and the Social Security death index (deaths after 1936, but not all deaths). Published records that often cover a wide area include cemetery transcriptions, will and probate abstracts, deed and land grant abstracts, tax or jury lists, newspaper abstracts, statewide marriage records, statewide census indexes from 1790 forward, Bible records compiled as a statewide project, and indexes to statewide and regional genealogical periodicals. Try networking with other people working on the same family. Put a query in a regional or national genealogical periodical for information on the "lost" person or family. If you organize your plan of attack and work on it systematically, your search is more likely to yield results.

Several examples illustrate the variety of helpful sources. The case file (now in the National Archives) generated by one Shelby ancestor's purchase of public land gave us his earlier county of residence and a new place to search. A series of obituaries of one family of Preuss siblings helped us keep up with where the surviving brothers or sisters lived over a period of about forty years.

Alf Coleman was a bachelor and a carpenter by trade in 1882 when the Bolivar, Tennessee, *Bulletin* bade him farewell and good luck as he left for Texas with his "celebrated Gate Hinge." At the time we found this notice, the 1900 census had not yet been opened to the public. When that record did become public, the Soundex picked up Alf, still single and living in Dallas. However, we still don't know the fate of his gate hinge.

According to the 1850 Caddo Parish, Louisiana, census, great-grandmother Ann Robertson Croom had one brother, James, listed as T.J. Robberson in the 1860 census. We were not able to find him in the state in the 1870 or 1880 census. Working in the parish deed records for any Croom or Robertson data, we found Thomas J. Robertson of *Lafayette County, Arkansas,* selling his undivided interest held in common with other heirs of his deceased mother Elizabeth C. Croom and stepfather Isaac Croom. Lafayette County is just across the state line from the parish where he grew up. The search in the new location is complicated by the presence of apparently several men by the same surname and initials, but the search does go on, now that we have somewhere to look.

Census records can be very useful in this kind of search. More and more indexes are being published each year for censuses without Soundex (1790-1870, 1910). Two particular searches present special, but not unusual, problems.

Case I

Project: Working backward to find a hometown, county, or parent(s) for a blind ancestor, Luther White.

Information at hand: 1870 and 1860 censuses, in Texas, listed his birthplace as Mississippi. The 1860 census indicated, from the ages of the three children, that the family was probably in Illinois or Mississippi in 1850 and came to Texas after 1855.

Problem: Luther was not listed as head of household in the Illinois or Mississippi 1850 index. (Either living elsewhere or with another head of household.)

Plan: Copy all entries for heads of household named White from the Mississippi index.

There were Whites in sixty-four Mississippi counties in 1850! (At times like this, I must remember a favorite quotation from Shakespeare's *Henry V*, Act II, Scene 1: "Though Patience be a tired Mare, yet she will plod on.") With persistence and plodding, I read, entry by entry, all the Mississippi White families, taking the counties in alphabetical order since they are arranged on the microfilm in approximately that way. Almost at the end, in Pontotoc County, I found James White, age 59; Luther White, age 25 and blind; wife Tennessee (other censuses had listed her as Frances T.); and children Sarah and William. Persistence paid off. Perhaps it will help in taking James and Luther back ten more years.

Case II

William Francis Marion Holmes was easy to find in the 1860-1900 census records because he remained in one county.

Project: Working backward to 1850 to try to find parent(s) or other relatives, since he was about 21 years old in 1850.

Information at hand: Censuses from 1870 to 1900 gave his birthplace as Tennessee; 1860 census and secondary Bible records said he was born in Mississippi. The family had no parents' names to use in searching.

Problem: Indexes in Texas, Arkansas, Tennessee, and Mississippi did not show him; reading all Holmes families listed for Texas and Mississippi turned up nothing. At last, other sources gave a tentative name for his father: Isham Holmes. I decided to read all families with surnames beginning with *H* and with heads of household named Isham. I found the family listed and indexed as "Haynes" in Tishomingo County, Mississippi. Use of further sources showed that this was indeed the correct *Holmes* family.

Finding parents and families before 1850 is more difficult because the census names only heads of households. If the ancestor you are seeking was a head of household in 1840 and before, you may indeed find him in a given location; then you can use other sources to prove it is the same family. If the person you seek was listed in the 1850 or later censuses, you have at least a tentative state of birth in which to start a search.

Specialized sources, such as those described in chapter twelve, can help you locate people in a state or county at a given time. These are further sources which may help:

1. *The Consolidated Index of Claims Reported by the Commissioners of Claims to the House of Representatives from 1871-1880.* Washington, DC: United States House of Representatives, 1892. These records of the Southern Claims Commission, a federal agency, are in the National Archives, Record Group 217. The approved claims, filed by state and county, are petitions, testimony, and supporting testimony and documents submitted as evidence concerning property seized for use by the Union Army from "citizens in the Southern states who remained loyal to the Union." Disallowed claims are found in Record Group 233. Similar claims of "loyal citizens in loyal states" are in Record Group 92, in the Quartermaster General Claims. These files are available on microfilm.

2. Revolutionary War claims of civilians against the state for losses incurred during the war or, especially in South Carolina's accounts, soldiers or their heirs claiming back pay. In Virginia, see Public Service Claims from the Revolutionary War. In North Carolina, consult Revolutionary War Claims. In South Carolina, see Audited Accounts.

3. Loyalists.
   - *Loyalists in East Florida, 1774-1785.* Wilbur H. Siebert. New York: Irvington Publishers, reprint of 1929 edition.
   - *Loyalists in North Carolina During the Revolution.* Robert O. DeMond. Baltimore: Genealogical Publishing Company, 1979 reprint of 1940 edition.
   - *Loyalists in the Southern Campaign of the Revolutionary War: Officer Rolls of Loyalists. . . .* Murtie J. Clark. Vol. 1: Recruited From North and South Carolina, Georgia, Florida, Mississippi, and Louisiana. Vol. 2: Recruited From Maryland, Pennsylvania, Virginia, and Those Recruited From Other Colonies. Vol. 3: Recruited From Middle Atlantic Colonies With Lists of Refugees From Other Colonies. Baltimore: Genealogical Publishing Company, 1981.
   - *South Carolina Loyalists in the American Revolution.* Robert S. Lambert. Columbia: University of South Carolina Press, 1987.
   - *United Empire Loyalists.* Arthur G. Bradley. New York: AMS Press, reprint of 1932 edition.

4. *North American Immigration to Brazil: Tombstone Records of the "Campo" Cemetery, Santa Barbara, Sao Paulo State, Brazil.* Betty Oliveira. Brasilia: Graf. do Senado Federal, 1978. A number of Southerners moved to this community after the Civil War, including families from Chester County, South Carolina.

5. *Passports Issued by Governors of Georgia, 1785-1809* (Vol. 1) and *1810-1820* (Vol. 2). Mary G. Bryan and William Dumont. Washington DC: National Genealogical Society, 1959, 1964.
   Passports of Southeastern Pioneers, 1770-1823: Indian, Spanish and other land passports for Tennessee, Kentucky, Georgia, Mississippi, Virginia, North and South Carolina. Dorothy Williams Potter. Baltimore: Gateway Press, 1982.

6. Records of important gateways or "jumping off places" to frontier areas: Hagerstown, Maryland; Nashville, Tennessee; St. Joseph or Independence, Missouri; etc.

7. Quaker, Huguenot, Moravian records.

8. *George Rogers Clark and His Men: Military Records 1778-1784.* Margery Harding, comp. Frankfort, KY: Kentucky Historical Society, 1981.
   Virginia Colonial Soldiers, 1607-1775. Lloyd D. Bockstruck. Baltimore: Genealogical Publishing Company, 1988. Compiled from bounty rolls, enlistment rolls, etc.
   Other such compilations of military units, militia records, etc.

9. Books of early land grants, early landholders, early taxpayers, early officials in given areas. The following are examples.
   - California: *Spanish and Mexican Land Grants in California.* Rose H. Avina. Salem, NH: Ayer Company Publishers, 1976.

- Indiana: *Indiana Land Entries, 1801-1840* (Vol. 1) and *Indiana Land Entries: Vincennes District, Part 1, 1807-1877* (Vol. 2). Margaret Waters. Knightstown, IN: Bookmark, 1977.
- Kentucky: *Certificate Book of the Virginia Land Commission, 1779-1780.* Easley, SC: Southern Historical Press, 1981 reprint of 1923, Vol. 21, *Register of the Kentucky State Historical Society.*
- Louisiana: *Land Claims in the Eastern District of the Orleans Territory, Communicated to the House of Representatives, January 9, 1812.* Walter Lowrie. Easley, SC: Southern Historical Press, 1985.
- New Mexico and Colorado: *Spanish and Mexican Land Grants in New Mexico and Colorado.* John R. and Christine M. Van Ness, eds. Manhattan, KS: Sunflower University Press, 1980.
- New York. *Landholders of Northeastern New York, 1739-1802.* Fred Q. Bowman. Baltimore: Genealogical Publishing Company, 1983.
- Ohio: *First Ownership of Ohio Lands.* Albion M. Dyer. Baltimore: Genealogical Publishing Company, 1982 reprint of 1911 edition.
- Tennessee: *North Carolina Land Grants in Tennessee, 1778-1791.* Goldene Burgner. Easley, SC: Southern Historical Press, 1981.
- Virginia: *Mother Earth: Land Grants in Virginia, 1607-1699.* W. Stitt Robinson, Jr. Charlottesville: University Press of Virginia, 1957.

10. Anyone doing research in Virginia must become familiar with Earl Gregg Swem's *Virginia Historical Index*, 2 vols. (Magnolia, MA: Peter Smith, 1965 reprint of 1934 original). This "Swem Index" is a massive project from precomputer days which indexes the *Calendar of Virginia State Papers* (1652-1869); *Hening's Statutes at Large* (1619-1792); *Laws of Virginia, Supplement to Hening's (1700-1750)*; *The William and Mary Quarterly*, Series 1 and 2; *The Virginia Historical Register*; *Tyler's Quarterly*; the *Lower Norfolk County, Virginia, Antiquary*; and *The Virginia Magazine of History and Biography.*

OCCUPATION

The census records of 1850 and later asked for each person's occupation, and this is probably the best place to begin looking. By 1870, the instructions to the census takers emphasized accurate and precise recording of occupations, including those of children who contributed to the family support with a regular job. By 1900, unemployment during the year could be recorded as well as the person's status as employer, employee, or self-employed.

Other good sources for occupation information include old letters, diaries, interviews with older relatives and family friends, scrapbooks, local newspapers, city directories, employee records, union membership records, state unemployment records, and published histories of cities, counties, or companies. Occasionally wills or deeds mention a family business or the tools of one's trade. Papers of businessmen, doctors, and families of the area that have been deposited at a library or archives sometimes include accounts with their customers, other businessmen, or employees. In court minutes I learned that Elliott Coleman had worked for the county repairing the iron bridge and cutting the floor of the courthouse for the cistern. Also in court minutes, we learned that James Shaw owned the ferry across the Cumberland River in early Nashville.

Inventories, estate sales and settlements in the probate records can also be helpful. Many inventories of deceased retailers give detailed lists of their stock and accounts. Estate settlements sometimes report the profits of a family business or the receipts for sale of the crops.

POLITICAL AFFILIATION

Local newspaper stories and advertisements, especially during campaigns, give information about volunteer workers, supporters, and candidates. Interviews with older relatives and family friends, old letters, diaries, scrapbooks, photographs of campaign parades, and perhaps local or state party records may give you information. We of the twentieth century, who take the secret ballot for granted, may forget that voting was not always a private matter. Some deed books or other county record books have polling lists that show who voted for whom in various elections. In one Kentucky county, I stumbled across the election returns (lists of who voted for whom in each precinct) from the Presidential elections as far back as the 1820s. What a gold mine of information that the clerk's office had not even known they had!

HOUSING OR LIVING CONDITIONS

Sources include photographs in the possession of family members or local historical societies, scrapbooks, old letters, diaries, interviews with older relatives and family friends, local archives, and published books on houses of the area. Sometimes deed records describe or illustrate a house on a particular lot. Church records and parish vestry books sometimes describe the minister's house. If a business has been built on the site of a former family home, that company or the builders of the new building may have photographs of the site before construction. If the home is still standing, the current residents may talk with you, allow picture taking, or even let you visit inside. If the home is still standing, older residents of the community may be able to describe the interior floor plan or tell you what changes have been made over the years.

Inventories and estate settlements in county records often include lists of personal property and furnishings that give an idea of the family's lifestyle: the number of plates and bowls, silver teaspoons, mirrors and candlesticks, sometimes even window curtains, bedspreads, and quilts, or the books that the individual owned. In a will, an ancestor may specify certain pieces of personal property, furniture, or jewelry to be given to particular individuals.

The censuses of 1850, 1860, and 1870 recorded the value of one's real estate. The 1860 and 1870 returns also asked the value of one's personal estate. Beginning in 1890, the census asked whether homes and farms were rented, owned, or owned free of mortgage.

The Sanborn Company's fire insurance maps, available in larger public and university libraries and state historical societies or archives, provide information, such as size and shape, on buildings in many towns and cities on specific dates, mostly since 1867. The New Orleans Notarial Archives (at 421 Loyola Avenue) has several hundred nineteenth-century watercolor drawings of buildings, mostly in the city and nearby parishes, produced when the buildings were placed on the market. The drawings are of both commercial buildings and residences, and some include floor plans. Some newspaper advertisements of buildings for rent or for sale contain descriptions of the buildings as well as the names of owners or tenants.

COUNTRY OF ORIGIN

The more recent the immigration, the easier it will be to find information. Consult census records, naturalization papers, passenger lists, land records, death certificates, tombstones, obituaries, family Bibles and histories, family tradition, and elder family members to learn of immigration since the mid-nineteenth century. (See pages 32, 72-73.) Studies of surnames and their origins may suggest translations and alterations of names that have changed after immigration.

Studying the ethnic backgrounds of the area where your earliest ancestor in this country lived may suggest groups to which he might have belonged. Religious groups often traveled in a body, as did members of extended families, or neighbors. People migrated with relatives or friends. Maps in published histories and geographies may show migration patterns of particular ethnic and religious groups, which may give you clues.

Westland Publications, P.O. Box 117, McNeal, AZ 85617, has published a number of books and booklets on immigrants from the German provinces and France, including such titles as *Mercenaries from Hessen-Hanau Who Remained in Canada and the United States After the American Revolution* and *Mercenaries from Ansbach and Bayreuth, Germany, Who Remained in America After the Revolution*, both compiled by Clifford Neal Smith.

A source of current books on immigrants, or any other topic, is the latest *Books in Print* volumes, published by R.R. Bowker Company.

Another major source of genealogical books, including many that will help with a search for immigrant ancestors, is Genealogical Publishing Company, 1001 N. Calvert St., Baltimore, MD 21202. Listed here is only a sampling of the books from this publisher.

- Peter W. Coldham: *The Complete Book of Emigrants in Bondage, 1614-1775* (1988); *Emigrants from England to the American Colonies, 1773-1776* (1988); *The Complete Book of Emigrants, 1661-1699* (1990); and other books on English emigrants.
- David Dodson: *Directory of Scots Banished to the American Plantations, 1650-1775* (1986); *Directory of Scots in the Carolinas, 1680-1830* (1986); *Directory of Scottish Settlers in North America 1625-1825*, 6 vols. (1985-1986); and other books on Scottish emigrants.
- Albert B. Faust and Gaius M. Brumbaugh. *Lists*

of Swiss Emigrants in the Eighteenth Century to the American Colonies. (reprint 1991).

• Ira A. Glazier and Michael Tepper, eds. *The Famine Immigrants: Lists of Irish Immigrants Arriving at the Port of New York, 1846-1851.* 7 vols. (1983-1986).

• John Camden Hotten, ed. *The Original Lists of Persons of Quality . . . from Great Britain to the American Plantations, 1600-1700.* (reprint 1986).

• James Savage. *A Genealogical Dictionary of the First Settlers of New England.* 4 vols. (reprint 1990).

• Ralph Beaver Strassburger. William John Hinke, ed. *Pennsylvania German Pioneers: A Publication of the Original Lists of Arrivals in the Port of Philadelphia From 1727 to 1808.* (Norristown, PA: Pennsylvania German Society, 1934, 3 vols.; reprint of Vols. 1 and 3 by Genealogical Publishing Company, 1966).

• Michael Tepper: *American Passenger Arrival Records: A Guide to the Records of Immigrants Arriving at American Ports by Sail and Steam* (1988); *Passenger Arrivals at the Port of Baltimore, 1820-1834* (1982); and *Passenger Arrivals at the Port of Philadelphia, 1800-1819* (1986).

• John Wareing. *Emigrants to America: Indentured Servants Recruited in London, 1718-1733.* (1985).

• Don Yoder, ed.: *Pennsylvania German Immigrants, 1709-1786* (1989) and *Rhineland Emigrants: Lists of German Settlers in Colonial America* (1985).

• Gary J. Zimmerman and Marion Wolfert. *German Immigrants: Lists of Passengers Bound from Bremen to New York, 1847-1854, . . . 1855-1862, . . . 1863-1867.* (1986-1988).

Other publishers have added valuable sources for immigration research:

• P. William Filby: *Passenger and Immigration Lists Index: A Guide to Published Arrival Records. . . .* 3 vols. (Detroit: Gale Research, 1981). 12th annual supplement, 1993. Over two million names indexed. Preliminary Edition, 1980. *Passenger and Immigration Lists Bibliography 1538-1900* (Detroit: Gale Research, 2d ed., 1988). Companion to *Index* listed above.

• Ira A. Glazier and P. William Filby, eds: *Germans to America: Lists of Passengers Arriving at United States Ports,* 32 volumes by 1993, covering 1850-September, 1876 (Wilmington, DE: Scholarly Resources, 1988-); and *Italians to America: Lists of Passengers Arriving at United States Ports, 1880-1899* (Wilmington, DE: Scholarly Resources, 1992-).

• Nils W. Olsson. *Swedish Passenger Arrivals in New York, 1820-1850.* (Chicago: Swedish Pioneer Historical Society, 1967).

• Robert P. Swierenga, comp. *Dutch Immigrants in the United States Passenger Manifests, 1820-1880.* 2 vols. (Wilmington, DE: Scholarly Resources, 1983).

Ethnic historical and genealogical societies are sources of information on immigrations from particular countries or regions. A few are listed in Appendix C. Others may be identified in the *Encyclopedia of Associations* or through advertisements in genealogical periodicals such as *The Genealogical Helper.* Through such societies you may be able to learn where your surname of interest originated. You may find society members descended from people of your surname(s). Although you may not find data on your specific ancestral family, you may gain from networking with other searchers.

For those whose ancestors immigrated to New England on the ship *Mary and John* in the early seventeenth century, the Mary and John Clearing House sponsors conferences and tours to the English West Country and publishes books. You can contact Burton Spear, 5602 305th St., Toledo, OH 43611. Also involved in these tours and conferences is Family Society Tours, Ltd., 62 Weston Rd., Weston, CT 06883. Write for information on tours to other ancestral locations in the British Isles.

More than 115,000 passengers arriving at the port of Galveston between 1836 and 1921 are now part of a database available to the public at the city's Texas Seaport Museum. Entries give arrival date, country of origin or embarkation, and destination.

Once you have enough clues to lead to tentative searches into the country of origin, you have many sources to check, but the problems include accessibility, language, difference in types of records, obscure place names, and time or money for travel. The Family History Library in Salt Lake City and a number of public libraries around the country are acquiring more and more foreign records each year, from deeds, wills, and other public records to church and parish registers.

The Everton Publishers, Inc., of Logan, Utah, has published a number of guides to searching in other countries, such as Austria, Norway, Denmark, Central Europe, Scandinavia, England and Wales, Italy, Germany, and Hungary. You can contact this company at P.O. Box 368, Logan, Utah 84321.

The Genealogical Publishing Company in Baltimore also has published several books on research in other countries:

- Angus Baxter: *In Search of Your Canadian Roots* (1989), *In Search of Your German Roots* (reprint 1992), *In Search of Your European Roots* (reprint 1992), *In Search of Your British and Irish Roots* (reprint 1992).
- Rosemary A. Chorzempa. *Polish Roots.* (1993).
- Margaret D. Falley. *Irish and Scotch-Irish Ancestral Research.* (reprint 1988).
- John Grenham. *Tracing Your Irish Ancestors.* (1993).

The accepted practice among genealogists when writing letters with genealogy requests is to enclose a self-addressed, stamped envelope (SASE) for a reply. When we write to individuals, libraries, or societies in foreign countries, however, we cannot enclose an SASE. The accepted method of providing for their reply is to send *International Reply Coupons*, which can be purchased at the post office. One coupon provides one ounce of surface mail; an airmail reply may require two coupons. Ask your local post office for guidance; different destinations may need different provisions for replies. The post office also sells aerograms, which are lightweight airmail paper on which you can write a message, then fold up and address on the outside. They are actually cheaper than sending a letter overseas in an envelope. However, enclosures are not allowed inside aerograms.

CHAPTER FOURTEEN

What's in a Date?

WRITING DATES

There are generally two methods of writing dates. The more common one combines month/day/year: 6/6/76 or June 6, 1976. The other system is used in Europe, in military notation, and increasingly by researchers as it eliminates commas and helps prevent confusion in reading. It simply notes day/month/year: 6 June 1976 or 6/VI/76 in which the month is written in Roman numerals. Each writer is usually consistent, so you can tell in a moment which system is in use. In 5/31/15, it is obvious the month is being placed first since there are not 31 months. If you send a questionnaire to someone to fill out, it would be wise to give them blanks to fill out as you want it done:

It is wise to write out or abbreviate clearly the month instead of using numbers. This practice prevents confusion.

READING DATES

In older newspapers or documents, writers sometimes used shortcuts in noting dates. These shortcuts deserve explanation. A person writing on 17 February 1841 and referring to *your letter of the 8th instant* meant *your letter of 8 February. Instant* means *this month.* Reference to *your letter of the 28th ultimo* meant *your letter of 28 January,* or last month. Likewise, someone writing in January 1841 about an event on *the 28th ultimo* meant 28 December, last month, which was also in the previous year.

Tuesday last meant the most recent Tuesday, and *Thursday next* meant the nearest Thursday to come. *September last* was the most recent September, even if it was in the previous calendar year.

OLD STYLE VERSUS NEW STYLE DATES

The Julian calendar, the Old Style, was introduced in Rome in the year we would call 46 B.C. and into the Christian world in A.D. 325. It gave the year 12 months and 365 days, with a leap year of 366 days every fourth year, similar to our system today. However, it became obvious to some that the calendar and suntime were not synchronized as they should be. Man's calendar was gradually getting behind the sun's natural calendar, like a clock losing a little time each day. In other words, each calendar day was a few minutes too long. These few minutes added up to three days over a period of 400 years or ten days by the year 1582. This discrepancy meant that the first day of spring, the vernal equinox, fell on March 11 instead of March 21, and the church's calculations for the date of Easter, which are governed by that equinox, were not right. Therefore, in March 1582, Pope Gregory XIII revised the calendar to be in accordance with the sun. He "made up for lost time" by moving over those ten days rather rapidly to catch up with the sun; and the day after 4 March 1582 became March 15 instead of March 5.

To keep the calendar accurate and prevent the loss of three more days in succeeding 400 years, we now omit three leap year days every 400 years. To simplify the process, the Pope chose the double-zero years, the century dividers. The rule is that the double-zero years that can be divided evenly by 400, with no remainder, *will* be leap years: 1600, 2000. The ones in between, which cannot be divided evenly by 400, will *not* be leap years: 1700, 1800, 1900, 2100, etc.

The Pope made one other change, and this is the one which really affects genealogists. New Year's Day had fallen on March 25. Thus 24 March 1532 was followed the next day by 25 March 1533. However, from 1582 on, New Year's Day would be January 1, as it is today.

The changes were confusing to a number of people, and some thought the Pope was trying to shorten their lives by ten days! Even more confusing, however, was the fact that only Spain, Portugal, Poland, France, and parts of Italy made the change in 1582. When it was December 12 in Rome that year, it was December 2 in London. The German Catholic states, Belgium, and parts of Holland followed in 1583-84; Hungary, by 1587. However, for over a century, the countries of Europe, as well as their territories in the New World, operated under two different calendars.

Various protestant states of central and northern Europe adopted the Gregorian calendar between 1699 and 1701, leaving Great Britain stubbornly clinging to the old Julian calendar for another half century. By then, the difference between the two systems was eleven days instead of ten because the year 1700 had been leap year, with an extra day, in Britain but not in Rome. Much of Eastern Europe and Asia remained under the Julian calendar or their own system until the twentieth century.

Further complicating the situation, some British individuals (and therefore some American colonists) adopted the Gregorian calendar on their own. Thus, you cannot always tell which calendar was used in the particular records you are reading, but it seldom really matters. You can make the distinction in your own notes as necessary or desirable by adding after the date *O.S.* (Old Style or Julian) or *N.S.* (New Style or Gregorian). If you find a date written with a double day, 5/16 April 1704, you know that under the old calendar the date would be April 5; under the new style, it would be April 16. Likewise, you may find a double year written in an early record, but only for the months of January, February, or March. They could come under either of two years depending on which calendar the recorder used. Thus, 9 January 1688/89 would mean 1688 for a person using the old calendar or 1689 for one using the new or Gregorian system. Technically, George Washington's birth date could be written 11/22 February 1731/32, which covers both calendars.

When you work with early records, you may find what otherwise may seem to be discrepancies or inaccuracies which can actually be explained by the difference in calendars. If a record is dated "the 5th day of the 5th month of 1729," it could be May 5 under the new calendar but July 5 under the old one, March being counted as the first month in the Julian system.

My own ancestor Patty Field Allen, according to the Bible record, was born on 25 August 1746. Her sister Obedience was born on 1 March 1747. It becomes obvious that the family was not using the Gregorian calendar, for a baby born in August is not followed by another born barely six months later. According to the Julian calendar, still the official calendar of Britain and the colonies, the March following Patty's birth was still 1746. March 25 ushered in 1747; so, 1 March 1747 was another twelve months away, actually eighteen months after Patty's birth. Obedience, therefore, could write her birth date 1 March 1747/48, meaning 1747 under the old system or 1748 under the new one.

Finally, in 1750, Parliament agreed to make the official change to the Gregorian calendar. The day after 2 September 1752 was September 14 instead of September 3, making up for the eleven days' difference in the two systems. Furthermore, the new year would begin on January 1 instead of March 25.

WHAT DAY OF THE WEEK?

The five-day work week with a weekend for family and social activities is, of course, a relatively recent phenomenon. Today's predominance of Saturday weddings is surely related to this pattern. On what day of the week did weddings occur in your family's past? Why did Grandma and Grandpa choose Wednesday for their wedding? At least one couple chose that day because the groom, who worked six days a week, found someone who would work for him Wednesday and Thursday. His only free day was Sunday, but no one in that community at that time would have considered having a wedding on Sunday.

Another prospective groom was asked when the wedding would be. The young farmer answered, "Sometime between the peas and the wheat." Apparently any day of the week would do so long as it fell within the slack season.

Some almanacs publish a perpetual calendar by which you can find the day of the week for many dates in the past or future. However, you can figure it yourself with easy arithmetic. The formula on page 90 gives a correct day of the week for any date after 14 September 1752, the day on which Britain and the colonies converted to the Gregorian calendar. Actually, you could use the formula for dates before this, if you then convert them to the old calendar. Below are two examples, using two actual wedding dates.

Just for the fun of it, practice the formula using 14 September 1752, the day of the great calendar switchover. Can you imagine the trauma of trying that kind of change in our culture on *that* day of the week? Even

Formula: What Day of the Week?	*Example 1* 9 December 1824	*Example 2* 8 August 1781
Step 1. Begin with the last 2 digits of the year.	24	81
Step 2. Add ¼ of this number, disregarding any remainder.	6	20
Step 3. Add the date in the month.	9	8
Step 4. Add according to the month: January 1 (for leap year, 0); February 4 (for leap year, 3); March 4; April 0; May 2; June 5; July 0; August 3; September 6; October 1; November 4; December 6	6	3
Step 5. Add for the 18th century 4; 19th century 2; 20th century 0; 21st century 6	2	4
Step 6. Total the numbers.	47	116
Divide by 7. Check the remainder against this chart to find the day of the week: 1 = Sunday; 2 = Monday; 3 = Tuesday; 4 = Wednesday; 5 = Thursday; 6 = Friday; 0 = Saturday	6 with remainder of 5. The wedding took place on Thursday.	16 with remainder of 4. The wedding took place on Wednesday.

daylight saving time goes into effect in the early hours of Sunday so as to give the least possible confusion. Imagine our making a daylight-saving-time change on the same day of the week that the whole calendar changed!

USING DATES

Dates are a useful tool for the genealogist. There are many ways to use them for purposes other than just vital statistics.

Here are some actual cases which illustrate the use and misuse of dates.

Case I

Notes taken from two tombstones in one family read as follows:

Infant daughter
4 September 1891-10 September 1891

Talmadge Ward Campbell
12 January 1892-26 November 1894

Do you see the discrepancy? And this has nothing to do with the old calendar. A daughter born in September and a son born four months later? Hardly. The first note seemed to be correct: The baby girl lived only a few days and was not named. The other was probably copied wrong. It could have been June 1892, or January of 1890 or 1893. The tombstone was studied again; the stone actually read June instead of January 1892. The copy contained the error.

Case II

Another tombstone clearly reads:

To the sacred memory of
Rev. William Harrison
who departed this life
20th November 1814 . . .

However, his will, which is dated May 1812, is recorded in the January 1814 probate records, and the year 1814 is clearly written three times on the page. So the tombstone must be incorrect and should probably read 1813. His will cannot have been probated before he died. Chances are that he died the November prior to the probate, or November 1813.

Case III

The original marriage bond in the archives of the Virginia State Library, showing the intent of William Daniel to marry Patty Field Allen, is clearly dated 28 March 1768, as is the attached consent of the bride's father, Samuel Allen. Under a Virginia law of October 1748, if either bride or groom was under 21 and not formerly married, consent of the father or guardian of "every such infant shall be personally given before the said clerk" of the county, with two witnesses (Hening's Statutes of Virginia, vol. 6, p. 82). According to the published Bible record of Patty's brother Archer Allen, Patty's birth date was 25 August 1746 (Bible record of Archer Allen, *The William and Mary Quarterly*, Series 1, vol. 22, p. 95). This date would make Patty 21 years and 7 months old when she married, and not really needing the consent of her father to marry.

At that time in Virginia, it was the law for a wife to be brought to the courthouse when her husband sold land to which she had a claim. The Justice of the Peace or another official took her aside, explained the deed of sale to her, and asked if she willingly signed it. Was the signature hers? Did she wish to retract it? By agreeing to the sale, she relinquished her dower rights to that property. (See page 52.)

William Daniel sold a tract of land in August 1761, and no dower right or wife was mentioned. Probably, William was not married at the time. Then in 1763, at least by September 27 when the deed was recorded, William sold 200 acres, also in Cumberland County, to John Daniel. No dower right or wife was mentioned at that time. However, in the spring of 1765, John Daniel sold this same tract, and William sold 375 acres in another tract. Seven months later, 28 October 1765, John's wife Elizabeth and William's wife Martha appeared in court and relinquished their dower rights to the 200 acres that John was selling, and Martha consented to the sale of William's 375 acres (Cumberland County, Virginia, Deeds, Bk. 3, p. 193, 416; Bk. 4, p. 60, 67). Why would Martha have any claim to relinquish on John's land unless she was married to William at the time he sold it to John? That sale was in 1763, and this document suggests that William and Martha were married by that time, and certainly by 1765 when the dower rights were relinquished. Yet the marriage record clearly shows their marriage in 1768.

The dates of these documents clearly present a dilemma, and perhaps they cannot be reconciled. A possible answer is that William was married to another Martha before he married Patty, who in later records continued to be called Martha rather than Patty. If this were so, the first Martha would have died in 1766 or 1767, leaving no children. Another possibility, although less likely in light of other county records and family histories, is that another couple named William and Martha were in the county in the 1760s. This is an example of one of the great puzzles of genealogy.

Case IV

After collecting information from many sources, it is helpful to chart what you know and study the possibilities. An outline of the life of any ancestor, provides convenient space in which to chart the information you have gathered on a particular person. At a glance and in chronological order, you have such information as birth and baptism, education, marriage, military service, moves from one home to another, the birth of children, real estate transactions, court appearances, voting records, and other puzzle pieces that you may obtain from public and family records. The outline helps keep these events in perspective, provides a quick review of what you know and what you lack, helps you catch discrepancies, and helps you formulate questions for your next search effort. Your notes, of course, contain the source and documentation for each piece of information transferred to the outline. An example is shown in Figure 13.

Here are some questions which arise from the outline of William Harrison's life:

1. The large gap between his birth and his ordination is an opportunity for study, for search. Where was he educated? Where did he grow up?

2. Did he actually go to North Carolina between 1756 and 1760?

3. Do Surry County records shed any light on his life around 1760-62?

4. Where did he go during his eleven-month leave of absence in 1772? Perhaps to England? Perhaps to Barbados? For further education?

5. Events between 1774 and 1780, especially in Virginia, must have troubled him greatly, for he resigned his pastorate and switched sides. Are there Cornwallis papers or Governor Nelson papers which might shed light on his change in loyalty from the American side to the British side?

6. The court records which may have included Harrison's trial no longer exist. Did a trial take place? What other sources may help us?

7. We know he left Virginia and later returned to his home. Where did he go? For how long? When did he leave? Immediately or in 1786 when Lucy was "about to leave this State" and could not appear in court?

8. When did Lucy die? What more can we learn about her? These deeds are the only mention of her that has been found so far.

Many more questions can arise as the search continues. They may or may not ever be answered, but looking for an answer is part of the fascination of genealogy.

Each ancestor presents a different set of questions and challenges to work on. To correlate the questions and the search for answers, I have found it helpful to use a Problem Search Record, as shown in Figure 14. It provides a central place to keep records of the search for particular information. As shown in the example, three problems presented by William Harrison's outline in Figure 13 are being "attacked."

An effort has been made to discover his birthplace and place of education. The various letters which have been written are listed here along with a summary of the answer from each source. This information is especially useful for those of us who have to put intervals of weeks or months between our opportunities to search. Over a period of time away from your subject, it is easy to forget what you have already accomplished if you do not write it down. Proper use of this chart can help you begin again where you had to stop the time before.

The questions or problems for which the Problem Search Record is most useful are those which require the use of a number of sources or writing a number of letters.

OUTLINE OF THE LIFE OF WILLIAM HARRISON
name of ancestor

Note: Fill in information on marriage(s), children, education, military service, illnesses, religious milestones, jobs, migrations, family events, deaths, etc.

YEAR	EVENT
c 1730	Born at Barbados (Info from Lambeth Palace Library-London)
19-21 Dec 1756	Ordained deacon & priest by Bishop of London & licensed to officiate in North Carolina, where he proposed to set up a public school.
1760	Minister in Southwark Parish, Surry Co, Va.
22 Nov 1762	Rector of Bristol Parish, Blandford Church, Petersburg, Dinwiddie Co, Va.
Sept 1772	11 months leave of absence – Where did he go?
27 May 1774	Signed the Association protesting closing of the port of Boston
4 Feb 1780	Resigned as rector of Bristol Parish, after 18 years
19 Oct 1781	Captured with Cornwallis, surrender at Yorktown
21 Oct 1781	Gov. Nelson wrote Lord Cornwallis: Harrison has been delivered to civil authorities to stand trial – we can't prevent it.
13 Feb 1782	Gov. Harrison wrote to Attorney for the State in Gloucester Co mentioning an order to prosecute Harrison on charge of high treason.
17 May 1782	Gov. Harrison wrote to Attorney General asking him to be present at trial of Harrison.
Nov 1784-Jan 1786	Wife Lucy joins him in selling Ravencroft lots in Petersburg.
10 Feb 1786	Lucy "being about to leave the state & cannot conveniently attend court."
26 Mar 1789	Marriage agreement of William with Nancy Ann Vaughan, dau. of David & Winnefred Vaughan.
c. 1792 — 1804 or so	5 children born to William & Nancy Ann – living in Petersburg
1810	Census: William's household in Petersburg, p126 of Dinwiddie Co, including 5 children
29 May 1812	Wrote his will
20 Nov* 1813	Death. Burial place his home, Porter Hill. (Later moved to front of Blandford Church)
3 Jan 1814	Will probated. *(Tombstone shows 1814 as death date – Court records indicate he died before 1814 – either 1812 or 1813.)

FIG. 13: OUTLINE OF LIFE OF WILLIAM HARRISON

PROBLEM SEARCH RECORD

THE SEARCH FOR Rev. William Harrison

name of ancestor

PROBLEM	SOURCES TO TRY/ QUESTIONS TO ANSWER
Origin, Birthplace, + Education	1. Registrar at Cambridge Univ. - no record of him 2. Registrar at Oxford - no record of him 29 June 1976 3. Registrar, Barbados - birth certificate search, April, 1976 - no record of him 4. Guildhall Library, London - June 1976 - referred me to Registrar, Barbados. 5. Bishop of London ★ Lambeth Palace Library - found ordination papers - 1756 - gave Barbados as birthplace & educated in England. 6. Church Commissioners, London, June 76 - referred me to Lambeth Palace Library. 7. Society for the Propogation of the Gospel - no record of him but helpful suggestions. ★
Cornwallis Papers which might shed light on his appt as chaplain, 1781, especially Orderly Book for August, 1781.	Library of Congress, Ms Division - April 1976 referred me to Clements Library, Ann Arbor Michigan. Clements Library - does not have Orderly Book. Suggested Pub. Rec. Office, London. Guildhall Library - June '76 - suggested Pub. Rec. Office, London. Public Records Office, London - does not do any searching - must hire searcher - alas!
Education, Birth cont'd.	Registration Office, Bridgetown, Barbados - no record of him, suggested their achives. 2 baptism certificates: 1688 too early & 1747 too late. Codrington College, Barbados - opened 1830, too late. Suggested Central Grammar School & Codrington Grammar School - Sent addresses. Write them.
1774 - "Association protesting closing port of Boston"	Is this the same William Harrison? Were there 2? Was the Rev ever a Burgess?

FIG. 14: PROBLEM SEARCH RECORD

CHAPTER FIFTEEN

Fitting the Pieces Together

Putting together a family history puzzle involves many strategies, sources, and people. One interview with a major figure probably will not be enough. You may contact the same person time and time again over a period of years. Likewise, use of the public records may call for several visits to the same courthouse as you learn more and ask more questions. It takes repeated use of all these sources to make your puzzle as complete and interesting as possible. Here is an example of an actual search as it began. Notice the combined use of family and public sources.

In a brief visit with a friend's Aunt Leona and Mama Edna, we started the family group sheet, with Grandma and Grandpa White as the husband and wife. Their eighteen children and stepchildren were not in chronological order, we listed them as we thought of them and numbered them later. In a few cases, we listed nicknames, leaving space for the full names when we found them. We had time to add three or four spouses and learn that all the children on the chart were born in the same Texas county. We learned that Grandpa had a brother named Wallace and a sister, and that both grandparents had lost spouses before marrying each other. The visit had to end, but we planned another soon.

Now we had two families to follow, two searches to pursue: Grandpa's family, the Whites, and Grandma's family whom we had not yet identified. Between visits, I read the 1880 federal census for their county. I found Grandpa and his first wife with brother Wallace and sister Olivia. This census gave their ages, birthplaces, and relationship to Grandpa who was head of the household. The census said that Grandpa was born in Illinois! The blanks for birthplaces of his parents were marked "unknown."

Finding that Wallace and Olivia were both born in Texas, I decided to try the 1870 census to see if I could find them with their parents. Since the older brother cared for the younger brother and sister, and no living relative knew of any others, what family were they part of? The 1870 census showed Grandpa, Wallace, two parents (Luther and Frances), two more sisters, and another brother! And Great-grandpa Luther was blind! Since Olivia was nine years old in the 1880 census, I did not expect to find her in 1870, and I didn't. She was born after the census was taken, either in late 1870 or 1871.

The immediate question was what happened to the rest of the family between 1870 and 1880? There are probably two alternatives: they moved away or they died. If they moved away, why did they leave the baby of the family with her older brother? Since none of the descendants have heard of any other relatives, chances are that the parents of the family died. The sisters could have married and lived in other counties. Was there an epidemic in the county that may have taken several family members in a short time? Some of these questions may never be answered. Meanwhile, we wrote them down, laid them aside, and continued the search for basic information.

Noticing in the 1870 census that one of Grandpa's sisters was born in Mississippi about 1856 and the next one in Texas about 1859, we could calculate the family's migration to Texas between 1856 and 1859. The next source we checked was the 1860 census of their county, and they were there. To round out the then-available census information, we read the 1900 census for Grandpa and his brother Wallace and their sister Olivia with their own households.

From the four census records we compiled the information shown at the top of page 97.

In the county records, we discovered marriage records for Grandpa, Wallace, and Olivia, and a second marriage for Great-grandpa Luther in 1873. So we knew that Frances died between December 1870, when Olivia was born (according to the 1900 census), and 1873. We found a deed record that showed Great-grandpa Luther still living in the county in 1878, but found no reference to him after that.

As Case I on page 82 illustrates, taking this family back to the 1850 census was a challenge and an exercise in patience. Information from other records suggested that they were probably in Illinois or Mississippi in 1850, but the 1850 census indexes did not show Luther as a head of household. With absolutely no other clues to go on, there was only one choice: read the several hundred entries for White families in sixty-four Mississippi counties. In Pontotoc County, there they were: James White (age 59), Luther (age 25 and blind), Felix (14), John (10), Tennessee (26), Sarah (5), and William (3). This gave us (1) James as a probable father of Luther, Felix, and John, born about 1791 in Tennessee; (2) his younger sons Felix and John, born in Mississippi about 1836 and 1840; (3) Frances Tennessee, Luther's wife; and (4) their children Sarah and William. Because Sarah did not appear in the 1860 and later censuses, chances are that she died before 1860.

The surprising information in the 1850 census was that Sarah's and William's birthplaces were both given as Mississippi, although all the other censuses said William was born in Illinois! Even in 1900, William and Olivia both said their *parents* were born in Illinois. This assumption is probably incorrect, but there may well be a clue in the fact that William's birthplace is given as Illinois during his entire adulthood and even once during his childhood. There are many possibilities: the family lived in Illinois only a short time during which William was born; he and Sarah were both born during a slightly longer stay in Illinois; the parents could have married there regardless of where their children were really born; they may have simply talked about moving to Illinois so much that it became fact in the minds of the children; one or both parents could have lived in Illinois during childhood; etc.

The family sources, for the time being, are exhausted, and the Texas sources are being examined. The Mississippi (and Tennessee and possibly Illinois) sources are, for the most part, untouched but promise a challenging search.

Meanwhile, the other part of the family, Grandma's, was even more intriguing because we knew nothing of it. We knew Grandma's maiden name (Cummings) from her first marriage record. Her second marriage record, of course, showed her as Mrs. E.L. Collier (Ella Lee) who married William J. White.

On the way to visit my friend's Aunt Leona a second time, we stopped at the county clerk's office in the courthouse and read marriage, deed, and probate records for Cummings, our "newest" family name. The only Cummings listed in the deed indexes was Moses Cummings, with his wife Adelia. This was possibly Ella Lee's (Grandma's) father, but we found no proof. The probate records gave us Moses's death date, 1903, at age 77, which suggests a birth year of 1826.

Our second interview with Aunt Leona was rewarding. We copied all information from the family Bible: marriages, births, and deaths, and found that Grandpa William White had died in 1910. No wonder the kids (the ones still living) didn't remember him; they were too small. We finished naming the eighteen children of Grandpa's and Grandma's combined families, and their spouses, on the family group sheet—as much as we could. We shared with Aunt Leona the surprises found at the library and the courthouse.

She guided us through the cemetery where she knew many of the family members were buried. As we copied names and dates, she identified each person: "Ida's husband," or "he was killed in a car wreck," or "an adopted son." She also listed for us the unmarked graves of family members known to be in the cemetery, including Grandpa and his first wife.

All afternoon we recorded stories as fast as she told them, and she was really wound up. Each question brought a 20-minute answer with tales of getting lost in the woods, having 75 to 100 relatives for Christmas, growing up in the tomato patch, a near-shotgun wedding, and the old aunt who griped when the kids fed scraps of biscuit dough to the chickens.

With Aunt Leona navigating, we drove to the old "home-place" where she had grown up, although the house is no longer there; to the school where all the kids got "edgicated"; down the road on which they used to walk to school; and by her Grandma Cummings's house! The real house! This opened a whole new area of the puzzle.

Aunt Leona's Grandma Cummings would be my friend's great-grandmother, Ella Lee's mother, but we call her Grandma now, slipping into Aunt Leona's generation. And we fired the questions:

1. What was your Grandma's name? *Grandma.*
2. When did she die? *She lived to be 93; the kids got out of school to go to the funeral.* (**Use this.** Leona was born in 1907 and started to school at six or seven, 1913 or 1914. Her grandma died when she was small

Name	1860 Age	1860 Birthplace	1870 Age	1870 Birthplace	1880 Age	1880 Birthplace	1900 Age	1900 Birthplace	Birth Date	Birthplace of parents
Luther White	35	Miss.	45	Miss.					c1824-25	
Fraces T. "	30	Tenn.	40	Tenn.					c1829-30	
William J. " (Grandpa)	12	Ill.	22	Ill.	32	Ill.	51	Ill.	Jan 1849	Ill.
Martha E. "	5	Miss.	14	Miss.					c1854-55	
Margaret A. "	1	Tx.	11	Tx.					c1858-59	
Wallace M.T. "			7	Tx.	18	Tx.	38	Tx.	Mar 1862	
James L. "			2	Tx.					c1867-68	
Olivia Frances "					9	Tx.	30	Tx.	Dec 1870	Ill.

but already in school, so after 1913 but possibly before 1920, when Leona was 13 and old enough to remember more about landmark events.)

3. Who were Grandma's children? *Mama and a brother Cumby.*

4. What was his real name? *I don't know.*

5. Was Grandma married more than once? *I don't know.*

6. Were there any stepchildren? Did Mama have half brothers and half sisters? (Note: from here on, we use Leona's names for these people. "Mama" was our Grandma Ella Lee; "Grandma" was our great-grandmother Cummings. It is easier for people being interviewed to identify relatives by the names they called them.) *Yes, Mama had a half brother, John Cummings.* (**Use this.** Grandpa Cummings married someone else before Grandma.)

7. We found a John Cummings in the 1880 census with a wife and a baby girl, Elnora. Is that the same John? *Yes, Nora was the only girl. She had eleven brothers, named for Bible characters, including Matthew, Mark, Luke, and John.*

8. Did Mama have other half brothers or half sisters? *I don't remember.*

9. What was Grandma Cummings's name? (again) *Grandma.* (again)

10. Did she live on "the place" a long time? *Yes, forty or fifty years. Grandma needed someone to look after her when she got old, and Mama had too many kids to be Mama and Papa to and run the farm and feed some of her grandkids, too. She simply could not take care of Grandma. So she deeded her half of the place to her brother, Cumby, if he'd look after Grandma.* (**Use this.** Grandma lived there many years, and Mama "deeded" her half. That means they owned the place; they didn't rent. In the deed index, the only Cummings listed was Moses. So Grandma is likely his wife.)

Now we made an effort to sort out what we knew about the Cummings family.

11. What road is the house on? *Old San Antonio Road.* (**Use this.** Moses had at least two pieces of land just outside town on the Old San Antonio Road, shown in deeds we just found at the courthouse.)

12. Did you ever know Grandpa Cummings? *No.* (We had found that Moses died in 1903, before Leona was born.)

13. What was his name? *Never heard anybody say.*

14. Could it have been Moses? *Don't have any idea.*

15. Could Grandma's name have been Adelia? *Hey, yes! But it was* Cor*delia. Yes, it had to be because sister Delia was named for her.* (Adelia in the deeds makes little difference; recorders can make mistakes.)

16. Moses was Adelia's husband. See these deeds of 1869 and 1870. Let's look at the marriages we copied at the courthouse. Here's M.H. Cummings (could be Moses) marrying Mrs. C.E. Everett (C could be Cordelia) in 1865. Your mama was born in 1867, so these could be her parents.

17. Look at some of the cemetery notes: Nina Cummings, 1872-1945; C.C. Cummings, 1865-1934; Alma Cummings, 1870-1878, daughter of M.H. and C.E. Cummings; Christopher Columbus Cummings, died in 1963, age 81. Can you identify these? *Well, Cumby's wife was Nina.* Could Cumby be a nickname for Christopher Columbus? *I don't know; I never heard his real name.*

We decided it could be: M.H. and C.E. married in March 1865. Their son Cumby, if the C.C. above, could still have been born in late 1865. The child Alma of M.H. and C.E. was born exactly three years to the day after Mama was born, but died young. Christopher

Columbus Cummings, born in 1882 and living 81 years, could be Cumby's son, a junior; or he could be a son of Cumby's half brother with eleven sons (but Christopher Columbus is hardly a Biblical name).

18. Do you know any of Cumby's kids or John's kids we could write to for further information? *Yes.* And she gave us a name and address.

The visit had to end. What next? Study notes taken so far. (I like to underline or star in bright-colored felt-tip pen the parts that pertain to the direct family.) Fill in the new information on the family group sheets. Write down questions that have come up and are still unanswered. Write the man Leona suggested. Recheck the 1880 census for Luther White's second wife Martha or Mattie, as a widow. Recheck the 1880 census for Moses and Cordelia Cummings. Leona's mama, their daughter Ella Lee, was still at home, unmarried, in 1880. Maybe this family was overlooked in first reading. Write Aunt Delia. She's 80 and unable to answer, but maybe her daughter will. Anyway, try. Plan to visit the courthouse again for the marriage dates of Ella Lee's eight Collier kids by her first husband and for the marriage of C.E. ____________ (Grandma) to a Mr. Everett, to find her maiden name and marriage.

That part of the search is now complete: Cordelia Huston Everett Cummings was the Grandma Cummings we first heard about from Aunt Leona. Her father, Almanzon Huston, was an innkeeper, stagecoach owner, and mail contractor, possibly of New York birth. Her mother was Elizabeth Newton, born in 1805, possibly in northern Pennsylvania. Grandma herself was one of their fourteen children. She was born in 1830, probably in Michigan, and came with the family to Texas prior to the Texas Revolution, in which her father served as Quartermaster General. Much remains to be gathered on this interesting family, who, contrary to persistent family tradition, was not "closely related" to General Sam Houston.

CHAPTER SIXTEEN

Read It Right

Reading handwriting from the past is a skill all genealogists use. Developing this skill is easier if you are aware of the pitfalls.

In the eighteenth and nineteenth centuries, most lowercase letters were formed about the same way they are today. Individual variations are found, of course, but there was a general pattern for writers to follow.

There were two styles of *r* and *t*, just as there are today:

Western fork of a branch running a northernly course

at my decease

all their future

Sometimes *u* and *n*, or *w* and *m*, looked alike. Like writers today, writers a century ago did not always dot their *i*s and cross their *t*s. Because of fading ink, yellowing paper, and the unevenness with which quill pens and pen staffs wrote, these and other strokes in the original are barely distinguishable to us today.

The most unusual characteristic of older handwriting is the double *s*, written as if it were *fs* or a sprawling *ps*. Here are some examples from the nineteenth century.

possessed

division [sic]

blessing

witnesseth

Clerk.

James Harriss, Clerk

Missouri

Missippi [sic]

Agness

Jessee

Miss Polly

Bass

One of these same writers made the *j* of *enjoyment* exactly the same as the first *s* in *blessing*. There is not confusion, however, because it is clear what word he is using.

in the enjoyment of

Another writer in 1903 used the same stroke, but for the letter *g* in *things*:

Some capital letters can confuse the modern reader. The *S* and *L* are very similar and sometimes the *T* is hard to distinguish from them.

Susannah, Sally &

Sister

Sons

Subject

Legacy

Levi

Lea

Lucy

Thomas

State of So Carolina

signed Thomas Smith

The *I* and *J* are almost identical. Perhaps this similarity is a carryover from the Latin and Greek alphabets in which the two letters were interchangeable, or in which there really was no *J*. Words which we spell with *J* often come from Latin or Greek stems beginning with *I*. A prominent example is the pair of Christian symbols *IHS* and *INRI*. The first is the beginning of the Greek spelling of *Jesus*. The second is an acronym from the Latin words for "Jesus of Nazareth, King of the Jews." The three *I*'s here stand for words we begin with *J*.

Another example is the variation of forms of the name *John*: the German *Johannes*, the French *Jean*, the Spanish *Juan*, the Russian *Ivan*, the Scandinavian *Jan*, and the Gaelic *Ian*. Many of the Biblical names used in the eighteenth and nineteenth centuries are of Hebrew or Aramaic origin and were originally spelled with an *I*. It was not until the seventeenth century that the *J* was clearly a separate letter in function and form. Is it any wonder then that handwriting reflected this double duty? Here are some examples showing the similarity of *I* and *J*.

January Sessions

I do

Isham

Isaac

Isaac

Joseph Harrisson

In the first place

J.B. Kirkland

Juliana

John

Isaac Johnston

James

Joshua

Many of the capital letters of the eighteenth and nineteenth centuries are similar to the script type, shown here:

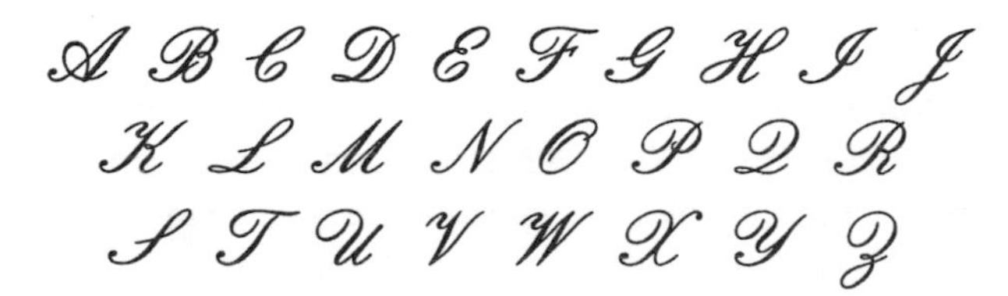

When you find problems in reading the handwriting, let your imagination play with the letters and try different combinations until you decide what the original says. If the letters individually create a problem, look at the word as a whole, or the phrase it is part of. What is the writer talking about? What is the logical word to fit the meaning? Is this the word he is using? Look at other letters of the same handwriting. Try to find the same letter or word written elsewhere by the same person. Can you guess it by comparing its shape with others you already know?

If you cannot decide, try copying the original as closely as possible or put a blank in your copy, indicating an illegible word. If you can narrow the possibilities, put the alternatives in your notes. An example is the two names Lemuel and Samuel, which are sometimes hard to tell apart. In your notes, put "Lemuel or Samuel" to indicate the problem and to let you know later that you could not tell which name it was.

Try some sample problems. This word looks frightful by itself. But when you put it with the whole phrase, there is only one possible reading: "Witness the following signatures and seals."

This is a signature on a marriage license from 1869:

We know the initial is *P* and the last name is *Mullally.* The first name looks like it ends in *is.* It cannot be *Morris* or *Travis.* The first letter is not shaped like the *M* in his last name, and there are too many humps for *Travis.* If you have access to another source, look to see how someone else wrote his name. His name is Francis.

Another signature to study is the one above Carter H. Trent's name on a contract. The initials are clearly *E.W.* There is a dot for an *i* and the last letter seems to be *s.* The beginning letter, as it turns out, is easily recognized as a large *s* as in the old-style double *s.* But it could give a reader an impression of *J* or maybe a fancy *T.* In this case, it cannot be compared with letters of the same shape on the document because this is a signature added to another man's instrument. But in the rest of the contract, the man's name appears several times, a little different each time:

By comparing three slightly different ways of writing the same name, we must conclude the man was E.W. Sims.

Seventeenth- and early-eighteenth-century writing looked very different from the later styles. It was much more square or rounded, not so sleek and flowing. Yet it was elaborate in its own way.

Steⁿ Hughes
Robert Hughes

mercy and merrits [sic] of my Lord

Daniel Croom

witnesses hereto

An excellent reference book for the very early American writing is E. Kay Kirkham's book, *How to Read the Handwriting and Records of Early America* (Salt Lake City: Deseret Book Co., 1961).

Copying older handwriting takes special care so that the message of the original is preserved. An example is found in a marriage record from Madison County, Tennessee. The bride's name is divided and on two lines of the original: Stur-devant. One copier saw only the first syllable and recorded, and published, the name as Steer. The original writing is tiny and the *u* could be read as two *e*s. But a more careful copier would have seen the rest of the name on the next line. Furthermore, one who had worked with the records of that county would have recognized Sturdevant as the name of several families in the county.

In copying a passage, copy it just as the original reads. If a letter or word has been omitted and you want to put it in, add it in brackets to indicate that you, rather than the original writer, supplied it. Another method is to write [*sic*] after the word. This is Latin for "thus." It indicates that you know something is wrong, but you've copied it exactly as it was.

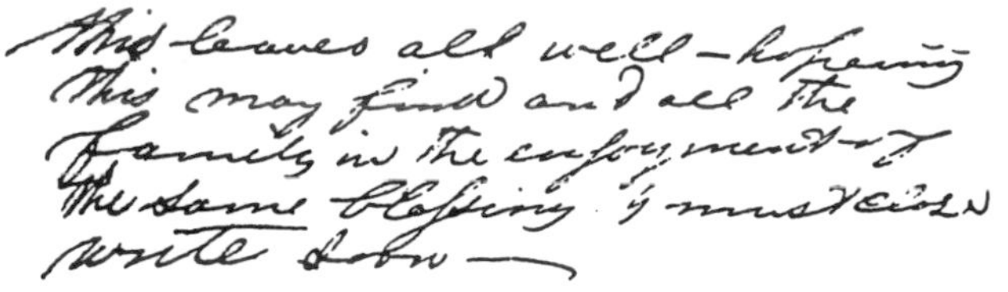

"This leaves all well—hopeing this may find [you] and all the family in the enjoyment of the same blessing. I must close write soon—"

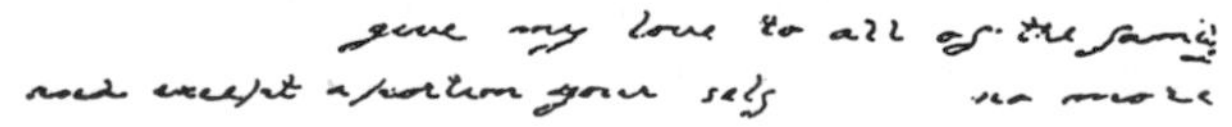

"give my love to all of the family
and except [*sic*] a portion your self no more."

Numbers written in the nineteenth century are very similar to numbers we write now. The major difference is that the older ones sometimes contain a few more flourishes.

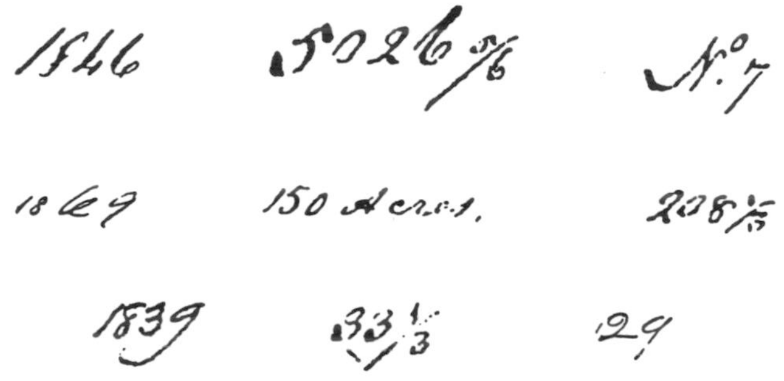

Reading old records can be quite enjoyable because clerks often had very polished, clear handwriting. It takes a lot more skill to duplicate their style than to read it. The care with which they wrote may remind us to review the legibility of our own scribbling.

CHAPTER SEVENTEEN

What About Computers?

Can you "do genealogy" without a computer? Absolutely. Genealogists researched and organized quite effectively before computers, and many work well today without a computer at home. However, with the tremendous sophistication and increased affordability of computer technology since the 1970s, the world of genealogy is forever changed.

Perhaps the first evidence many of us had that computers were at work in genealogy was the rapid increase of indexes for the voluminous federal census records. They have become such an integral part of census research that we wonder how we ever managed without them. Gradually, correspondence among us took on the "printout" appearance, and form letters were being sent to "Dear Friends Searching Jenkins Families." Soon these letters included family group and pedigree charts from the computer.

Have you ever spent hours looking up all the family addresses from the last three years' Christmas cards before sending out requests for information for family group sheets? Have you ever typed, retyped, cut and taped, and retyped a research paper or family history project, or written or indexed anything using little slips of paper in a house with children, pets, or ceiling fans? Have you ever spent an hour looking up one marriage record in your stack of notebooks in order to answer Cousin Grace's letter and, in the meantime, forgotten three times just which of Silas Brown's daugnters you were looking for? If you've had experiences similar to these, you will be receptive to the idea of computers in genealogy.

Computers can store and print address lists, speed our writing efforts, aid in indexing and organizing our files, and search for the information we give them. With special programs, computers can enhance our efforts with many kinds of charts, printouts, and even graphic images. They also allow us to communicate with people and computers by remote access. Of course, it takes time and concentration to learn computer skills, and this learning comes easier for some than for the rest of us. The process is especially frustrating when most instructional manuals are written by experts using a vocabulary seemingly from outer space. Nevertheless, even regular folks can take advantage of the benefits that computer technology has brought to genealogy.

COMPUTER GENEALOGY AT HOME

Genealogy Computer Programs

Genealogists have available a number of ways to use a computer at home. Among the options are genealogy programs, word processing, computer interest groups, and various long distance or "remote access" opportunities.

Many genealogy programs are available which can link related individuals into family groups, record vital statistics and notes, and print out charts. Some researchers even use several programs to take advantage of the strengths of each. No one program is "best." Your choice would depend on what you want to be able to do and for what price. These sources may help you make a choice:

1. *Archer's Directory of Genealogical Software.* George Archer. Bowie, MD: Heritage Books, Inc., 1994 or latest edition.
2. *Computer Genealogy: A Guide to Research Through High Technology.* Richard A. Pence, ed. Salt Lake City: Ancestry, 1991, revised edition.
3. *Guide to Genealogy Software.* Donna Przecha and Joan Lowrey. Baltimore: Genealogical Publishing Company, 1993 or latest edition.
4. *Genealogical Computing: A Quarterly Journal.* Salt Lake City: Ancestry. The July-August-September issue each year contains a software directory. Each issue contains articles on software programs.

5. *National Genealogical Society/Computer Interest Group Digest.* Arlington, VA: National Genealogical Society. This *NGS/CIG Digest* is part of the society's *Newsletter* that is issued six times a year. Each issue contains articles about software. One series comparing software features appeared in Volume 12, Numbers 2-5 (1993).

6. Articles and advertisements on computers and genealogy also appear in these general genealogical journals: *Heritage Quest Magazine*, published bimonthly by the American Genealogical Lending Library of Bountiful, Utah, and *Everton's Genealogical Helper*, published bimonthly by the Everton Publishers of Logan, Utah.

Genealogists sometimes want to add programs that will provide specialized information or functions, such as atlases, calendars, timelines, historical events on a given date, Soundex codes, or making maps and printing a variety of charts. These *utility* programs can be identified in basically the same publications as listed above:

1. *Archer's Directory of Genealogical Utility Software.* George Archer. Bowie, MD: Heritage Books, Inc., 1993 or latest edition.
2. *Guide to Genealogy Software.* Donna Przecha and Joan Lowrey. Baltimore: Genealogical Publishing Company, 1993 or latest edition. Contains a section on utility programs.
3. *Genealogical Computing: A Quarterly Journal.* Salt Lake City: Ancestry. The July-August-September issue's software directory includes utility and accessory programs.
4. *NGS/CIG Digest.* Arlington, VA: National Genealogical Society. Various issues contain articles and advertisements on utility programs.
5. Articles and advertisements in other genealogical and general periodicals.

Accessories such as scanners, digital cameras, and photos transferred to CD-ROM or floppy disk are among the new technologies that intrigue genealogists. The periodicals listed above often mention such new developments and their applications in genealogy.

Word Processing

A second option for a home computer in genealogy is word processing. Although I own and use a genealogy program, I often find that my word processing program does exactly what I need for studying a given family or individual. Whether I am researching some-

Fig. 15: Sample Word Processing Document
Thomas King, 1844-1891

1844, June 20—Thomas King born. His grandson AT King always said he was born in England. Census records of his only son give Ger (1900), Tx (1910), Eng (1920).	*Tombstone, Washington Cemetery, Houston, TX, gives date.*
1870, Feb 13—(?) a Thomas King mar. a Carrie McCain.	*Travis Co, TX, Mar. Bk 2:588.*
1870 census—Emilie Preuss & Wilhelm Rock with Paul & Clara Prusler household. Thomas King not yet found.	*Travis Co, TX, p 308.*
1872, Aug 17—Amelia Preuss m William Rock	*Travis Co, TX, Mar. Bk 3:200.*
1874, 1875—William Rock & (?) a Thomas King on tax roll	*Travis Co, TX, tax rolls, 1874-1875.*
1873, 1877-79—no mention of Thomas King in Houston.	*Houston city directories.*
1880 census—Thomas King not yet found. Amelia Rock, widowed or divorced, & 3 Rock children in house of Catherine Smith & sons, 160 Washington St.	*Houston, Harris Co, TX, ed 72, p 13. [full details in notebook]*
1880, Dec 3—Amelia Rock m Thomas King	*Harris Co, TX, H:391, #10278.*
1880-1881—Thomas King, carpenter, H&TC railroad shops, no home address given.	*Houston city directory.*

one else's family or my own, I like to create a word processing document, especially on the elusive ancestors, to show in chronological order each event as it is identified, along with the documentation for that information. This document then provides easy access for additions, study, and evaluation, especially if research turns up, for example, three different birthplaces, two maiden names for the first wife, or some other conflicting information. Figure 15 is part of such a document. Notice the mention of certain information that has *not* been found. When I find a person with the same name and can not yet tell whether he/she is my subject, I list the information but note the question of identity.

Computer Interest Groups

Computer users sometimes band together into computer interest groups (CIGs) to learn from each other about the use of the computer or of a particular genealogy software. The January-February-March issue of *Genealogical Computing* each year contains a computer interest group directory. Also contact George Archer, P.O. Box 6233, McLean, VA 22106, for information on such groups, or ask about a local *CIG* at your local genealogy society.

Remote Access—Communication

Some genealogists enjoy subscribing to a bulletin board system (BBS), to electronic mail (e-mail), to a newsgroup such as *soc.roots* (name change under consideration in late 1994), or to a mailing list such as ROOTS-L. These are all avenues of communication using the computer to contact other people with similar interests, to share research information and methods, to ask questions, and to look for other people researching in the same area or for the same surnames. Access to these systems requires a computer, a modem, a telephone, and telecommunications software. Some bulletin boards are free of charge to users; others, along with e-mail, newsgroups, and mailing lists, require paid subscriptions. Long-distance telephone charges may be involved as well.

Thousands of genealogy-related bulletin boards exist. To learn about access to one, ask local computer genealogists, or contact the National Genealogical Society bulletin board, home of the National Genealogy Conference, at 4527 Seventeenth St. N., Arlington, VA 22207-2399, or (703) 525-0050, or fax (703) 525-0052. You can also contact George Archer at P.O. Box 6233, McLean, VA 22106.

The 1994 issues of the *National Genealogical Society/Computer Interest Group Digest* (part of the NGS *Newsletter*) featured very informative articles by George Archer on bulletin boards and the other forms of electronic communication, "The Genealogist's Guide to the Internet" (*NGS/CIG Digest*, Volume 13). The Internet is a collection of thousands of smaller computer networks worldwide and is the means by which one connects with e-mail, the newsgroups (soc.roots) and mailing lists (ROOTS-L). It is accessible through many bulletin board systems, through commercial on-line services such as Delphi, CompuServe, GEnie, Prodigy, or America Online, or through an Internet service provider. Many genealogists have access through the computer systems where they work. For information on specific providers, consult the *NGS/CIG Digest* articles mentioned above or magazines in bookstores, such as *Computer Shopper* or *Boardwatch Magazine.* Various issues of *Genealogical Computing* contain helpful articles, such as "Researching with Freenets," by George L. Thurston in volume 13, number 2 (October 1993), pages 1, 22-26.

Remote Access—Library Catalogs

Many libraries have computerized their catalogs and all but retired their *card* catalogs. Some libraries have made their automated catalogs available to patrons, not only in-house but by remote access via computer and modem. Browsing in such a catalog can help genealogists learn of books and other media on a particular subject, in a particular location, or possibly available on interlibrary loan. This kind of searching broadens our knowledge of sources and assists in finding materials that could be helpful in a particular search. Public and university library catalogs are available on-line in such cities as New York City, Buffalo, Houston, Ft. Wayne, Miami, and others. Some of the on-line catalogs are available by direct dial; others require the use of a bulletin board system or the Internet.

In addition to individual library catalogs, it is possible to access the combined catalogs of a network of libraries, such as CARL (Colorado Alliance of Research Libraries), that includes a number of libraries both in and out of Colorado; MELVYL of the University of California system and state library; and HARLIC (Houston Area Research Library Consortium).

Perhaps the most important library accessible through the Internet is the Library of Congress. More than twenty-six million items, including books, serials, manuscripts, maps, and microforms, are cited in the

Library of Congress Information System (LOCIS), as well as references to other information sources, such as federal legislation (since 1973), copyright registrations (since 1978), and organizations.

Remote Access—Databases

Genealogical databases of various kinds are becoming accessible via home computers, and more and more will be added in the coming years. These can be fun to view, may give you important clues for searching, and sometimes yield concrete results. Some of the databases are surnames and pedigree linkages submitted by subscribers and/or readers. Some are more research oriented, with indexes to public records. In most cases, the databases do not represent complete coverage of the topic and should be considered finding tools only. Use of these databases may help you find a distant cousin working on the same family, a possible link to another generation, an ancestral family in a census record, or a marriage or death date. However, the information you gain from using these files does not replace the real research of reading the census microfilm, looking at the county or city marriage records, or gathering documents to prove the link to a new generation of ancestors. As with any transcription, information that had to be typed into the databases may contain errors.

The Bureau of Land Management's General Land Office Automated Records System is, at this writing, perhaps the best available source of remote access research using original records. Because it is a database, it is not only an index that can be searched by name or other categories of information, but it is also abstracts of the land office records themselves. The automated records system operates out of the Eastern States Office, 7450 Boston Blvd., Springfield, VA 22153, (703) 440-1600. This office holds original tract books and survey plats for the thirteen public land states within its jurisdiction: Alabama, Arkansas, Florida, Illinois, Indiana, Iowa, Louisiana, Michigan, Minnesota, Mississippi, Missouri, Ohio, and Wisconsin. (The other states in the eastern part of the country are state-land states and maintain their own original land transfer records. See chapter twelve for further discussion.) These tract book records have been copied into the automated system for nine of the thirteen states. Plans are to complete the remaining four (Illinois, Indiana, Iowa, and Missouri [1995]) by the end of the decade.

By opening an account with the Eastern States Office, an individual can search the pre-1908 homestead and cash entry patents from home or office. Most genealogists would request patents in the name of an ancestor in a given state. Any record found will provide the legal description and size (acreage) of the property, the land office that handled the sale, the date of the transaction, other identifying data, and the document (or entry) number, which is the number needed to access the land entry case file at the National Archives. This is an exciting development for genealogists, title companies, and others who research land records.

Gradually, these GLO records are being published on CD-ROM. By early 1995, Arkansas, Florida, Louisiana, Michigan, and Wisconsin were available in this medium. The disks are for sale to the public through the Government Printing Office, P.O. Box 371954, Pittsburgh, PA 15250-7954, (202) 512-2250. Many libraries that are federal documents depositories are also receiving the disks for their collections.

Everton's On-Line Search is a bulletin board system of the Everton Publishers of Logan, Utah, (800) 443-6325, whose magazine *Everton's Genealogical Helper* is well-known among genealogists. Since 1992, On-Line Search has offered primarily the publisher's "Roots" Cellar, Family File (family group sheets), Pedigree Library (four-generation charts), and GEDSRCH (linked pedigrees submitted on floppy disk), all of which are furnished by readers and subscribers. Their "Roots" Cellar is a database of ancestors' names, each with one event (birth, marriage, death, residence), its date and location, and the identity of the submitter. The first three databases in the list are also being made available for purchase on microfiche and CD-ROM. More recent additions to the On-Line Search include the 1851 English census, 1871 Canadian census, and an extensive Kentucky death index from 1911 forward. More acquisitions are planned.

The American Genealogical Lending Library, (801) 298-5446, of Bountiful, Utah, began its bulletin board system in February 1994. Among the databases available for searching are federal census indexes, marriage indexes, the Social Security death index, and the AGLL catalog. The census indexes include mostly heads of household in 1870 for Baltimore, Chicago, New York City, Philadelphia, St. Louis, and a growing number of states. Scattered indexes for 1820, 1860, and 1910 are also available. The marriage records, from Liahona Research, provide early and partial coverage for about nineteen states at this time and are also available on floppy disk and CD-ROM. Inquire about additions to the bulletin board system.

The Reference Desk **BBS of the Atchison, Kansas, Public Library**, (913) 367-0859, tel: (913) 367-1902, provides a database of tombstone inscriptions, mostly from Atchison County, and plans to add other information of genealogical interest.

Automated Archives, Inc., of Orem, Utah, (801) 226-6066, has an extensive catalog of CD-ROM products, which are available for individuals and libraries to purchase. The databases published on these disks include census and tax list indexes, marriage record indexes, family history books and indexes, the Social Security death index, the Everton Publishers' databases mentioned above, some mortality schedule indexes, birth and cemetery indexes, the BLM automated land records, and an index to Irish censuses, 1831-1841. Some of these databases are also for sale on floppy disk. Their marriage record indexes are mostly from the Hunting for Bears database, abstracted from selected counties in many states and representing only partial coverage of available records. These databases are good finding tools but do not take the place of research into the documents themselves.

An exciting "high-tech" item in their catalog, released late in 1994, is a CD-ROM of military volunteers between the Revolutionary War and the War of 1812, providing graphic images of the original records. Other graphic image disks are planned, but the company will not announce specifics until each project is ready for release.

The Family History Library of Salt Lake City in 1994 was testing the feasibility of making their FamilySearch databases available for home use. This set of databases is available in most of their branch family history centers. It includes primarily the Social Security death index, the military (Korean War and Vietnam) death index, their Ancestral File, the International Genealogical Index (IGI), and the massive catalog of the Family History Library.

The Geographic Names Information System (GNIS) of the United States Geological Survey is a huge database of place names, including many which no longer exist. If you need help finding a particular ancestral community, cemetery, or landmark that does not appear on current maps, you can access the database via the Internet or you can write to the GNIS at USGS, Branch of Geographic Names, 523 National Center, Reston, VA 22092, (703) 648-4544. Extensive searches may incur a small fee.

COMPUTERIZED DATABASES AWAY FROM HOME

Libraries

Even genealogists who do not have computers in their homes can take advantage of the technological revolution that makes some aspects of research quicker and easier. Many libraries have computerized their catalogs for use in-house even if they are not available by remote access. Although not all libraries have completed entering older materials in their collections, they gradually are replacing the old card catalogs with the computerized versions. In addition, a number of libraries with genealogy and history collections are acquiring CD-ROM publications such as those from Automated Archives, the American Genealogical Lending Library, and the Bureau of Land Management. Other reference sources available on CD-ROM in larger public and university libraries include the index called ERIC (Educational Resources Information Center) and the index and abstracts of *America: History and Life*.

Bureau of Land Management, General Land Office Records

As discussed earlier, the Bureau of Land Management Eastern States Office has automated over a million land records of the states within their jurisdiction. This computerized system can be searched at their public research room, 7450 Boston Blvd., Springfield, VA 22153. One feature of on-site use that is not available to remote users is the ability to receive the actual document images in addition to the extracted data. By mail, however, long-distance searchers can get photostatic copies of patents, survey plats, and tract book pages.

Galveston's Texas Seaport Museum Database

In 1991, the Texas Seaport Museum opened in Galveston. A popular feature among visitors is the database of immigrants who entered through Texas ports between 1846 and 1948. The database has more that 130,000 names, with whatever information the original record contained: arrival date, ship's name, port of embarkation and date, destination in the United States, and often personal information such as age, nationality, and occupation. The great majority of records are from the passenger arrival lists, but other sources are used as they come to light. The museum staff does make every effort to verify additions before they are entered into the database. As is the case with any set of old records, some of these passenger records are missing, especially for the years 1871 to 1894. Nevertheless, the database is a valuable tool that gives many people easy access to important immigration information.

Ellis Island Immigration Records

Another database of immigration information is the project under way for the Ellis Island Family History Center in New York City. The primary source of information is the passenger arrival lists in the National Archives, many of which are not indexed. Such a database, therefore, provides not only an index but the extracted information as well. The first phase of the project will include mostly German, Irish, and Italian immigrants, but plans are to include, from the earliest records to the twentieth century, all nationalities and all ports of entry, not just Ellis Island, which was established in 1892. The project coordinators include the Ellis Island Restoration Commission of the National Park Service and the Balch Institute's Center for Immigration Research at Temple University, Philadelphia. They hope to have the first phase open to the public during 1995 and the project complete before the end of the decade. Plans do include eventual remote access via computer and modem. Again, remember that, for many reasons, the original records are not complete but are an extremely valuable research source.

Civil War Soldiers System

The National Archives and National Park Service, along with several other organizations and many volunteers, are engaged in an ambitious project to create a computerized database of some 3.5 million to 5 million Civil War soldiers from both sides of the conflict and descriptions of major battles. By late 1994, Shiloh National Battlefield in Tennessee and Antietam National Battlefield in Maryland had test systems with about 70,000 names for visitors to access. Information for the database comes primarily from the index to service records in the National Archives, as well as from military prison records, national cemeteries, and other sources. Because it is, for the most part, a volunteer project, the completion date for the first stage is difficult to predict, but project officials hope that data entry can be finished by the end of 1996.

The initial data includes whatever is available on the National Archives index to compiled service records, and this information varies from person to person. It most often includes name, rank(s), and unit(s); dates of service; hometown or location from which the serviceman enlisted; and, sometimes, death and burial information. The project committee hopes to include unit and battle information so that one could follow the footsteps of a particular unit through the battles in which it participated. Plans call for the database to be installed for visitor use at Civil War event sites and, eventually, to be available on CD-ROM.

Family History Library Databases

At the family history centers, branches of the Family History Library of the Church of Jesus Christ of Latter-day Saints, researchers can use several large databases. Two of these come from government files: the Social Security death master index and the index to U.S. military personnel who died in Korea or Vietnam. The Ancestral File is a database of linked individuals, contributed by church members and nonmembers. The International Genealogical Index (IGI) is an index to millions of names contained in a database of births and marriages. The information comes from both individual researchers and a program of extraction from church and other records. Because the individually contributed information is not verified for accuracy before being added to the database, searchers are advised to exercise caution in using and accepting data found on ancestors in these files. Using these two databases may help identify other searchers working on the same family and may provide clues for further research. They do not replace research into original records.

Since the 1980s, we have seen a rapid increase in software and utility programs for genealogy; in floppy disk, CD-ROM, and graphic imaging products with genealogy applications; and in on-line services and databases with a genealogical emphasis. Even if you choose not to work on a computer at home, your research capabilities are being expanded by these developments, and you can benefit by using many of the printed and on-line products of that technology in libraries and other centers. We are indeed entering an exciting era for searching.

CHAPTER EIGHTEEN

Sharing Your Family History

Once you have gathered as much information as you want or as much as is available, you will probably want to share the results with the family at large. Notebooks and clippings may fascinate those who gathered them, but they may not entertain those who have not shared in the search. What then?

WRITING A FAMILY HISTORY

One approach is to write in narrative form all the information on one family, from its earliest proven ancestor to the present generations. Each chapter is a biography of an ancestor or ancestral couple, from birth to death, including marriage and family. (Be sure to include your documentation for the facts you report.) Each chapter also includes the general history of the area and period in which they lived. This material you can find in county, state, and regional histories. Social histories and reprints of contemporary books and articles can tell you about the customs, clothing, and everyday life of the period in which the ancestors lived.

You can set the stage for your ancestor's arrival by describing the family that he or she was born into: the number and ages of the older children, the ages of parents and other adults in the household, the house the family lived in, and what you have learned about their living conditions or community, etc.

So often we tend to think of all people of the past living in one large generation at the same time, or we tend to consider those who became famous as always being famous. We forget that they began life more or less as the rest of us did. It is fun to find some of those famous individuals who were contemporaries of your ancestor, some who were adults when he was born and some who were children. Mentioning them adds some perspective and interest to your stage-setting. Information of this kind can be found in such books as the *Dictionary of American Biography*, 13 vols., Dumas Malone, et al., eds. (New York: Charles Scribner's Sons, 1928-1974) and the *Encyclopedia of American History*, Richard B. Morris, ed. (New York: Harper and Row, 1965). These books and other standard reference books can give you information about events which took place in the community or nation at the time when your ancestor was born. Perhaps he was born during the Civil War in Vicksburg, Mississippi. Do a little extra research to find out whether he was born during the siege of Vicksburg. If he was, he and his family probably had a rough time. A number of primary sources tell the experiences of many of the city residents at that time. You may not find your family mentioned in these sources, but you can relate in your account what their fellow citizens experienced and suggest that your family may have had similar experiences. Word your account carefully so that you don't claim as fact something that is only an educated guess.

Here is one way of introducing an ancestor's biography. It was an effort to add some perspective on the year of his birth and on the family at the time of his birth. The facts were used to suggest what could have happened in the family as the new baby arrived on the scene.

> *In 1829, Andrew Jackson was serving his first year as President of the 24 United States. Sam Houston was governor of Tennessee, and U.S. Grant was an Ohio 7-year-old. Robert E. Lee graduated from West Point that year, and 20-year-old Abe Lincoln lived on his family's farm in Indiana. That year Stephen Foster was a Pennsylvania 3-year-old, and Charles Goodyear was going bankrupt in his hardware business in Connecticut. Daniel Boone, Thomas Jefferson, and John Adams were now names of the past; James Madison and James Monroe were retired elder statesmen; and Samuel Clemens, Andrew Carnegie, and Joel Chandler Harris were still names of the future.*

November 22 of 1829 was a Sunday, and possibly a cold one, in Caldwell County, Kentucky. If Hiram and Celestine Brelsford were regular churchgoers, they probably did not go that day, for during the day Celestine gave birth to their fourth child and third son, whom they named Samuel Black Brelsford, after Celestine's father. Grandparents Samuel and Keturah Black probably admired their new grandson that day along with his big sister, Mary Jane, who would be 4 the next Friday, and brothers Marjoram (2½) and William (1½).

Grandmother Keturah must have worked in double time that week. She still had five children at home. The youngest, John Thomas, was just a toddler. Dorcas was 18 now, and may have had to babysit with John and Mary Jane, Marjoram, and William. Keturah may have sent her to Celestine's house to help out for a while. It was customary for the grandmother to go to her son's or daughter's home, or for the new mother and baby to be at the grandmother's house. But Keturah had only four days left to finish preparations for Mary Katherine's wedding, next Thursday.

At the close of each biographical chapter, it is helpful to include a family group outline or family group sheet listing the subject, children, and perhaps grandchildren, similar to the one in Figure 16 (see page 111). Other sheets can be added to update each branch of the family.

Some genealogists compile an extensive outline which lists each descendant of the common ancestor with an individual identification number. This system has merit, but if family history is to mean anything, it must be more than just lists of names and dates. A narrative is perhaps the best way to share the stories and letters, or to set the family into the society in which they lived.

Many family histories are written using letters or diaries as a foundation. They are tied together with editorial comments and explanations by the researcher. In this case, the searcher has preserved the flavor of the original but has interpreted it for the present and future generations.

Perhaps you do not consider yourself "a writer," but still you want to share the history you have found. Compile copies of the actual documents that have taught you about your ancestors and add a little explanation here and there as well as copies of your charts.

When your presentation is in its final form, you may want to consider these options:

a. If the local or state library, historical society or university library in your research area has a file of area family genealogies, send them a copy of yours, especially if you used their materials in your search.

b. The Family History Library in Salt Lake City collects family histories from everywhere. Send them a copy of yours.

c. Present your gift in honor of or in memory of special relatives. I prefer to give something "in honor of" the person while he or she is living as a way of saying "Thank you" or "You are special to me."

OUTLINE FOR A FAMILY HISTORY PROJECT

Even while you are working on the more complete family history, you can collect, preserve, and organize valuable and interesting family data. This project is an exciting way to share the more recent family history of three to five generations. It makes great Christmas, birthday, or anniversary gifts for other family members and may stimulate interest in your larger genealogy effort. Grandparents can prepare it for children and grandchildren; aunts can give it to nieces and nephews; brothers or sisters can share it with parents and siblings.

The items suggested in the outline are ideas. The collection certainly can contain whatever you want to include. Once the pages are arranged, you can photocopy them and bind each set into booklets or folders for family members. You can also use plastic sheet protectors for inserting any original documents, photos, or double-sided keepsakes you include. When you put together a collection of this kind and want it to last for future generations, why not spend a little more and use materials that are made to last, such as acid-free, chemically stable, archival quality paper, binders, sheet protectors, and storage containers. One good source for these materials is the Preservation Emporium, P.O. Box 226309, Dallas, TX 75222-6309 (2600 Stemmons Freeway, Suite 131, Dallas, TX 75207, catalog available).

Contents are listed in a random order; arrange yours however you wish.

1. **Title Page.** List title, your name as compiler, date, perhaps your address, or any dedication statement.

Family of Elliott G. Coleman I

Elliott G. Coleman—born by 1764, Cumberland Co., Virginia, married 23 November 1789, died 1822, Cumberland Co., Va.

Elizabeth W. Daniel—born c1773, died c1853, daughter of William and Patty Field (Allen) Daniel. Born and died in Cumberland Co., Va.

Children:

1. Newton H. Coleman

   Probably eldest son since he was first executor of his father's estate. Died September 1829, unmarried.

2. Ferdinand Glen Coleman

   Born c1794, Cumberland Co., married c3 January 1822, Elizabeth A. Phillips, daughter of Peter Talbot and Elizabeth A. (Allen) Phillips. 14 children.

3. Mary D. Coleman

   Married John A. Allen, 14 January 1817; died by 1825. Children: Cary Allen; Archer Allen, who married Caroline _____ and had son Cary. Archer died in July 1852.

4. Elliot R. Coleman

   Died between 1841 and 1850, apparently. No evidence of marriage found.

5. Archer Allen Coleman

   Died October 1829, unmarried. Under 21 in 1818.

6. Creed D. Coleman

   Born c1800-1810, under 21 in 1818; elected delegate to Virginia House of Delegates, 1859-1860; living in 1860.

7. John Henry Coleman

   Born c1810, living in 1860.

8. William Pride Coleman

   Under 21 in 1818, died November 1829, unmarried.

9. Martha Coleman

10. Susan E. Coleman

    Married February 1848, William P. Miller, moved to Hollysprings, Mississippi. Son Daniel Miller, born 1849.

Information gathered from Cumberland County, VA, wills, census records, family records and letters, marriage records, deeds.

FIG. 16: SAMPLE FAMILY GROUP SHEET

2. **Table of Contents.** Items can be grouped by topic, generation, surname, decade or any way you think best. You may want to leave blank sheets at the end for notes and additions.

3. **Foreword.** Write a note or letter to your family, preferably in your own handwriting, or at least signed, explaining what the collection is and why you want to share it, or what you hope it will mean to the family in years to come—whatever you want to say.

4. One or more **five-generation charts**, filled with whatever information you have, from personal experience, documents in your possession, research that represents facts that can be proved. You can begin the chart with your children or grandchildren or with yourself.

5. **Family Group Sheets,** which list parents and children of each generation:
   - you, your spouse, and your children,
   - your parents and their children,
   - your spouse's parents and their children,
   - your child, his/her spouse, their children (one sheet for each of your children),
   - your grandparents and their children (one sheet for each set of grandparents),
   - your spouse's grandparents and their children (again, two sets of grandparents),
   - great-grandparents and their children if you have that information,
   - your brothers and sisters with their spouses and children (one sheet for each couple).

6. **Names and addresses** of living relatives who may be on the family group sheets, especially any who have worked on family history or have information on the family's past.

7. **Biographical sketches** or outlines, one person to a page. See page 158. You should include yourself, your spouse, one or both parents, your spouse's parents, etc. It might be helpful to include the residence of the subject in the census years: 1920, 1910, 1900, 1880, etc.

8. **Interesting tidbits** which you have available. The idea here is not to make a complete, comprehensive history, but that certainly can be your ultimate goal. This is a collection of "spice" that adds interest and personality to all the names and dates on the charts. These items might be arranged topically and may not take more than a few lines each.
   - *Church history:* who belonged to what denominations or congregations.
   - *Occupational history:* any working women in the family history, occupations of the men. Who were the farmers? teachers? ministers? any doctors? salesmen? elected officials? craftsmen? etc.
   - *Medical and genetic history:* causes of death, diseases or physical problems which have repeated themselves, longevity, occurrence of twins or triplets (one family identified 14 sets of twins!), physical characteristics which "run in the family," predominant hair color or other physical features.
   - *Educational history:* who went where, especially college attendance and degrees.
   - *Military history:* who fought where in which war, peacetime service, any family members who are members of Daughters of the American Revolution (DAR), Sons of the American Revolution (SAR), United Daughters of the Confederacy (UDC), etc.
   - *Talents or outstanding characteristics of family members:* musical ability, authors, artists, terrific cooks, seamstresses; sense of humor, gentleness, meanness; beauties, those who excel in sports, etc.
   - *How we got our names:* who was named for whom, nicknames and real names, anything unusual about the surnames represented.
   - *Special traditions and customs:* Christmas traditions, birthday celebration traditions, vacations the family has taken; oral traditions about family history—where ancestors came from, why they immigrated to this country, why they settled where they did (relatives, job, stationed there, etc.).
   - *Hobbies* and pastimes of family members, especially of previous generations; pets.
   - *Favorites,* especially of previous generations: favorite foods, sports, books, movies, authors, teams, music, performers, places to visit, cars, pets, color, hymn, scripture, friend, etc. Interesting habits of family members, especially previous generations. Sayings or expressions that family members use(d).

9. **Keepsakes and collectibles** (originals or copies):

- *Documents:* birth certificates, marriage licenses, diplomas, degrees, awards, report cards, transcripts, driver's licenses, poll tax receipts, voter registration cards, ration books, newspaper clippings, funeral cards and announcements, etc.
- *Photographs*, labeled with name(s), approximate date, place.
- *Letters* and cards from those who have gone before as well as from present family members, especially those in their own handwriting. A note from each living family member. One in my own family very characteristically wrote: "I've always wondered why I'm not rich since I'm so smart."
- *Recipes* (favorites), especially in the cook's own handwriting.
- *Handwriting samples*, especially signatures, from letters, cards, wills and other documents. These can be arranged in the form of a five-generation chart or as shown in Figure 17, page 115.
- Photos of *houses* in which family generations have lived. Sketches of the floor plans of family homes of the past, especially those which are no longer standing.
- Samples of *creativity* from family members: poetry, music, drawing, short story, parody, photos of items which cannot be included (furniture, paintings, sculpture, dollhouses, etc.).

10. **Memories**, a paragraph or one-page recollection or story handed down. Topics could include a *memorable* Christmas, vacation, wedding, storm, fire, job, friendship, pet, relative, experience, anything *unusual* or *comical* that happened, stories of the Depression or war or college years; *childhood* memories. *Bits of information* which could help someone in researching family history later: your great-grandmother lived in Oklahoma City when she died; your great-grandmother was married five times and outlived all her husbands; towns the family lived in; great-grandfather was one of 15 children. *Interviews* such as the one in Figure 5, page 28. Separate *biographical cassette tape* to give along with the booklet. Memories of *firsts:* first car, first movie, first television, first date, first apartment, first home, first day of school, first telephone, first baby, first solo, first job, etc.

11. **Map** of state or United States (Appendix F). See Figure 9, page 44, showing residences of the family in certain years, or movement of one family over the years.

Tape interviews with grandparents and great-grandparents about their childhood, their own parents and grandparents, family stories, and their memories, using the questions suggested in chapters seven, eight, and nine. Such tapes preserve the history as well as special memories of the subject for those who will hear the tapes in the future. One year when I was teaching American history, I invited an eighty-year-old family friend to be our guest in class and talk with us about his growing up in the 1890s. I taped the session and have a delightful memento of the visit. After his death several years later, I sent a copy of the tape to his son. He was thrilled and was making copies for everyone in the family because everybody wanted one! They now have not only his voice but many family stories and a few vital statistics as well.

Show-and-tell reunion. Another way of sharing family mementos and history is to have a "show-and-tell" reunion, to which everybody brings their old family pictures, family Bible, or other objects for display. Such an occasion is a good opportunity to identify unlabeled pictures, to share and tape-record stories about common ancestors or the "good old days," to take group pictures, to make videotapes, to collect autographs or recipes, to serve food made from old family recipes, to furnish updated vital statistics on each part of the family, and to renew old acquaintances.

Family history makes special gifts:

- Give a book to the local history or genealogy library in the name of a friend or relative.
- Give friends or relatives some of their own family history that you or someone else has gathered: a book by or about an ancestor, tapes of interviews with or about an ancestor, photographs, antiques, or collectibles that have been in the family.
- Give a book on the history or genealogy of the county where their ancestor lived, or the family church, university, hometown, etc.
- Give a subscription to a family association newsletter or membership in such an organization.
- Give a subscription to a genealogical periodical, especially one from their favorite research locale.

- Especially for a genealogist, consider giving a genealogy resource book, such as a guide to research in a particular state, or the holdings of a particular collection that could be helpful in their search.
- For family history searchers, a copy of *Unpuzzling Your Past* or *The Genealogist's Companion & Sourcebook*, by Emily Croom (Cincinnati: Betterway Books, 1994).

Regardless of how you share your material, it can have meaning for the family only when it is shared. Whether done formally or informally, published or photocopied from a typed original, it holds insight and fascination for the whole family for years to come.

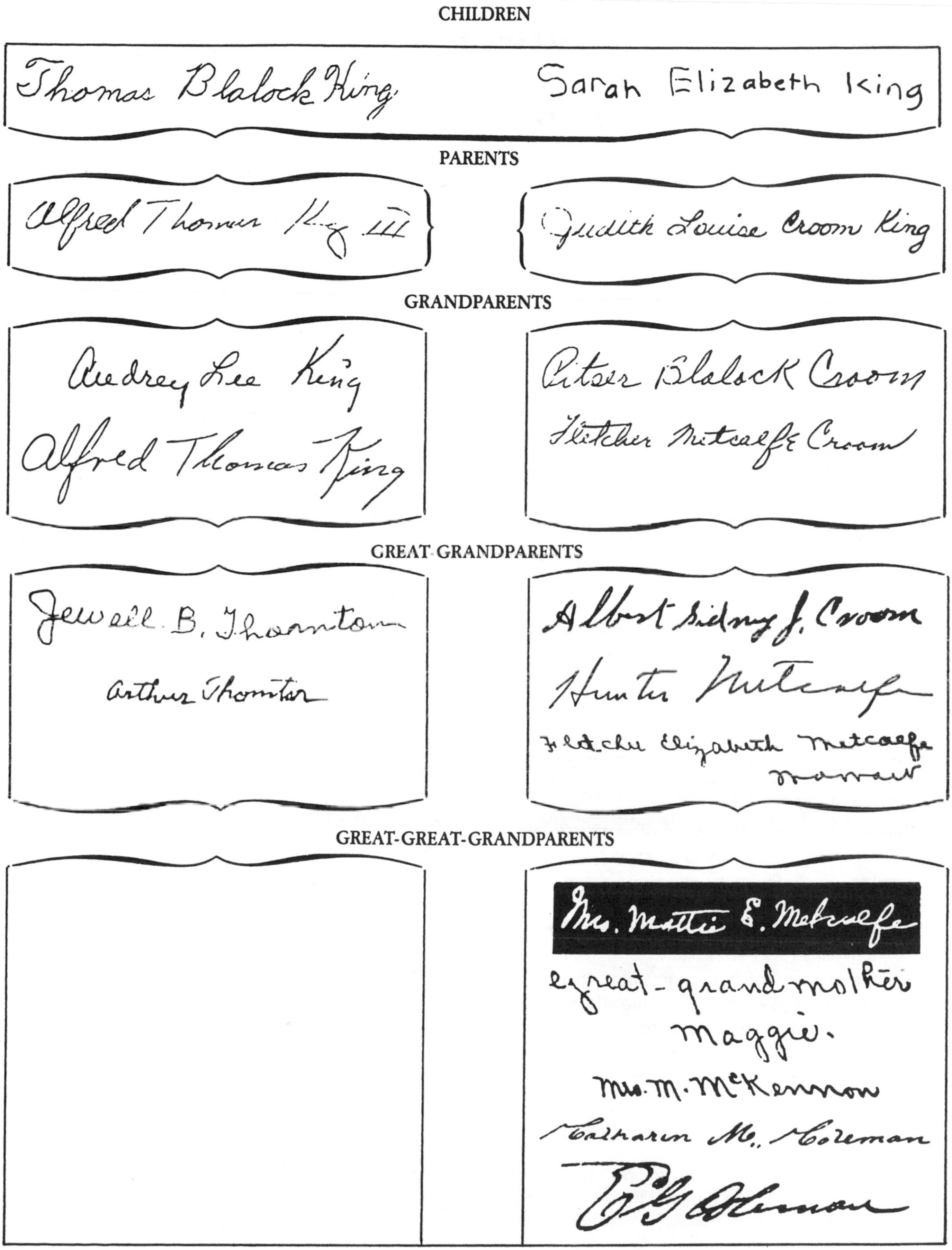

CHILDREN

Thomas Blalock King — Sarah Elizabeth King

PARENTS

Alfred Thomas King III — Judith Louise Croom King

GRANDPARENTS

Audrey Lee King
Alfred Thomas King

Pitser Blalock Croom
Fletcher Metcalfe Croom

GREAT-GRANDPARENTS

Jewell B. Thornton
Arthur Thornton

Albert Sidney J. Croom
Hunter Metcalfe
Fletcher Elizabeth Metcalfe

GREAT-GREAT-GRANDPARENTS

Mrs. Mattie E. Metcalfe
great-grandmother
Maggie.
Mrs. M. McKennon
Catharine M. Coleman

FIG. 17: SIGNATURE COLLECTION

APPENDIX A

Glossary

Additional references include the following:

Black's Law Dictionary. 6th ed. Henry Campbell Black. St. Paul: West Publishing Co., 1990.

Colonial American English. Richard M. Lederer, Jr. Essex, CT: Verbatim, 1985.

Concise Genealogical Dictionary. Maurine and Glen Harris. Salt Lake City: Ancestry, 1989.

The New A to Zax: A Comprehensive Genealogical Dictionary for Genealogists and Historians. 2nd ed. Barbara Jean Evans. Champaign, IL: the author, 1990.

What Did They Mean By That?: A Dictionary of Historical Terms for Genealogists. Paul Drake. Bowie, MD: Heritage Books, Inc., 1994.

Abstract—summary of important points of a text, especially deeds and wills.

Administrator—person appointed to manage or divide the estate of a deceased person. *feminine:* administratrix.

Alien—*noun:* a foreigner, citizen of another country; *verb:* to transfer property to another.

Ancestor—person from whom you are descended; a forefather; a forebear.

Ancestry—the lineage of all ancestors of a person, from parents backward in time.

Archives—records of a government, organization, institution; the place where such records are stored.

Attest—to affirm; to certify by signature or oath.

Banns—public announcement of an intended marriage.

Bequeath—to give personal property to a person in a will. *noun:* bequest.

Bond—a binding agreement to perform certain actions or duties or be required to pay a specified sum of money as a penalty; at different times required of estate administrators or executors, grooms, certain elected officials. A bondsman, often a relative, acted as surety.

Bounty land—land promised as reward or inducement for enlisting in military service.

Christian name—the name given at christening or baptism, the *given* name.

Codicil—addition to a will.

Common ancestor—one shared by any two or more people.

Confederacy—Confederate States of America, the southern states which seceded from the U.S. in 1860-61. *adjective:* confederate.

Consort—wife or husband whose spouse is living.

Conveyances—deeds.

Cousin—child of one's aunt or uncle in any generation; once used informally for any close relative or friend.

Deceased—dead.

Declaration of Intention—first paper, sworn to and filed in court, by an alien stating the desire to become a citizen.

Deed—transfer of ownership of and title to property.

Descendancy—a person's offspring: children, grandchildren, and succeeding generations.

Descendant—offspring of a person, even into remote generations.

Devise—to give property, usually land, in a will.

Devisee—one to whom property is given in a will.

Devisor—one who gives property in a will.

Dissenter—one who did not belong to the established church, especially the Church of England.

Dower—legal right or share which a wife acquired by marriage in the real estate of her husband, allotted to her after his death for her lifetime.

Emigrant—one leaving a country and moving to another.

Enfeoff—to grant property in fee simple. In deeds, the sellers "do grant, bargain, sell, alien, enfeoff, release, and confirm unto" the buyer certain property.

Enumeration—listing or counting, such as a census.

Estate—all property and debts belonging to a person.

Executor—one appointed in a will to carry out its provisions. *feminine:* executrix.

Fee Simple—absolute ownership of a piece of land, to sell or devise as the owner chooses.

Friend—member of the Religious Society of Friends; a Quaker.

Given name—name given to a person at birth or baptism; one's first and middle names.

Grantee—one who buys property or receives a grant.

Grantor—one who sells property or makes a grant.

Great-aunt—sister of one's grandparent.

Great-uncle—brother of one's grandparent.

Guardian—person appointed to care for and manage property of minor orphan or adult incompetent of managing his own affairs.

Half brother or sister—child by another marriage of one's mother or father; the relationship of two people who have only one parent in common.

Heir—one entitled by law or by terms of a will to inherit property from another.

Illegitimate—born to a mother who was not married to the child's father.

Immigrant—one moving into a country from another.

Indentured servant—one bound into the service of another person for a specified number of years, often in return for transportation to this country; a redemptioner.

Infant—*law.* one who is under legal age.

Instant—*archaic.* of the current month; of this month.

Intestate—*noun:* one who dies without a will; *adjective:* dying without a will.

Issue—offspring; children; descendants; progeny.

Late—recently deceased; now deceased.

Legacy—property or money left to someone in a will.

Legatee—one who inherits money or property through a will.

Lineage—ancestry; direct descent from a specific ancestor. *adjective:* lineal.

Loyalist—Tory; an American colonist who supported the British side in the American Revolution.

Maiden name—a girl's surname before marriage.

Maternal—related through one's mother. Maternal grandmother is the mother's mother.

Microform—reproduction of images, reduced in size, in one of several ways: microcard, microfiche, or microfilm.

Militia—citizens of a state who are not part of the national military forces but who can be called into military service in an emergency; a citizen army, apart from the regular military forces.

Minor—one who is under legal age; not yet a legal adult; an infant.

Mortality—death; death rate.

Namesake—person named after another person.

Necrology—listing or record of persons who have died recently.

Nee—*French.* born. Used to identify a woman's maiden name: Mrs. Susan Jones nee Smith.

Orphan—person who has lost one or both parents by death.

Patent—grant of land from a government to an individual.

Paternal—related through one's father. Paternal grandmother is the father's mother.

Pedigree—family tree; ancestry; lineage.

Pension—money paid regularly to an individual, especially by a government as reward for military service during wartime or upon retirement from government service.

Pensioner—one who receives a pension.

Poll—list or record of persons, especially for taxing or voting; one "head" or taxable person.

Prenuptial agreement (antenuptial agreement)—legal document made by a couple before marriage, usually involving property.

Primogeniture—*law.* the right of the eldest child, usually the eldest son, to inherit the entire estate of the parents.

Probate—legal process of determining that a will is valid before authorizing distribution of the estate, appointing someone to administer an intestate

estate, and overseeing the settlement of estates. See *succession.*

Progenitor—a direct ancestor.

Proximo—*Latin, archaic.* in the following month, the month after the present one.

Public domain—land owned by the government.

Quitclaim deed—transfer of claim or title (usually to land) without guarantee of valid title.

Relict—*archaic.* widow.

Section—640 acres; one of 36 divisions of a township.

Sibling—person having one or both parents in common with another; brother or sister.

Sic—*Latin.* thus; copied exactly as the original reads. Often suggests a mistake or surprise in the original.

Statute—law.

Stepbrother, stepsister—child of one's stepmother or stepfather by a previous marriage.

Stepchild—child of one's husband or wife by a previous marriage.

Stepfather—husband of one's mother by a later marriage.

Stepmother—wife of one's father by a later marriage.

Succession—especially in Louisiana, the process of determining a will's validity, identifying heirs, ordering inventory of the estate, ordering family meetings to determine the best interest of minor heirs, putting heirs in possession of the estate. *Probate* in other states. *Succession* as a legal term in other states is the transfer of property to legal heirs of an intestate estate. The right to inherit and to what degree is determined by the state's laws of descent and distribution.

Surname—family name; last name.

Territory—area of land owned by the United States, not a state, but having its own legislature and governor.

Testator—person who makes a valid will before death.

Tithable—taxable; a person who owes tax to a specified jurisdiction.

Tithe—formerly, money due as a tax for support of the clergy or church.

Tory—Loyalist; one who supported the British side in the American Revolution.

Township—division of U.S. public land that contains 36 sections, or 36 square miles. Also a subdivision of the county in many states.

Tutor—*Louisiana, civil law.* guardian of minor children. *feminine:* tutrix.

Ultimo—*Latin, archaic.* in the month before this one; last month.

Union—the United States; also the North during the Civil War, the states which did not secede.

Vital records—records of birth, death, marriage, divorce.

Vital statistics—data dealing with birth, death, marriage, divorce.

Warranty deed—deed in which the seller of the property guarantees a clear title to the buyer.

Will—document declaring how a person wants his/her property divided after death.

ABBREVIATIONS
(commonly used in genealogy or in documents)

b—born

B—black; Negro

c, ca—about, approximately; from Latin *circa.*

co—county, or company.

col—"colored"; black; Negro.

CSA—Confederate States of America, the association of southern states which seceded from the U.S. in 1860-61.

d—died.

dau—daughter.

dea—deacon.

decd or dec'd—deceased.

et al—Latin *et alii,* meaning "and others."

etc—Latin *et cetera,* meaning "and other things."

F—female.

fmc—free man of color.

fwc—free woman of color.

govt—government.

ibid—Latin *ibidem,* meaning "in the same place." Used in footnotes to mean the same work as just cited.

IOOF—Independent Order of Odd Fellows, fraternal organization.

IS—Interim Supply, meaning that a minister is appointed as full-time minister to the congregation but on an interim or temporary basis.

JP—Justice of the Peace.

LDS—The Church of Jesus Christ of Latter-day Saints, the Mormons.

LE—Local Elder.

LS—Latin *locus sigilli*; on documents, the place where a man's seal is placed.

M—male.

m—married.

m1—married first.

m2—married second.

ME South, ME North—Methodist Episcopal Church South, or North.

MG—Minister of the Gospel.

Mu—Mulatto, person of mixed Caucasian and Negro ancestry.

nd—no date given.

n m—never married.

np—no page or publisher given.

NS—New Style, referring to the Gregorian calendar.

OM—Ordained Minister.

OS—Occasional Supply, referring to a minister appointed to serve when needed, not on a regular basis.

OS—Old Style, referring to the Julian calendar.

pp—pages.

SS—Stated Supply, referring to a minister appointed as regular minister of a congregation.

unm—unmarried.

VDM—Latin *Verbi Domini Ministerium*, minister of the Word of God.

W—white; Caucasian.

(w) or wit— witness.

RELATIONSHIP CHART

Instructions for using the chart on page 120 to identify the relationship between any two people.

1. Identify the common ancestor of the two people. Locate the box in the upper left corner for the common ancestor.
2. Across the top row of the chart, find the relationship of one of the two people to their common ancestor.
3. Down the left edge of the chart, find the relationship of the second person to their common ancestor.
4. Read down the column of the first person and across the chart on the row of the second person. Where the two rows intersect is the box which identifies the relationship.

Example:

1. The common ancestor is Elliott Coleman.
2. Judith is the great-great-granddaughter of Elliott, four generations away from him. Read down column #4.
3. Word is the grandson of Elliott, two generations away from him. Read across row #2.
4. Column #4 and row #2 intersect at the box which reads "1 cou 2 R," or first cousin two generations removed. Judith and Word are first cousins twice removed.

RELATIONSHIP CHART

	1	2	3	4	5	6	7	8	9
	COMMON ANCESTOR	**SON / DAU.**	**GRAND-SON**	**GREAT GRAND-SON**	**G-G GRAND-SON**	**G-G-G GRAND-SON**	**4G GRAND-SON**	**5G GRAND-SON**	**6G GRAND-SON**	**7G GRAND-SON**
1	SON / DAU.	BRO / SIS.	NEPHEW / NIECE	GRAND NEPHEW	GREAT GRAND-NEPHEW	G-G GRAND-NEPHEW	G-G-G GRAND-NEPHEW	4G GRAND-NEPHEW	5G GRAND-NEPHEW	6G GRAND-NEPHEW
2	GRAND-SON	NEPHEW / NIECE	1ST COUSIN	1 COU 1 R	1 COU 2 R	1 COU 3 R	1 COU 4 R	1 COU 5 R	1 COU 6 R	1 COU 7 R
3	GREAT GRAND-SON	GRAND NEPHEW	1 COU 1 R	2ND COUSIN	2 COU 1 R	2 COU 2 R	2 COU 3 R	2 COU 4 R	2 COU 5 R	2 COU 6 R
4	G-G GRAND-SON	GREAT GRAND-NEPHEW	1 COU 2 R	2 COU 1 R	3RD COUSIN	3 COU 1 R	3 COU 2 R	3 COU 3 R	3 COU 4 R	3 COU 5 R
5	G-G-G GRAND-SON	G-G GRAND-NEPHEW	1 COU 3 R	2 COU 2 R	3 COU 1 R	4TH COUSIN	4 COU 1 R	4 COU 2 R	4 COU 3 R	4 COU 4 R
6	4G GRAND-SON	3G GRAND-NEPHEW	1 COU 4 R	2 COU 3 R	3 COU 2 R	4 COU 1 R	5TH COUSIN	5 COU 1 R	5 COU 2 R	5 COU 3 R
7	5G GRAND-SON	4G GRAND-NEPHEW	1 COU 5 R	2 COU 4 R	3 COU 3 R	4 COU 2 R	5 COU 1 R	6TH COUSIN	6 COU 1 R	6 COU 2 R
8	6G GRAND-SON	5G GRAND-NEPHEW	1 COU 6 R	2 COU 5 R	3 COU 4 R	4 COU 3 R	5 COU 2 R	6 COU 1 R	7TH COUSIN	7 COU 1 R
9	7G GRAND-SON	6G GRAND-NEPHEW	1 COU 7 R	2 COU 6 R	3 COU 5 R	4 COU 4 R	5 COU 3 R	6 COU 2 R	7 COU 1 R	8TH COUSIN

ABBREVIATIONS

BRO = brother
SIS = sister
DAU = daughter
COU = cousin
R = removed (generations removed)
G-G = great-great
GRANDSON = grandson or granddaughter
SON = son or daughter
NEPHEW = nephew or niece

The chart may be extended in either direction for identifying more distant relationships.

FIG. 18: RELATIONSHIP CHART

APPENDIX B

Additional References

CHAPTER 5

Bardsley, Charles W. *A Dictionary of English and Welsh Surnames with Special American Instances.* Reprint of 1901 ed. Baltimore: Genealogical Publishing Company, 1980.

Benson, Morton, ed. *Dictionary of Russian Personal Names.* Philadelphia: University of Pennsylvania Press, 1964.

Black, George F. *Surnames of Scotland: Their Origin, Meaning and History.* Reprint of 1946 ed. New York: New York Public Library, 1986.

Chuks-Orji, Ogonna. *Names from Africa.* Chicago: Johnson Publishing Co., 1972.

Coghlan, Ronan. *Pocket Guide to Irish First Names.* St. Paul, MN: Irish Books and Media, 1985.

Ewen, Cecil. *A Guide to the Origin of British Surnames.* Reprint of 1938 ed. Detroit: Gale Research Co., 1969.

———. *A History of Surnames of the British Isles.* Reprint of 1931 ed. Baltimore: Genealogical Publishing Company, 1968.

Foreign Versions of English Names: And Foreign Equivalents of U.S. Military and Civilian Titles. Document No. M-131. Reprint of 1973 ed. Detroit: Gale Research Co., 1980.

Grehan, Ida. *Pocket Guide to Irish Family Names.* St. Paul, MN: Irish Books and Media, 1985.

Gruffudd, Haini. *Welsh Personal Names.* Willits, CA: British American Books, not dated.

Hanks, Patrick and Flavia Hodges. *A Dictionary of First Names.* Oxford; New York: Oxford University Press, 1990.

———. *A Dictionary of Surnames.* Oxford; New York: Oxford University Press. 1988.

Hook, J.N. *Family Names: How Our Surnames Came to America.* New York: Macmillan, 1982.

Kolatch, Alfred J. *The Complete Dictionary of English and Hebrew First Names.* Middle Village, NY: Jonathan David Publishers, 1984.

Lower, Mark A. *English Surnames.* 2 vols, 4th ed. Reprint of 1875 ed. Detroit: Gale Research Co., 1968.

O'Corrain, Donnchadh, and Fidelma Maguire. *Gaelic Personal Names.* Wolfeboro, NH: Longwood Publishing Group, 1981.

Room, Adrian. *Dictionary of Translated Names and Titles.* New York: Methuen, Inc., 1985.

Shankle, George E. *American Nicknames.* 2d ed. Bronx, NY: H.W. Wilson, 1955.

Stewart, George R. *American Given Names: Their Origin and History in the Context of the English Language.* New York: Oxford University Press, 1979.

White, C. Pawley. *A Handbook of Cornish Surnames.* New York: State Mutual Books, 1985.

Woods, Richard C., comp. *Hispanic First Names: A Comprehensive Dictionary of 250 Years of Mexican-American Usage.* Westport, CT: Greenwood, 1984.

CHAPTER 10

Beattie, Jerome Francis, ed. *The Hereditary Register of the United States.* The Hereditary Register Publications, Inc., latest edition.

Encyclopedia of Associations: A Guide to National and International Organizations and *Encyclopedia of Associations: A Guide to Regional, State and Local Organizations.* Detroit: Gale Research Co., latest edition.

The Genealogical Helper. Logan, UT: The Everton Publishers, Inc., 6 issues per year.

Wheeler, Mary Bray, ed. *A Directory of Historical Organizations in the United States and Canada.* Nashville: American Association for State and Local History, latest edition.

CHAPTER 11

Berry, Ellen T., and David A. Berry, *Our Quaker Ancestors: Finding Them in Quaker Records.* Baltimore: Genealogical Publishing Company, 1987.

Brown, Mary J., comp. *Handy Index to the Holdings of the Genealogical Society of Utah.* Logan, UT: The Everton Publishers, Inc., 1971.

Filby, P. William. *A Bibliography of American County Histories.* Baltimore: Genealogical Publishing Company, 1985.

Kemp, Thomas J. *International Vital Records Handbook.* Baltimore: Genealogical Publishing Company, 1994.

Peterson, Clarence S., comp. *Consolidated Bibliography of County Histories in Fifty States in 1961. . . .* Baltimore: Genealogical Publishing Company, 1961.

Stemmons, John D., and E. Diane Stemmons, comp. *The Vital Record Compendium.* Logan, UT: The Everton Publishers, Inc., 1979.

Where to Write for Vital Records: Births, Deaths, Marriages, and Divorces. Hyattsville, MD: U.S. Department of Health and Human Services, Public Health Service, 1993 or latest edition.

CHAPTER 12

Croom, Emily. *The Genealogist's Companion & Sourcebook.* Cincinnati: Betterway Books, 1994.

Dubester, Henry J., comp. *State Censuses.* Washington, DC: Library of Congress, Census Library Project, 1948.

Eichholz, Alice, ed. *Ancestry's Red Book: American State, County and Town Sources.* Salt Lake City: Ancestry, 1992.

Lainhart, Ann S. *State Census Records.* Baltimore: Genealogical Publishing Company, 1992.

Lancour, Harold, comp. *A Bibliography of Ship Passenger Lists, 1538-1825.* 3rd ed. Revised by Richard J. Wolfe. New York: New York Public Library, 1963.

Neagles, James C. *The Library of Congress: A Guide to Historical and Genealogical Research.* Salt Lake City: Ancestry, 1990.

Stemmons, John, comp. *United States Census Compendium.* Logan, UT: The Everton Publishers, 1973.

Thorndale, William, and William Dollarhide. *Map Guide to US Federal Censuses, 1790-1920.* Baltimore: Genealogical Publishing Company, 1991.

CHAPTER 13

United States Department of Commerce, Bureau of the Census. *Age Search Information.* Washington, DC: 1990. Available from Superintendent of Documents, Government Printing Office, Washington, DC 20402.

See also under chapters eleven and twelve.

CHAPTER 16

Kirkham, E. Kay. *How to Read the Handwriting and Records of Early America.* Salt Lake City: Deseret Book Co., 1961.

CHAPTER 18

Malone, Dumas, et. al., eds. *Dictionary of American Biography.* 13 vols., including supplements. New York: Charles Scribner's Sons, 1928-1974.

Morris, Richard B., ed. *Encyclopedia of American History.* New York: Harper and Row, 1965.

ADDITIONAL REFERENCES

Askin, Jayne. *Search: A Handbook for Adoptees and Birthparents.* New York: Harper and Row, 1982. Includes help groups, agencies. Discusses twentieth-century U.S. sources.

Beard, Timothy Field, with Denise Demong. *How to Find Your Family Roots.* New York: McGraw-Hill, 1977. Comprehensive. Suggests sources in many foreign countries.

Bentley, Elizabeth Petty. *The Genealogist's Address Book.* Baltimore: Genealogical Publishing Company, 1992.

DePlatt, Lyman. *Genealogical Historical Guide to Latin America.* Gale Genealogy and Local History Series. Detroit: Gale Research Co., 1978.

Doane, Gilbert. *Searching for Your Ancestors.* Minneapolis: University of Minnesota Press, 1948. Especially helpful for New England records.

Eakle, Arlene, and Johni Cerny, eds. *The Source: A Guidebook of American Genealogy.* Salt Lake City: Ancestry, Inc., 1984.

Everton, George B., Sr., and Gunnar Rasmuson. *Handy Book for Genealogists.* Logan, UT: The Everton Publishers, Inc., latest edition.

Groene, Bertram Hawthorne. *Tracing Your Civil War Ancestor.* Winston-Salem: John F. Blair, 1973.

Helmbold, F. Wilbur. *Tracing Your Ancestry.* Birmingham: Oxmoor House, Inc., 1976.

Law, Hugh T. *How to Trace Your Ancestors to Europe: 117 Stories, Procedures, and Sources to Use for 24 Countries.* Salt Lake City: Cottonwood Books, 1987.

Lederer, Richard M., Jr. *Colonial American English: A Glossary.* Essex, CT: A Verbatim Book, 1985.

Miller, Olga K. *Genealogical Research for Czech and Slovak Americans.* Detroit: Gale Research Co., 1978.

Punch, Terrence M. *Genealogical Research in Nova Scotia.* Halifax: Petheric Press, Ltd., 1978.

Sale, Randall D., and Edwin D. Karn. *American Expansion: A Book of Maps.* Lincoln: University of Nebraska Press, 1962.

Schreiner, Bette, ed. *Genealogical and Local History Books in Print.* Springfield, VA (now in Maine, NY): GBIP, latest edition.

Stevenson, Noel C. *Search and Research.* Salt Lake City: Deseret Book Co., 1959.

Valentine, John F., ed. *Handbook for Genealogical Correspondence.* Logan, UT: Cache Genealogical Library, 1963.

Wellauer, Maralyn A. *A Guide to Foreign Genealogical Research.* Milwaukee, 1976.

Westin, Jeane Eddy. *Finding Your Roots.* New York: Ballantine Books, 1978.

SOME PUBLISHERS OF GENEALOGICAL MATERIALS

Ancestral Genealogical Endexing Schedules (AGES), P.O. Box 2127, Salt Lake City, UT 84110. Formerly Accelerated Indexing Systems International.

Ancestry, Inc., P.O. Box 476, Salt Lake City, UT 84110.

Boyd Publishing Co., P.O. Box 367, Milledgeville, GA 31061.

Clearfield Company, 200 E. Eager St., Baltimore, MD 21202.

The Everton Publishers, Inc., P.O. Box 368, Logan, UT 84323.

Genealogical Books in Print, P.O. Box 394, Maine, NY 13802-0394.

Genealogical Publishing Company and Gateway Press, 1001 N. Calvert St., Baltimore, MD 21202.

Heritage Books, Inc., 1540-E Pointer Ridge Pl., Bowie, MD 20716.

Margaret M. Hofmann, P.O. Box 446, Roanoke Rapids, NC 27870.

Iberian Publishing Company, 548 Cedar Creek Dr., Athens, GA 30605-3408. Specializes in Virginia reference and research.

Marietta Publishing Company, 2115 N. Denair Ave., Turlock, CA 95380.

The Reprint Company Publishers, P.O. Box 5401, Spartanburg, SC 29304.

Byron Sistler and Associates, 1712 Natchez Trace, P.O. Box 120934, Nashville, TN 37212. Specializes in Tennessee materials.

Southern Historical Press, Inc., P.O. Box 1267, Greenville, SC 29602-1267.

Westland Publications, P.O. Box 117, McNeal, AZ 85617.

In addition, many university presses, public libraries, historical and genealogical societies publish books. Most publishers will make their catalogs available on request.

APPENDIX C

Libraries and Archives

This appendix of libraries and archives will help you identify research facilities near your home and in your research areas. The libraries listed here are, by no means, all the libraries with genealogy or related collections, and the ones listed vary considerably in size and scope.

Many public libraries and local historical societies focus their genealogy collections on local or county residents. Others have genealogy materials for the state, region, nation, or foreign countries. The location of the largest genealogical collections varies from state to state. These collections may be in public or university libraries, in historical society libraries, or at the state library or archives. In some states, such as Virginia and South Carolina, the state library and archives have large collections of primary and secondary sources for genealogical research. In other states, such as Rhode Island and Washington, the state libraries are not really genealogical centers. In some states, the state historical society has a very small reference collection, but elsewhere the historical society is a major research facility in the state.

In addition, hundreds of public, historical society, and university libraries have a local or regional history collection. Although these collections may not have family histories, censuses, and genealogical periodicals, they may have newspapers, maps, manuscripts, business and family papers, documents, and other sources that genealogists find very beneficial. Although it is beyond the scope of this appendix to list these local history collections, genealogists need to recognize their value and use them.

To locate additional genealogy and local history collections in libraries near your home or in your research areas, consult the following references:

American Library Directory. Jacques Cattell Press, ed. New York: R.R. Bowker Co., latest edition.

Directory of American Libraries With Genealogical or Local History Collections. P. William Filby, comp. Wilmington, DE: Scholarly Resources, 1988.

Directory of Archives and Manuscript Repositories in the United States. National Historical Publications and Records Commission. 2nd ed. Phoenix: Oryx Press, 1988.

A Directory of Historical Organizations in the United States and Canada. Mary Bray Wheeler, ed. Nashville: American Association for State and Local History, latest edition.

Encyclopedia of Associations. National Organizations of the United States and *Encyclopedia of Associations: Regional, State and Local Organizations.* Detroit: Gale Research Co., latest edition.

Everton's Genealogical Helper. Logan, UT: The Everton Publishers, Inc. Each July-August issue contains a directory of genealogical societies, libraries, and periodicals.

The Official Museum Directory. Washington, DC: American Association of Museums, latest edition.

A Preliminary Guide to Church Records Repositories. August R. Suelflow, comp. St. Louis (now Chicago): Society of American Archivists, 1969.

Yearbook of American and Canadian Churches. Nashville: Abingdon Press, latest edition.

AMERICAN LIBRARIES AND ARCHIVES

ALABAMA

A number of libraries have local history or genealogy collections.

Anniston—Public Library of Anniston and Calhoun County, 108 E. 10th St., 36201.

Auburn—Auburn University Library, Auburn, 36830-3501.

Birmingham—Birmingham Public Library, 2100 Park Pl., 35203.

—Birmingham-Southern College Library, Arkadelphia Rd., P.O. Box A-20, 35254-9990. (Alabama Methodism and Alabama history)
—Samford University Library, 800 Lakeshore Dr., 35229. (genealogy and Baptist history)
Decatur—Wheeler Basin Regional Library, Decatur Public Library, 504 Cherry St. NE, P.O. Box 1766, 35602.
Florence—Florence-Lauderdale Public Library, 218 N. Wood Ave., 35603.
Gadsden—Gadsden-Etowah County Library, 254 College St., 35999-3101.
Huntsville—Huntsville-Madison County Public Library, Heritage Room, 915 Monroe, P.O. Box 443, 35804.
Mobile—Mobile Public Library, 701 Government St., 36602.
Montgomery—Alabama Department of Archives and History, 624 Washington Ave., 36130-0100.
—Huntingdon College Library, 1500 E. Fairview Ave., 36194. (United Methodist history—Alabama/West Florida)
Tuscaloosa—Tuscaloosa Public Library, 1801 River Rd., 35401.
University—Special Collections, Gorgas Library, University of Alabama, 35486.

ALASKA

Anchorage—Anchorage Municipal Library, 3600 Denali, 99503-6093.
—Anchorage Museum of History and Art, Archives, 121 W. 7th Ave., 99501.
Juneau—Alaska Archives and Records Management, 141 Willoughby Ave., 99801-1720.
—Alaska Historical Library and Museum, State Office Bldg., P.O. Box G, 99811-0571.
—Alaska State Library and Archives, P.O. Box 110571, 99811. (limited genealogy)

ARIZONA

Kingman—Mohave County Historical Society, Mohave Museum Library, 400 W. Beale St., 86401.
Phoenix—Arizona Dept. of Library, Archives and Public Records, 1700 W. Washington, 85007.
—Phoenix Public Library, 12 E. McDowell, 85004. (Arizona history)
Prescott—Prescott Historical Society Library, 415 W. Gurley St., 86301.
Tucson—Arizona Daily Star Library, 4850 S. Park Ave., P.O. Box 26807, 85726. (*Daily Star* newspaper from 1877, city directories)
—Arizona Historical Society Research Library, 949 E. 2nd St., 85719.
—University of Arizona Library, Special Collections, 85721. (Arizona history)

ARKANSAS

A number of libraries have local history or genealogy collections.

Conway—Hendrix College Library, Washington and Front Sts., 72032. (Arkansas Methodism)
El Dorado—Union County Libraries, Barton Library, 200 E. 5th St., 71730.
Fort Smith—Fort Smith Public Library, 61 S. 8th St., 72901.
Little Rock—Arkansas Democrat Gazette News Library, 112 W. 3rd, P.O. Box 1821, 72203. (newspaper issues from 1819)
—Arkansas History Commission Archives, One Capitol Mall, 72201.
—Arkansas State Library, One Capitol Mall, 72201.
—Little Rock Public Library, 700 Louisiana St., 72201.
North Little Rock—Laman Public Library, 2801 Orange St., 72114-2296.
Pine Bluff—Pine Bluff and Jefferson County Library, 200 E. 8th Ave, 71601. (Southern genealogy)
Texarkana—Texarkana Public Library, 600 W. 3rd St., TX 75501.
Washington—Southwest Arkansas Regional Archives, Old Washington Historic State Park, P.O. Box 134, 71862.

CALIFORNIA

A number of libraries have local history or genealogy collections.

Bakersfield—Kern County Library, Beale Memorial Branch, 701 Truxtun Ave., 93301-4816.
Berkeley—Western Jewish History Center, 2911 Russell St., 94705. (Western Jewish Americana)
—Bancroft Library, University of California at Berkeley, 94720.
Colma—Archdiocese of San Francisco, 1500 Old Mission Rd., 94014. Write to Chancery Archives, P.O. Box 1799, Colma, 94014. (Catholic history in San Francisco area)
Glendale—Sons of the Revolution Library, 600 S. Central Ave., 91204.
Huntington Beach—Huntington Beach Public Library,

7111 Talbert Ave., 92648. (Orange County Genealogical Society collection)

Long Beach—Long Beach Jewish Community Center Library, 3801 E. Willow, 90815. (Southwest Jewish history)

Los Angeles—Hebrew Union College Library, 3077 University Ave., 90007 (West Coast Jewish Archives)

—Jewish Federation Council of Greater Los Angeles, Library, 6505 Wilshire Blvd., 90048. (Los Angeles area Jewish history and archives)

—Los Angeles Public Library, 630 W. 5th St., 90071-2097.

Mission Hills—Roman Catholic Archdiocese of Los Angeles, Library & Museum, 15151 San Fernando Mission Blvd., 91345.

Modesto—Stanislaus County Free Library, 1500 I St., 95354.

Riverside—Riverside Public Library, 3581 7th St., P.O. Box 468, 92502.

Sacramento—California State Archives Library, 1020 O St., 95814.

—California State Library, 914 Capitol Mall, Library-Courts Building, P.O. Box 942837, 94237-0001.

—Sacramento Public Library, Genealogy collection at Carmichael Regional Library, 5605 Marconi Ave., Carmichael, CA 95608.

San Carlos—Ragusan Press, Yugoslav-Croatian-Serbian-Slovene Immigration Library, 2527 San Carlos Ave., 94070.

San Diego—San Diego Historical Society, 1649 El Prado, Balboa Park, P.O. Box 81825, 92138.

San Francisco—California Genealogical Society Library, 300 Brannan St., 94142.

—California Historical Society Library, 2099 Pacific Ave., 94109-2235.

—San Francisco African-American Historical and Cultural Society, Inc., Library, Ft. Mason Center Building C, No. 165, 94123. (black history and African descendants)

—San Francisco Public Library, Civic Center, 94102.

—Society of California Pioneers Library, 456 McAllister St., 94102.

—Sutro Library, Branch of California State Library, 480 Winston Dr., 94132.

Santa Barbara—Santa Barbara Genealogical Society Library, Box 1303, 93116.

—Santa Barbara Historical Society Library, 136 E. De La Guerra St., P.O. Box 578, 93102.

—Santa Barbara Mission Archives Library, Old Mission, 2201 Upper Laguna St., 93105. (Catholic diocese archives)

Stockton—Stockton-San Joaquin County Public Library, 605 N. El Dorado St., 95202.

—United Methodist Church Research Library, University of the Pacific, 3601 Pacific Ave., 95211. Open by appointment. (West Coast Methodist history and genealogy)

Thousand Oaks—Thousand Oaks Public Library, 1401 E. Janss Rd., 91362.

Whittier—Whittier College, Wardman Library, 7031 Founders Hill Rd., 90608. (Quaker collection)

COLORADO

Boulder—Carnegie Branch of Boulder Public Library, 1125 Pine, 80302.

Denver—Colorado Historical Society Library, 1300 Broadway, 80203.

—Colorado State Archives and Public Records, 1313 Sherman St., 80203.

—Denver Public Library, 1357 Broadway, 80203. (Consult Social Science-Genealogy branch.)

—Iliff School of Theology Library, 2201 S. University Blvd., 80210. (archives of the Rocky Mountain Conference of the United Methodist Church)

Greeley—Greeley Public Library, 919 7th St., 80631. (genealogy and German-Russian collection)

Pueblo—Pueblo Library District, 100 E. Abriendo Ave., 81004.

Steamboat Springs—Werner Memorial Library, Routt County Collection Library, 1289 Lincoln Ave., P.O. Box 774568, 80477.

CONNECTICUT

Many local public libraries have local history or genealogy collections.

Bloomfield—St. Thomas Seminary Library, 467 Bloomfield Ave., 06002. (early Catholic Americana)

Fairfield—Fairfield Historical Society Library, 636 Old Post Rd., 06430.

Glastonbury—Connecticut Society of Genealogists, P.O. Box 435, 06033-0435.

Groton—Groton Public Library, 52 Route 117, New Town Rd., 06340.

Hartford—Connecticut Historical Society Library, One Elizabeth St., 06105.

—Connecticut State Library, 231 Capitol Ave., 06106.

—Episcopal Diocese of Connecticut, 1335 Asylum

Ave., 06105. (Connecticut Episcopal Church archives)

Middletown—Godfrey Memorial Library, 134 Newfield St., 06457.

—Middlesex County Historical Society Library, 151 Main St., 06457.

Milford—Milford Public Library, 57 New Haven Ave., 06460.

New Haven—New Haven Colony Historical Society Library, 114 Whitney Ave., 06510.

—Yale University Library, 120 High St., P.O. Box 1603 A, Yale Station, 06510. (family history, New England history, etc.)

Southport—Pequot Library, 720 Pequot Ave., 06490-1496.

Stamford—Stamford Genealogical Society, Inc., and Public Library, One Public Library Plaza, 06904.

—Stamford Historical Society Library, 1508 High Ridge Rd., 06903.

Tolland—French-Canadian Genealogical Society of Connecticut Library, P.O. Box 45, 06084.

Torrington—Torrington Historical Society Library, 192 Main St., 06790.

Windsor—Windsor Historical Society Library, 96 Palisado Ave., 06095.

DELAWARE

A number of public libraries have local history collections.

Dover—Delaware Bureau of Archives and Records Management, Hall of Records, P.O. Box 1401, 19903.

Wilmington—Historical Society of Delaware Library, 505 Market Street Mall, 19801.

—Holy Trinity (Old Swedes) Church Foundation Library, 606 Church St., 19801. (Swedish and Delaware history and genealogy)

—Wilmington Institute Library, 10th and Market St., 19801. (Delawareana)

DISTRICT OF COLUMBIA

Library of Congress, Independence Ave. at 1st St. E., 20540.

National Archives, Pennsylvania Ave. at 8th St. NW, 20408.

National Society, Colonial Dames XVII Century, Library, 1300 New Hampshire Ave. NW, 20036.

National Society, Daughters of American Colonists Library, 2205 Massachusetts Ave. NW, 20008.

National Society, Daughters of the American Revolution Library, 1776 D St. NW, 20006.

Wesley Theological Seminary Library, 4500 Massachusetts Ave. NW, 20016. (early American Methodist history)

FLORIDA

Daytona Beach—Volusia County Public Library, City Island, 32114-4484.

Gainesville—Gainesville-Alachua County Public Library, 401 E. University Ave., 32601.

—Yonge Library of Florida History, University of Florida, Library East, 32611.

Jacksonville—Jacksonville Public Library, 122 N. Ocean St., 32202.

Largo—Largo Library, 351 E. Bay Dr., 34640-3793.

Lutz—Genealogical Center, Inc., 16512 N. Florida Ave., P.O. Box 17695, Tampa, 33682.

Miami—Miami-Dade County Public Library, 101 W. Flagler St., 33130-1523.

Miami Beach—Reed Institute Library, 1015 W. 47th St., 33140.

Ocala—Central Florida Regional Library, 15 SE Osceola Ave., 32671.

Orlando—Orlando Public Library, 101 E. Central Blvd., 32801.

Pensacola—Pensacola Historical Society Library, 405 S. Adams St., 32501.

—West Florida Regional Library, Pensacola Public Library, 200 W. Gregory, 32501.

St. Augustine—St. Augustine Historical Society Library, 271 Charlotte St., 32084.

St. Petersburg—St. Petersburg Public Library, 3745 9th Ave. N., 33713.

Tallahassee—Florida State Library and Florida Bureau of Archives, R.A. Gray Building, 32399-0250.

Tampa—Hillsborough County Historical Commission Museum Library, Second Floor, County Courthouse, 401 Pierce St., 33602.

—Tampa-Hillsborough County Public Library System, 900 N. Ashley Dr., 33602.

GEORGIA

Many public and regional libraries have local history and genealogy collections.

Athens—Athens Regional Library, 120 W. Dougherty, 30601.

Atlanta—Atlanta Public Library, One Margaret Mitchell Square NW, 30303.

—Emory University Library, Central Library, 1364 Clifton Rd. NE, 30322. (family papers, Methodist history)
—Georgia Department of Archives and History, 330 Capitol Ave. SE, 30334.
Augusta—Richmond County Historical Society Library, Reese Library, Augusta College, 2500 Walton Way, 30910.
Columbus—Chattahoochee Valley Regional Library, 1120 Bradley Dr., 31995.
Macon—Washington Memorial Branch Library, 1180 Washington Ave., P.O. Box 6334, 31208-6334.
Marietta—Genealogical Center Library (rental library), P.O. Box 71343, 30007-1343.
Rome—Shorter College Library, P.O. Box 5, 30161. (Georgia Baptist history)
Savannah—Georgia Historical Society Library, 501 Whitaker St., 31499.
Thomasville—Thomas College Library, 1501 Millpond Rd., 31792. (Southern history and church histories)

HAWAII

Honolulu—D.A.R. Memorial Library, 1914 Makiki Heights Dr., 96822.
—Hawaii Chinese History Center Library, 111 N. King St., Rm. 410, 96817.
Hawaii State Archives, Iolani Palace Ground, 96813.
—Hawaiian Historical Society Library, 560 Kawaiahao St., 96813. (Ask for their directory of historical records repositories.)

IDAHO

Boise—Idaho Historical Society Library, Library and Archives Building, 450 N. 4th St., 83702.
—Idaho State Library and State Archives, 325 W. State St., 83702.
Moscow—Latah County Historical Society Library, 327 E. 2nd St., 83843.
—University of Idaho Library, 83843-4198. (Idaho history)
Rexburg—Ricks College Library, 83460-0405.
Salmon—Salmon Public Library, 204 Main St., 83467.

ILLINOIS

Many public libraries have local history and genealogy materials.

Arlington Heights—Arlington Heights Memorial Library, 500 N. Dunton Ave., 60004.
Belleville—Belleville Public Library, 121 E. Washington St., 62220.
Berwyn—Czechoslovak Heritage Museum Library, 2701 S. Harlem Ave., 60402.
Bloomington—McLean County Historical Society Library, 201 E. Grove St., 61701.
—United Methodist Church Central Illinois Conference Library, P.O. Box 515, 61702. (Methodist history; staff genealogist/historian)
Chicago—Balzekas Museum of Lithuanian Culture, Library, 6500 S. Pulaski Rd., 60629. (Lithuanian genealogy, history)
—Chicago Historical Society Library, North Ave. and Clark St., 60614.
—Chicago Public Library, 400 N. Franklin St., 60610.
—Chicago Public Library, Special Collections Dept., 78 E. Washington St., 60602.
—Jesuit-Krauss-McCormick Library, 1100 E. 55th St., 60615. (Merged collections of McCormick Theological Seminary and Lutheran School of Theology; Presbyterian and Lutheran church history, archives)
—Lithuanian Research and Studies Center, Inc., 5620 S. Claremont Ave., 60636. (Lithuanian Historical Society)
—Naes College Library, 2838 W. Peterson, 60659. (American Indian tribal histories)
—National Huguenot Society, 9027 S. Damen Ave., 60620.
—Newberry Library, 60 W. Walton St., 60610. (genealogy; American Indian collection)
—Polish Museum of America Library, 984 N. Milwaukee Ave., 60622.
—Spertus College of Judaica, Library, 618 S. Michigan Ave., 60605. (Chicago Jewish history)
—Swedish-American Historical Society, Swedish-American Archives, 5125 N. Spaulding Ave., 60625. (Chicago Swedes, Swedish immigration history)
—University of Chicago Library, 1100 E. 57th St., 60637. (Kentucky-Ohio River Valley history, English manorial records of Norfolk, Suffolk)
—University of Illinois at Chicago, Special Collections Library, 801 S. Morgan St., P.O. Box 8198, 60680. (pre-fire Chicago manuscripts, Hull House papers, Immigrants' Protective League and other organization and business collections)
Deerfield—Trinity Evangelical Divinity School, Library, 2065 Half Day Rd., 60015. (Evangelical Free Church of America archives)
Dixon—Dixon Public Library, 221 Hennepin Ave., 61021.

Edwardsville—Edwardsville Public Library, 112 S. Kansas, 62025.
Elgin—Church of the Brethren General Board, Brethren Historical Library and Archives, 1451 Dundee Ave., 60120. (Brethren history, archives)
Elmwood Park—E.R. Sadowski, Masonic Historical Library, 1924 N. 74th Ct., 60635. (Masonic history, records)
Eureka—Eureka College Library, 300 College Ave., 61530. (Disciples of Christ church archives)
Kankakee——Kankakee County Historical Society Library, 8th and Water St., 60901.
Moline—Moline Public Library, 504 17th St., 61265.
Oak Forest—Slovak Catholic Culture Center Library, 5900 W. 147th St., 60452.
Peoria—Peoria Public Library, 107 NE Monroe St., 61602.
Rock Island—Swenson Swedish Immigration Research Center Library, Augustana College, College Box 175, 61201.
Rockford—Rockford Public Library, 215 N. Wyman St., 61101.
South Holland—South Suburban Genealogical and Historical Society Library, 320 E. 161st Pl., P.O. Box 96, 60473.
Springfield—Daughters of Union Veterans of the Civil War, 503 S. Walnut St., 62704.
—Illinois State Archives, Archives Bldg., 62756.
—Illinois State Historical Library, Old State Capitol, 501 S. 2nd, 62701.
Urbana—Urbana Free Library, 201 S. Race St., 61801.

INDIANA

Many public libraries have local history and genealogy collections.

Anderson—Anderson and Stony Creek Township Public Library, 111 E. 12th, 46016.
Bloomington—Indiana University Library, 10th St. and Jordan Ave., 47405.
Evansville—Willard Library of Evansville, 21 1st Ave., 47710.
Ft. Wayne—Allen County-Ft. Wayne Historical Society Library, 302 E. Berry, 46802.
—Allen County-Ft. Wayne Public Library, 900 Webster St., P.O. Box 2270, 46801-2270.
Franklin—Franklin College Library, 46131. (Indiana Baptist collection)
Gary—Gary Public Library, 220 W. 5th Ave., 46402.
—Roman Catholic Diocese of Gary, 668 Pierce St., 46402. (Catholic archives, NW Indiana)
Greencastle—DePauw University Library, Box 137, 46135. (Indiana United Methodism archives)
Hanover—Hanover College Library, P.O. Box 287, 47243. (Indiana Presbyterian archives)
Indianapolis—American Legion National Headquarters Library, 700 N. Pennsylvania St., P.O. Box 1055, 46206. (local, state, national American Legion archives)
—Indiana Historical Society, 315 W. Ohio St., 46202.
—Indiana State Archives, 140 N. Senate Ave., 46204-2215.
—Indiana State Library, Genealogy Division, 140 N. Senate Ave., 46204-2296. (houses state historical society library)
Lafayette—Tippecanoe County Historical and Genealogical Associations, Library, 909 South St., 47901.
—Tippecanoe County Public Library, 627 South St., 47901. (local newspapers from 1831)
Plainfield—Western Yearly Meeting of Friends, Library, 203 S. East St., P.O. Box 70, 46168. (W. Indiana-E. Illinois Quaker records)
Richmond—Earlham College Library, 47374-0027. (Quaker archives and genealogy)
—First Friends Meeting House, E. Main and 15th St., 47374. (Ohio, Michigan, Indiana Quaker records; open by appointment)
—Wayne County, Indiana Historical Museum Library, 1150 N. A St., 47374.
South Bend—Northern Indiana Historical Society Library, 112 S. Lafayette St., 46601.
—Saint Joseph County Public Library, 304 S. Main, 46601.
Valparaiso—Porter County Public Library, 107 Jefferson St., 46383.
Vincennes—Vincennes University, Lewis Historical Collections Library, 1002 N. 1st St., 47591. (Northwest Territory Genealogical Society)

IOWA

Many public libraries have local history or genealogy collections.

Decorah—Vesterheim Norwegian American Museum, 502 W. Water St., 52101.
Des Moines—Episcopal Diocese of Iowa, 225 37th St., 50312. (Iowa Episcopal archives, vital records)
—Iowa Genealogical Society Library, 6000 Douglas Ave., Suite 145, P.O. Box 7735, 50322.
—State Historical Society of Iowa, Library Archives

Bureau, Capitol Complex, 600 E. Locust, 50319.
—State Library of Iowa, E. 12th and Grand Ave., 50319.
Dubuque—Telegraph Herald Library, 8th Ave. and Bluff, P.O. Box 688, 52001.
—University of Dubuque Library, 2000 University, 333 Wartburg Pl., 52001. (American Lutheran Church Archives)
Iowa City—State Historical Society of Iowa Library, 402 Iowa Ave., 52240-5391.
LeMars—Teikyo Westmar University Library, 51031. (United Methodism collection)
Marshalltown—Marshalltown Public Library, 36 N. Center St., 50158. (Central Iowa Genealogical Society)
Mt. Pleasant—Iowa Wesleyan College Library, 52641. (Iowa Methodist archives)
Pella—Central College Library, 812 Peace St., 50219. (Collection on Dutch in America and Iowa)
Sioux City—Catholic Diocese of Sioux City, 1821 Jackson St., 51105. (twentieth-century vital records from all its parishes; parish histories)
—Sioux City Public Library, 529 Pierce St., 51101-1203.
Waterloo—Grout Museum of History and Science, Library, 503 South St., 50701.

KANSAS

Many public libraries have genealogy and local history collections.

Kansas City—Archdiocese of Kansas City, 2220 Central Ave., 66102. (vital records of diocese parishes)
—Kansas City Public Library, 625 Minnesota Ave., 66101. (Wyandotte Indian collection)
Lawrence—Kansas and Special Collections, Kenneth Spencer Research Library, University of Kansas, 66045.
Manhattan—Riley County, Kansas Genealogical Society Library, 2005 Claflin, 66502.
North Newton—Bethel College, Mennonite Library and Archives, P.O. Drawer A, 67117. (German, Dutch genealogy; Mennonite and Anabaptist history)
Shawnee Mission—Johnson County Library, 8700 Shawnee Mission Pkwy., Box 2901, 66201.
Topeka—Kansas State Historical Society Library and Archives, Memorial Building, 120 W. 10th, 66612.
—Topeka Genealogical Society Library, 2717 Indiana St., P.O. Box 4048, 66604.
Wichita—Midwest Historical and Genealogical Society, Inc., Library, 1203 N. Main, P.O. Box 1121, 67201.
—Wichita Public Library, 223 S. Main, 67202.
—Wichita State University Library, P.O. Box 68, 67208. (local and state history)

KENTUCKY

A number of city and county public libraries have local history and genealogy collections.

Bowling Green—Bowling Green Public Library, 1225 State St., 42101.
—Western Kentucky University, Kentucky Library, 42101-3576.
Covington—Kenton County Public Library, 502 Scott St., 41011.
Frankfort—Kentucky Department for Libraries and Archives, 300 Coffee Tree Rd., P.O. Box 537, 40602.
—Kentucky Historical Society Library, 300 W. Broadway, P.O. Box H, 40602.
Lexington—Herald-Leader Company Library, 100 Midland Ave., 40508. (newspapers)
—Lexington Public Library, 140 E. Main, 40507.
—Transylvania University Library, 300 N. Broadway, 40508. (Kentucky collection)
—University of Kentucky, King Library, 40506-0039. (Kentucky and Appalachia collection)
Louisville—Filson Club, 1310 S. 3rd St., 40208.
—Louisville Free Public Library, 301 York St., 40203.
—National Society, Sons of the American Revolution, Genealogical Library, 1000 S. 4th, 40203.
Murray—Murray State University Library, 42071.
Owensboro—Kentucky Wesleyan College Library, 3000 Frederica St., P.O. Box 1039, 42302. (Kentucky Methodism)
—Owensboro-Daviess County Public Library, 450 Griffith Ave., 42301.

LOUISIANA

A number of parish and university libraries have genealogy and/or local history collections.

Alexandria—Alexandria Historical and Genealogical Library, 503 Washington, 71301.
—Louisiana State University at Alexandria, Library, 8100 Hwy. 71 S, 71302.
Baton Rouge—East Baton Rouge Parish Library, 7711 Goodwood Blvd., 70806-7699.
—Louisiana Office of the Secretary of State, Archives and History Library, 3851 Essen Lane, P.O. Box 94125, 70804.

—Louisiana State Library, P.O. Box 131, 760 Riverside Mall, 70821. (state history)
—Louisiana State University, Middleton Library, Special Collections, 70803.
—Southern University Library, Southern Branch Post Office, 70813. (black history and archives)
Lafayette—Lafayette Public Library, 301 W. Congress, P.O. Box 3427, 70502-3427.
Lake Charles—Calcasieu Parish Public Library, 3900 Ernest St., 70605.
Metairie—Jefferson Parish Library Dept., Lobby Branch, 3420 N. Causeway Blvd., 70002, and Belle Terre Branch, 5550 Belle Terre Rd., Marrero, 70072.
Monroe—Ouachita Parish Public Library, 1800 Stubbs Ave., 71201.
New Orleans—Historic New Orleans Collection Library, 533 Royal St., 70130.
—Howard-Tilton Library, Louisiana Collection, Tulane University, 6823 St. Charles Ave., 70118.
—Louisiana State Museum, Historical Center, 400 Esplanade Ave., P.O. Box 2448, 70176. (New Orleans area history, by appointment only)
—New Orleans National Archives, Civil Court Bldg., 421 Loyola Ave.
—New Orleans Public Library, 219 Loyola Ave., 70140. (city archives, state history)
Shreveport—Ark-La-Tex Genealogical Association, P.O. Box 4462, 71134.
—Shreve Memorial Library, 424 Texas, P.O. Box 21523, 71120.
Thibodaux—Nicholls State University Library, 70310. (local history, including papers from area sugar plantations)

MAINE

Many town libraries and historical societies have genealogy or local history collections.

Augusta—Maine State Library and Archives (LMA Building), State House Station 64, 04333.
Bangor—Bangor Public Library, 145 Harlow St., 04401.
New Gloucester—Shaker Library, Sabbathday Lake, Rt. 26, 04274. Mailing address: RR1, P.O. Box 640, Poland Spring, 04274. (Shaker history)
Orono—University of Maine, Fogler Library, 04469. (Maine newspapers)
Portland—Maine Historical Society Library, 485 Congress St., 04101.
—Portland Public Library, 5 Monument Sq., 04101. (oral history and newspapers)
York—Old York Historical Society Library, York St., P.O. Box 312, 03909.

MARYLAND

A number of public libraries have genealogy or local history collections.

Annapolis—Maryland State Archives Library, 350 Rowe Blvd., 21401.
—Maryland State Law Library, Court of Appeals Building, 361 Rowe Blvd., 21401. (Maryland newspapers from 1745)
Baltimore—Archdiocese of Baltimore, Catholic Center, 320 Cathedral St., 21202. (diocese archives)
—Jewish Historical Society of Maryland, Library, 15 Lloyd St., 21202.
—Johns Hopkins University, Peabody Library, 17 E. Mt. Vernon Pl., 21202.
—Maryland Historical Society Library, 201 W. Monument St., 21201.
—Ner Israel Rabbinical College Library, 400 Mt. Wilson Lane, 21208. (collections of Hebrew newspapers of Europe, 1820-1937)
—Enoch Pratt Free Library, Maryland Room, 400 Cathedral St., 21201.
—Saint Mary's Seminary and University, School of Theology Library, 5400 Roland Ave., 21210. (early Catholic Americana)
—Sojourner-Douglass College Library, 500 N. Caroline St., 21205. (African and African-American history)
—United Methodist Historical Society, Lovely Lane United Methodist Church Museum Library, 2200 St. Paul St., 21218. (Methodist history, archives of Baltimore Conference)
Bowie—Bowie State College Library, Jericho Park, 20715. (African-American experience, slave documents)
College Park—National Archives II, 8601 Adelphi Rd., 20740.
—University of Maryland, McKeldin Library, Maryland Room, 20740.
Emmitsburg—Mount Saint Mary's College and Seminary Library, 21727. (Early Catholic Americana)
Hagerstown—Washington County Free Library, 100 S. Potomac St., 21740.
Leonardtown—Saint Mary's County Historical Society Library, P.O. Box 212, 20650.
Rockville—Montgomery County Historical Society Li-

brary, 103 W. Montgomery Ave., 20850.

Silver Spring—Roman Catholic Archdiocese for the Military Services, 962 Wayne Ave., 20910.

MASSACHUSETTS

Numerous town libraries and historical societies have genealogy and/or local history collections.

Beverly—Beverly Historical Society Library, 117 Cabot St., 01915.

Boston—American Congregational Association, Congregational Library, 14 Beacon St., 02108. (Congregational church history, archives)

—Boston Public Library, Copley Square, 02116.

—Episcopal Diocese of Massachusetts Library and Archives, 138 Tremont St., 02111.

—Massachusetts Historical Society, 1154 Boylston St., 02215.

—Massachusetts State Archives, State House, Beacon Hill, 02133.

—New England Conference Historical Depository, Boston University School of Theology Library, 745 Commonwealth Ave., 02215. (New England United Methodist history)

—New England Historic Genealogical Society Library, 101 Newbury St., 02116.

—State Library of Massachusetts, State House, Beacon Hill, 02133.

Brighton—Roman Catholic Archdiocese of Boston, 2121 Commonwealth Ave., 12135. (diocese archives and registers)

Cambridge—Harvard University, Houghton Library, 02138. (rare books and manuscripts)

Haverhill—Haverhill Public Library, 99 Main St., 01830.

Lynn—Lynn Historical Society Museum Library, 125 Green St., 01902.

—Lynn Public Library, 5 N. Common St., 01902.

New Bedford—New Bedford Free Public Library, 613 Pleasant St., 02740.

Newton Centre—Andover Newton Theological School Library, 169 Herrick Rd., 02159. (New England Baptist and Congregational Church records and history)

Pittsfield—Berkshire Athenaeum, Pittsfield Public Library, One Wendell Ave., 01201.

Springfield—City Library, 220 State St., 01103. (New England and French-Canadian genealogy)

—Connecticut Valley Historical Museum Library, 194 State St., 01103.

Taunton—Old Colony Historical Society Library, 66 Church Green, 02780.

Waltham—American Jewish Historical Society Library, 2 Thornton Rd., 02154.

Worcester—American Antiquarian Society Library, 185 Salisbury St., 01609.

MICHIGAN

A number of public libraries have local history and genealogy collections.

Albion—Albion College Library, 602 E. Cass St., 49224. (Western Michigan Conference, United Methodist Church archives)

Ann Arbor—University of Michigan, Bentley Historical Library, 1150 Beal Ave., 48109.

—University of Michigan, Clements Library, 909 S. University Ave., 48109.

Detroit—Detroit Public Library, 5201 Woodward Ave., 48202. (Michigan, Northwest Territories history and genealogy)

Flint—Genesee District Library, G-4195 W. Pasadena Ave., 48504.

Grand Rapids—Grand Rapids Public Library, 60 Library Plaza NE, 49503.

Hancock—Finnish-American Historical Archives, Suomi College, 601 Quincy St., 49930.

Holland—Herrick Public Library, 300 S. River Ave., 49423. (Dutch and local genealogy)

—The Joint Archives of Holland, Hope College Library, 49423.

—Western Theological Seminary Library, 85 E. 13th, 49423. (history, Reformed Church in America)

Kalamazoo—Kalamazoo College Library, Thompson and Academy Sts., 49007. (Michigan Baptist history)

Lansing—French-Canadian Heritage Society Library, P.O. Box 30007, 48909.

—Library of Michigan, 717 W. Allegan, P.O. Box 30007, 48909.

—Michigan Department of State, State Archives, 717 W. Allegan, 48909.

Marquette—Marquette County Historical Society Library, 213 N. Front St., 49855.

Midland—Dow Memorial Library, 1710 W. St. Andrews Dr., 48640.

Saginaw—Public Library of Saginaw, 505 Janes St., 48605.

Saint Joseph—Palenske Memorial Library, Genealogy Collection, 500 Market St., 49085.

MINNESOTA

A number of libraries and historical societies have genealogy collections.

Arden Hills—Bethel Theological Seminary Library, 3949 Bethel Dr., 55112. (Baptist General Conference archives and history)
Chisholm—Iron Range Research Center, Highway 169W, P.O. Box 392, 55719.
Duluth—Duluth Public Library, 520 W. Superior St., 55802. (area history)
—Northeast Minnesota Historical Center Archives, University of Minnesota Library 375, 55812.
Minneapolis—American-Swedish Institute Library, 2600 Park Ave., 55407.
—Minneapolis Public Library, 300 Nicollet Mall, 55401. (various history collections)
—United Methodist Church Archives and Historical Library, 122 W. Franklin Ave., Room 400, 55404. (Minnesota Conference)
Northfield—St. Olaf College Library, 1510 St. Olaf Ave., 55057. (Norwegian-American Historical Association collection and Norwegian Lutheran collection)
St. Paul—Minnesota Historical Society, Division of Library and Archives, 345 Kellogg Blvd. W., 55102. (state archives)
—Orphan Voyage, Kamman Dale Libraries, 57 N. Dale St., 55102.
—St. Paul Public Library, 90 W. 4th St., 55102. (area history)
—University of Minnesota Library, Immigration History Research Center and Manuscript Collection, 826 Berry St., 55114.

MISSISSIPPI

A number of public libraries have local history and genealogy collections.

Biloxi—Biloxi Public Library, 139 Lameuse St., 39530.
Clinton—Mississippi Baptist Convention Board, Mississippi Baptist Historical Commission, P.O. Box 51, 39060. (Mississippi Baptist history)
—Mississippi College Library, P.O. Box 127, 39056. (Mississippi Baptist Convention archives, history)
Hattiesburg—University of Southern Mississippi, McCain Library, P.O. Box 5148, Southern Station, 39406.
Jackson—Belhaven College, Hood Library, 1500 Peachtree St., 39202. (Presbyterian records)
—Millsaps College Library, 39210-0001. (Mississippi Methodism)
—Mississippi State Department of Archives and History, 100 S. State St., P.O. Box 571, 39205.
—Reformed Theological Seminary Library, 5422 Clinton Blvd., 39209. (Southern Presbyterianism)
Meridian—Meridian Public Library, 2517 7th St., 39301.
Mississippi State—Mississippi State University Library, P.O. Drawer 5408, 39762.
University—University of Mississippi Library, 38677.
Vicksburg—Vicksburg and Warren County Historical Society, McCardle Library, Old Court House Museum, 39180.

MISSOURI

A number of libraries have genealogy and local history collections.

Columbia—State Historical Society of Missouri, University Library Bldg., 1020 Lowry St., 65201-7298.
—University of Missouri, Western Historical Manuscript Collection, 23 Ellis Library, 65201.
Fayette—Central Methodist College Library, 411 Central Sq., 65248. (Missouri Methodism)
Independence—Mid-Continent Public Library, 15616 E. 24 Highway, 64050.
Jefferson City—Missouri State Archives, 1001 Industrial Dr., 65101; P.O. Box 778, 65102.
—Missouri State Library, 2002 Missouri Blvd., P.O. Box 387, 65102-0387.
Kansas City—Heart of America Genealogical Society Library, 311 E. 12th, 64106.
—Kansas City Public Library, 311 E. 12th St., 64106.
—University of Missouri, Western Historical Manuscript Collection, 302 Newcomb Hall, 5100 Rockhill Rd., 64110.
Liberty—Missouri Baptist Historical Society, Wiliam Jewell College, Curry Library, 500 College Hill, 64068. (Missouri Baptist history)
Marshall—Missouri Valley College Library, 500 E. College, 65340. (Archives, Cumberland Presbyterian Church)
Springfield—Springfield-Green County Library, 397 E. Central, P.O. Box 760, 65801.
St. Louis—Concordia Historical Institute Library, Missouri Synod of the Lutheran Church, 801 DeMun Ave., 63105.
—Diocese of Missouri Archives, Episcopal Church, 1210 Locust St., 63103.

—Missouri Historical Society, 225 S. Skinker Blvd., P.O. Box 11940, 63112-0940.
—St. Louis Public Library, 1301 Olive St., 63103.

MONTANA

A number of public libraries have local history, Indian history, or genealogy collections.

Billings—Parmly Billings Library, 510 N. Broadway, 59101.
—Rocky Mountain College Library, 1511 Poly Dr., 59102-1796. (Montana Methodist history)
Bozeman—Montana State University Library, 59717. (Montana history)
Glendive—Glendive Public Library, 106 S. Kendrick, 59330. (German-Russian immigrations)
Great Falls—Great Falls Genealogy Society Library and Cascade County Historical Society Library and Archives, 1400 1st Ave. N., Paris Gibson Square, 59401.
Helena—Montana Historical Society Library, 225 N. Roberts, 59620-9990. (state archives, genealogy, state newspapers)
—Montana State Library, 1515 E. 6th Ave., 59620.
Missoula—University of Montana, Mansfield Library, 59812. (Montana history)

NEBRASKA

A number of towns have local history or genealogy collections.

Grand Island—Grand Island Public Library, 211 N. Washington, 68801.
—Stuhr Museum of the Prairie Pioneer, Research Library, 3133 W. Highway 34, 68801.
Hastings—Adams County Historical Society Archives, 1330 N. Burlington Ave., P.O. Box 102, 68902.
Lincoln—American Historical Society of Germans from Russia, Library, 631 D St., 68502.
—Historical Center of the United Methodist Church Library, Nebraska Wesleyan University, 5000 St. Paul Ave., 68504. (United Methodist clergy and history)
—Nebraska State Historical Society Library, 1500 R St., P.O. Box 82554, 68501.

NEVADA

Carson City—Nevada State Library and Archives, 100 Stewart St., 89710.
Elko—Northeastern Nevada Historical Society Museum Research Library, 1515 Idaho St., P.O. Box 2550, 89801.
Reno—Nevada Historical Society Museum-Research Library, 1650 N. Virginia St., 89503.
—University of Nevada Library, 89557. (state history and newspapers)

NEW HAMPSHIRE

A number of libraries and historical societies have local history or genealogy collections.

Concord—New Hampshire Historical Society, 30 Park St., 03301.
—New Hampshire Records and Archives Center, 71 S. Fruit St., 03301-2410.
—New Hampshire State Library, 20 Park St., 03301.
Dover—Dover Public Library, 73 Locust St., 03820.
Hanover—Dartmouth College, Baker Memorial Library, 03755. (state and Congregational Church history)
Keene—Historical Society of Cheshire County, Archive Center, 246 Main St., P.O. Box 803, 03431.
—Keene Public Library, 60 Winter St., 03431.
Manchester—American-Canadian Genealogical Society, P.O. Box 668, 03015.
—Manchester City Library, 405 Pine St., 03104. (state history)

NEW JERSEY

A number of libraries and historical societies have local history and genealogy collections.

Atlantic City—Atlantic City Free Public Library, One N. Tennessee Ave., 08401.
Camden—Camden County Historical Society Library, Park Blvd. at Euclid Ave., 08103.
Madison—Commission on Archives and History, United Methodist Church, 36 Madison Ave., P.O. Box 127, 07940. (United Methodist and Evangelical United Brethren history)
Morristown—Joint Free Public Library of Morristown and Morris Township, New Jersey History and Genealogy Department, One Miller Rd., 07960.
New Brunswick—New Brunswick Theological Seminary, Library, 21 Seminary Pl., 08901. (Archives of Reformed Church in America)
—Rutgers University, Alexander Library, Special Collections, 169 College Ave., 08903.
Newark—New Jersey Historical Society Library, 230 Broadway, 07104.

—Newark Public Library, New Jersey Dept., 5 Washington St., P.O. Box 630, 07101-0630.

Rutherford—Fairleigh Dickinson University, Messler Library, 207 Montross Ave., 07070-2299. (New Jersey room)

Trenton—New Jersey State Archives, 185 W. State St., 08625-0520.

—New Jersey State Library, 185 W. State St., CN520, 08625-0520.

Vineland—Historical and Antiquarian Society Library, 108 S. 7th St., P.O. Box 35, 08360.

Woodbury—Gloucester County Historical Society Library, 17 Hunter St., P.O. Box 409, 08096.

NEW MEXICO

Albuquerque—Albuquerque Public Library, Special Collections, 423 Central Ave. NE, 87102.

—University of New Mexico Library, 87131. (maps, newspapers, history)

Las Cruces—New Mexico State University Library, P.O. Box 3475, 88003-3475.

Roswell—Roswell Public Library, 301 N. Pennsylvania Ave., 88201.

Santa Fe—Library of the Museum of New Mexico, 110 Washington Ave., P.O. Box 2087, 87504-2087.

—New Mexico State Commission of Public Records and Archives, 404 Montezuma St., 87503.

—New Mexico State Library, 325 Don Gaspar, 87503-1629.

NEW YORK

Many public libraries and county historical societies have local history collections.

Albany—Albany Institute of History and Art, McKinney Library, 125 Washington Ave., 12210.

—New York State Library, Cultural Education Center, Empire State Plaza, 12230. (Dutch colonial records, Shaker collection, New York history)

Auburn—Foundation Historical Association, Inc., Library, Seward House, 33 South St., 13021.

Brooklyn—Brooklyn Historical Society Library, 128 Pierrepont and Clinton St., 11201.

—World Jewish Genealogy Organization, 1533 60th St., P.O. Box 420, 11219.

Buffalo—Buffalo and Erie County Historical Society Library, 25 Nottingham Ct., 14216.

Huntington—Huntington Historical Society Library, 209 Main St., 11743.

New Paltz—Huguenot Historical Society Library, 88 Huguenot St., P.O. Box 339, 12561.

New Rochelle—Huguenot-Thomas Paine Historical Association Library, 983 North Ave., 10804. (area history)

New York City—American Federation of Jews from Central Europe, Research Foundation for Jewish Immigration, Library, 570 7th Ave., 3rd Floor, 10018.

—American-Irish Historical Society Library, 991 5th Ave., 10028. (Irish & Scotch-Irish in NY & colonies, by appointment only)

—Holland Society of New York, Library, 122 E. 58th St., 10022. (genealogy in Dutch Settlements)

—Huguenot Society of America Library, 122 E. 58th St., 10022.

—New York Genealogical and Biographical Society, 122 E. 58th St., 10022-1939.

—New York Historical Society Library, 170 Central Park W., 10024-5194.

—New York Public Library, Genealogy Division, 5th Ave. and 42nd St., 10018.

—Religious Society of Friends, New York Yearly Meeting, Haviland Records Room, 222 E. 16th St., 10003. Write to 15 Rutherford Pl., New York, NY 10003. Open by appointment, tel. (212) 673-5750.

—Sons of the (American) Revolution in the State of New York, c/o Frances Tavern Museum, Broad and 54 Pearl St., 10004.

Rochester—American Baptist Historical Library, 1106 S. Goodman St., 14620. (archives of the American Baptist Convention, English Baptist history)

Syracuse—Onondaga County Public Library System, 447 S. Salina St., 13202-2494.

Troy—Troy Public Library, 100 2nd St., 12180-4005.

NORTH CAROLINA

Many public libraries have local history and genealogy collections.

Chapel Hill—University of North Carolina, Wilson Library, Special Collections, 27514.

Charlotte—Public Library of Charlotte and Mecklenburg County, 310 N. Tryon St., 28202-2176.

Durham—Duke University, Perkins Library, 27706-2597. (newspapers, Methodist collection, supplemental census schedules)

Elon College—Elon College Library, P.O. Box 187, 27244-2010. (United Church of Christ, Southern Conference history)

Gastonia—Gaston County Public Library, 1555 E. Garrison Blvd., 28054.

Greensboro—Guilford College Library, 5800 W. Friendly Ave., 27410. (genealogy, Quaker collection)

Montreat—Presbyterian Church (USA) Department of History, 318 Georgia Terr., P.O. Box 849, 28757. (Presbyterian churches of the southern U.S.)

Raleigh—North Carolina Dept. of Cultural Resources, State Library, 109 E. Jones St., 27611.

—North Carolina Division of Archives and History, 109 E. Jones St., 27611.

Winston-Salem—Forsyth County Public Library, 660 W. 5th St., 27101.

—Moravian Church in America, Southern Province Archives and Research Library, 4 E. Bank St., 27101.

NORTH DAKOTA

Bismarck—North Dakota State Library, Liberty Memorial Building, 604 E. Boulevard Ave., 58505.

—State Historical Society of North Dakota, North Dakota Heritage Center, 612 E. Boulevard Ave., 58505.

Fargo—North Dakota State University Library, N.D. Institute for Regional Studies, S.U. Station, P.O. Box 5599, 58105. (North Dakota history and pioneer reminiscences)

Fort Yates—Standing Rock College Library, 58538. (Sioux Indian collection)

Grand Forks—Grand Forks Public Library, 2110 Library Cir., 58201. (local history)

—University of North Dakota, Chester Fritz Library, 58202. (North Dakota and Western history)

Minot—Minot Public Library, 516 2nd Ave. SW, 58701.

—Minot State University Memorial Library, 500 University Ave. NW, 58701. (Indians of North Central States, Dakota territory and state history)

OHIO

Many public libraries have local history or genealogical collections.

Bluffton—Mennonite Historical Library, Musselman Library, Bluffton College, 45817. (Mennonite & Amish history)

Bowling Green—Bowling Green State University Libraries, Center for Archival Collections, 43403.

Canton—Malone College, Cattell Library, 515 25th St. NW, 44709. (Quaker collection)

—Stark County District Library, 715 Market Ave. N, 44702.

Cincinnati—Cincinnati Historical Society Library, 1301 Western Ave., 45203.

—Hebrew Union College Library, 3101 Clifton Ave., 45220. (Jewish Americana to 1850)

—Public Library of Cincinnati and Hamilton County, 800 Vine St., 45202.

—University of Cincinnati, Central Library, ML King and Campus Dr., 45221. (German-Americana)

Cleveland—Cleveland State University Library, 1860 E. 22nd St., 44115. (city and county history)

—Western Reserve Historical Society Library, 10825 East Blvd., 44106. (Genealogy, Shaker history)

Columbus—Ohio Historical Society Library, 1982 Velma Ave., 43211-2497.

—State Library of Ohio, State Office Bldg., 65 S. Front St., 43266. (genealogy section)

Dayton—Wright State University Library, 7751 Col. Glenn Highway, 45435. (family and business papers, area county records, Miami Valley Genealogical Society library)

Delaware—Ohio Wesleyan University, Beeghly Library, 43 University Ave., 43015. (Methodist historical collection)

Findlay—Findlay-Hancock County Public Library, 206 Broadway, 45840.

Lima—Allen County Historical Society Library, 620 W. Market St., 45801.

Mansfield—Ohio Genealogical Society Library, 34 Sturges Ave., P.O. Box 2625, 44906.

Marietta—Ohio Historical Society Library, Campus Martius Museum Library, 601 2nd St., 45750.

Mentor—Library of Henry J. Grund, 4897 Corduroy Rd., Mentor Headlands, 44060. Write for appointment.

Middletown—Middletown Public Library, 125 Broad St., 45044.

Newark—Licking County Genealogical Society Library, 743 E. Main St., P.O. Box 4037, 43055.

Toledo—Toledo Public Library, 325 Michigan St., 43624.

Youngstown—Public Library of Youngstown and Mahoning County, 305 Wick Ave., 44503.

Zanesville—Muskingum County Genealogical Society Library, Ohio University Library, Herrold Hall, 1425 Newark Rd., 43701.

OKLAHOMA

A number of libraries have genealogy, local history, or American Indian collections.

Bartlesville—Bartlesville Public Library, 3001 SE Frank Phillips, 74006.

Lawton—Lawton Public Library, 110 SW 4th St., 73501.

Norman—University of Oklahoma, Western History Collection, Monnet Hall, 630 Parrington Oval, 73019.

Oklahoma City—Oklahoma Division of Archives and Records, 109 State Capitol, 73105.

—Oklahoma Historical Society, Historical Bldg., 2100 N. Lincoln Blvd., 73105. (the major genealogy collection in the state)

Shawnee—Oklahoma Baptist University Library, 74801. (state Baptist history, archives)

Stillwater—Stillwater Public Library, 206 W. 6th Ave. at Husband, 74074.

Tahlequah—Cherokee National Historical Society, Inc., Library, Cherokee National Museum, TSA-LA-GI, P.O. Box 515, 74465.

Tulsa—Rudisill North Regional Library, 1520 N. Hartford, 74106.

OREGON

Eugene—Lane County Museum Library, 740 W. 13th, 97402. Open by appointment.

—University of Oregon Library, Newspaper Microfilming Project, 97403.

Newburg—George Fox College Library, 97132. (archives, Northwest Yearly Meeting, Society of Friends)

Portland—Genealogical Forum of Oregon Library, 1410 SW Morrison St., Suite 812, 97205.

—Oregon Historical Society Museum & Library, 1230 SW Park Ave., 97205.

Roseburg—Douglas County Museum Library, County Fairgrounds, P.O. Box 1550, 97470.

Salem—Oregon State Archives, 800 Summer St. NE, 97310.

—Oregon State Library, 250 Winter St. NE, 97310-0640.

PENNSYLVANIA

Many libraries and historical societies have genealogy and local history collections.

Allentown—Lehigh County Historical Society Library, Old Courthouse, 5th and Hamilton St., P.O. Box 1548, 18105.

Annville—Lebanon Valley College Library, 17003. (Pennsylvania German collection)

Bethlehem—The Archives of the Moravian Church, 41 W. Locust St., 18018.

Erie—Erie County Historical Society Library, 417 State St., 16501.

—Erie County Library System, 3 S. Perry Sq., 16501.

Harleysville—Mennonite Historians of Eastern Pennsylvania, P.O. Box 82, 565 Voder Rd., 19438.

Harrisburg—Pennsylvania State Archives, 3rd and North Sts., P.O. Box 1026, 17108.

—Pennsylvania State Library, Walnut St. and Commonwealth Ave., P.O. Box 1601, 17105.

Haverford—Friends Historical Association, Haverford College Library, 19041. (Quaker collection, Yearly Meeting archives)

Indiana—Historical and Genealogical Society of Indiana County, 200 S. 6th, 15701.

Lancaster—Archives of the Evangelical and Reformed Historical Society and of the United Church of Christ, Lancaster Theological Seminary, 555 W. James St., 17603. (Pennsylvania and nearby states)

—Lancaster County Historical Society Library, 230 N. President Ave., 17603.

—Lancaster Mennonite Historical Society Library, 2215 Mill Stream Rd., 17602. (Southeast Pennsylvania, Mennonite, Amish history, genealogy)

Overbrook—Archdiocese of Philadelphia, Archives and Historical Collections, 1000 E. Wynnewood Rd., 19096. (Catholic immigration, newspapers)

Philadelphia—American-Swedish Historical Museum Library, 1900 Pattison Ave., 19145.

—Archives of the American Catholic Historical Society of Philadelphia, 263 S. 4th St., P.O. Box 84, 19105.

—Balch Institute for Ethnic Studies, Library, 18 S. 7th St., 19106. (Archives of Scotch-Irish Society of the U.S.A.; Philadelphia Jewish archives; immigration history)

—Free Library of Philadelphia, Logan Square, 19th and Vine St., 19103. (map and newspaper collections)

—Genealogical Society and Historical Society of Pennsylvania, Library, 1300 Locust St., 19107. (separate organizations at the same address)

—Germantown Historical Society Library, 5501 Germantown Ave., 19144.

—Lutheran Theological Seminary Library, 7301 Germantown Ave., 19119. (New Jersey, Pennsylvania Lutheran records)

—Masonic Library and Museum of Pennsylvania, One N. Broad St., 19107-2598.

—Methodist Historical Center, 326 New St., 19106.

(Historical Society of Eastern Pennsylvania Annual Conference, archives, includes records of closed churches in this conference)
—Philadelphia City Archives, 401 N. Broad St., Suite 942, 19108.
—Philadelphia Maritime Museum Library, 321 Chestnut St., 19106.
—Presbyterian Church U.S.A., Presbyterian Historical Library, 425 Lombard St., 19147.
—Temple University, Paley Library, Berks and 13th Sts., 19122.
Pittsburgh—Carnegie Library of Pittsburgh, 4400 Forbes Ave., 15213. (local history, newspapers)
—Historical Society of Western Pennsylvania, Library, 4338 Bigelow Blvd., 15213.
Reading—Historical Society of Berks County, Library, 940 Centre Ave., 19601.
Scranton—Lackawanna Historical Society Library, 232 Monroe Ave., 18510.
Swarthmore—Friends Historical Library of Swarthmore College, 19081. (Quaker records, archives)
University Park—Pennsylvania State University, Pattee Library, 16802. (some family papers, archives from area labor unions)
West Chester—Chester County Archives & Records Services Library, 117 W. Gay St., 19380.
—Chester County Historical Society Library, 225 N. High St., 19380.
York—York County Historical Society Library, 250 E. Market St., 17403.

RHODE ISLAND

A number of libraries have local genealogy or history collections.

Kingston—University of Rhode Island, Library, 02881. (records of Episcopal Diocese of Rhode Island, state history)
Newport—Newport Historical Society, 82 Touro St., 02840.
Pawtucket—American-French Genealogical Society, 78 Earl St., 02895.
—Pawtucket Public Library and Regional Library Center, 13 Summer St., 02860. (Polish collection, local and state history)
Providence—Brown University, University Library and John Carter Brown Library, P.O. Box 1894, 02912.
—Providence College Library, River Ave. at Eaton St., 02918. (Rhode Island black history, papers)
—Rhode Island Historical Society Library, 121 Hope St., 02906. (New England genealogy, archives of New England Yearly Meeting, Society of Friends)
—Rhode Island Jewish Historical Association, 130 Sessions St., 02906.
—Rhode Island State Archives, 337 Westminster, 02903.
—Rhode Island State Library, State House, 82 Smith St., 02903.

SOUTH CAROLINA

Many city and county libraries have genealogy collections.

Central—Central Wesleyan College Library, 1 Wesleyan Dr., 29630. (Upstate South Carolina genealogy)
Charleston—Charleston Diocese Archives, 119 Broad St., 29401. (South Carolina Catholic history, archives)
—Charleston Library Society, 164 King St., 29401. (state history; South Carolina Jewish collection)
—Huguenot Society of South Carolina Library, 21 Queen St., 29401.
—South Carolina Historical Society Library, Fireproof Building, 100 Meeting St., 29401.
Columbia—South Carolina Department of Archives and History, Capitol Station, P.O. Box 11669, 29211.
—South Carolina State Library, 1500 Senate St., 29201, P.O. Box 11469, 29211.
—South Caroliniana Library, University of South Carolina, 29208.
Greenville—Furman University, Duke Library, 3300 Poinsett Highway, 29613. (South Carolina Baptist archives, history)
—Greenville County Library, 300 College St., 29601.
Richburg—Chester District Genealogical Society Library, P.O. Box 336, 29729. Open by appointment.
Rock Hill—Winthrop College, Dacus Library, 810 Oakland Ave., 29733-0001. (local history)
—York County Library-Rock Hill Public Library, 138 E. Black St., P.O. Box 10032, 29731.
Spartanburg—Wofford College Library, 429 N. Church St., 29301. (South Carolina Conference of the United Methodist Church)

SOUTH DAKOTA

Aberdeen—Aberdeen Public Library, 519 S. Kline St., 57401.
Pierre—South Dakota Historical Society Library and

State Archives, 900 Governors Dr., 57501-5070.
—South Dakota State Library, State Library Building, 800 Governors Dr., 57501-2294.
Sioux Falls—Augustana College Library, 57197. (Dakota and Norwegian collections)
—North American Baptist Seminary Library, 1321 W. 22nd St., 57105. (North American Baptist archives)
Vermillion—University of South Dakota, Weeks Library, 57069-2390. (archives and history collections)

TENNESSEE

Many public libraries in the state have local history and genealogy collections.

Chattanooga—Chattanooga-Hamilton County Library, 1001 Broad St., 37402.
Clarksville—Clarksville-Montgomery County Public Library, 329 Main St., 37040.
Columbia—Columbia State Community College, Finney Library, P.O. Box 1315, 38402. (area history)
Jackson—Jackson-Madison County Public Library, 433 Lafayette, 38301.
Knoxville—Knoxville-Knox County Public Library, 500 W. Church Ave., 37902.
Memphis—Memphis-Shelby County Public Library, 1850 Peabody Ave., 38104.
—Memphis State University Library, Southern Ave., 38152. (family papers; history of lower Mississippi Valley)
—Memphis Theological Seminary Library, 168 E. Parkway S., 38104. (Cumberland Presbyterian history, archives)
Nashville—Archives of the Jewish Federation of Nashville and Middle Tennessee, 801 Percy Warner Blvd., 37205.
—Disciples of Christ Historical Society Library, 1101 19th Ave. S., 37212.
—Historical Commission, SBC, Southern Baptist Historical Library & Archives, 901 Commerce, Suite 400, 37203. (Southern Baptist history and archives)
—Public Library of Nashville and Davidson County, 8th Avenue N. and Union, 37203.
—Tennessee Historical Society, Tennessee State Library Building, 403 7th Ave. N., 37243-0312.
—Tennessee State Library and Archives, State Library Building, 403 7th Ave. N., 37243-0312.
Sewanee—University of the South, DuPont Library, 37375. (Episcopal Church collection on twenty-two Southern dioceses)
—University of the South, School of Theology Library, 37375. (Protestant Episcopal Church)

TEXAS

Many public libraries have local history and genealogy collections.

Austin—Austin History Center, Austin Public Library, P.O. Box 2287, Austin, TX 78768-2287.
—Daughters of the Republic of Texas Library, 510 E. Anderson Ln., 78752.
—Library and Archives of the Episcopal Church Historical Society, 606 Rathervue Pl., 78768.
—Texas Catholic Historical Society, Catholic Archives of Texas Library, W. 16th at N. Congress, P.O. Box 13327, Capitol Station, 78711. (Texas Catholic archives, history)
—Texas State Library and Archives, 1200 Brazos St., P.O. Box 12927, Capitol Station, 78711.
—University of Texas, Barker History Center, SRH2.109, 78712.
Beaumont—Beaumont Public Library, Tyrrell History Library, 695 Pearl St., 77701.
Dallas—Dallas Public Library, 1515 Young St., 75201.
—Dallas Historical Society Research Center, Hall of State, Fair Park Station, P.O. Box 150038, 75315.
—Highland Park Library, 4700 Drexel Dr., 75205.
—Paul Quinn College Library, 3837 Simpson-Stuart Rd., 75241. (A.M.E. Church archives)
El Paso—El Paso Public Library, 501 N. Oregon, 79901. (local history)
Fort Worth—Fort Worth Public Library, 300 Taylor St., 76102.
—Southwestern Baptist Theological Seminary Library, 2001 W. Seminary Dr., 76115, P.O. Box 22000-2E, 76122. (Texas Baptist history)
Hillsboro—Confederate Research Center, Hill Junior College, 76645.
Houston—Clayton Center for Genealogical Research, 5300 Caroline, 77004.
—Rice University, Fondren Library, 6100 Main, 77005, P.O. Box 1892, 77251. (Civil War and Texas history and special collections)
Lubbock—Lubbock City-County Library, 1306 9th St., 79401.
San Antonio—Archdiocese of San Antonio, 2718 W. Woodlawn, P.O. Box 28410, 78284-4901. (Catholic archives)
—Daughters of the Republic of Texas Library, P.O. Box 1401, 78295.

—Episcopal Diocese of West Texas, Cathedral Library, 111 Torcido, P.O. Box 6885, 78209.
—San Antonio College Library, 1001 Howard St., 78284. (Southwestern Genealogical Society)
—San Antonio Public Library, History, Social Sciences, and General Reference Division, 203 S. St. Mary's, 78205.
Texarkana—See under Arkansas.
Waco—Baylor University, Texas Collection, P.O. Box 97142, 76798-7142.
—Masonic Grand Lodge of Texas AF & AM Library, 715 Columbus, P.O. Box 446, 76703.
—Waco-McLennan County Library, 1717 Austin Ave., 76701.

UTAH

Bountiful—American Genealogical Lending Library (AGLL), P.O. Box 244, 84011.
Salt Lake City—Family History Library, 35 North West Temple, 84150.
—Utah State Archives, Archives Bldg., State Capitol, 84114.
—Utah State Historical Society Library, 300 Rio Grande, 84101.
—Utah State Library, 2150 South 300 West, 84115.

VERMONT

A number of public libraries have local history collections.

Bennington—Bennington Museum, Genealogical Library, 05201.
Brattleboro—Brooks Memorial Library, 224 Main St., 05301.
Montpelier—Vermont Historical Society Library, Pavilion Building, 109 State St., 05609-0901. (center for genealogical research in Vermont) State library and state archives at the same address.

VIRGINIA

A number of public libraries and local museums have local history and genealogy collections.

Arlington—National Genealogical Society Library, 4527 17th St. N., 22207.
Ashland—Randolph Macon College Library, Virginia Conference of the United Methodist Church Historical Society, 23005. (Virginia Methodism)
Charlottesville—University of Virginia Library, 22903. (Virginia collection and personal papers)
Harrisonburg—Eastern Mennonite College and Seminary, Hartzler Library, 22801-2462. (Anabaptist/Mennonite history, genealogy, archives)
Radford—Radford University Library, 24142. (Southwest Virginia history, archives)
Richmond—Grand Lodge of Virginia Library, 4101 Nine Mile Rd., P.O. Box 27345, 23261.
—Museum of the Confederacy Library, 1201 E. Clay St., 23219. (Primary sources of the Confederacy and the South)
—Richmond Newspapers, Inc., Library, 333 E. Grace St., 23219.
—United Daughters of the Confederacy Library, 328 North Blvd., 23220.
—University of Richmond Library, P.O. Box 34, 23173. (Virginia Baptist Historical Society)
—Virginia Historical Society Library, 428 North Blvd., P.O. Box 7311, 23221.
—Virginia State Library and Archives, 12th and Capitol St., 23219.
Williamsburg—College of William and Mary in Virginia, Swem Library, 23187. (Virginia history)
—Colonial Williamsburg Foundation, Central Library, 415 N. Boundary St., P.O. Box C, 23187.
Wise—Clinch Valley College of the University of Virginia, Library, 24293. (Southwest Virginia archives, family and business papers)

WASHINGTON

Olympia—Olympia Public Library, 8th at Franklin, 98501.
—Washington Division of Archives, 12th and Washington, P.O. Box 9000, 98504.
—Washington State Library, Capitol Campus, P.O. Box 42460, 98504-2460. (Its genealogical materials are in the Seattle Public Library.)
Pullman—Washington State University Library, 99164-5610. (area history and Germans from Russia)
Seattle—Diocese of Olympia, Resource Center, 1551 10th Ave. E., P.O. Box 12126, 98102. (Episcopal Church in Washington)
—Seattle Genealogical Society Library, 1405 5th Ave., P.O. Box 1708, 98111.
—Seattle Public Library, Genealogy Section, 1000 4th Ave., 98104.
—University of Washington Library, FM-25, 98195. (Northwest history, manuscripts)
Spokane—Catholic Diocese Archives, 1023 W. Riverside, 99210-1453.

—Spokane Public Library, W. 906 Main Ave., 99201.
Tacoma—Tacoma Public Library, 1102 Tacoma Ave. S., 98402-2098. (city archives)
—Washington State Historical Society Library, 315 N. Stadium Way, 98403.

WEST VIRGINIA

Other public libraries have genealogy or local history collections.

Buckhannon—West Virginia Wesleyan College Library, 26201. (West Virginia Methodist history)
Charleston—West Virgina Archives and History Library, Cultural Center, State Capitol Complex, 25305.
—West Virginia Historical Society, Cultural Center, Capitol Complex, 25305.
Fairmont—Marion County Public Library, 321 Monroe St., 26554.
Huntington—Cabell County Public Library, 455 9th St. Plaza, 25701-1417.
—Marshall University, Morrow Library, Special Collections, 25755.
Morgantown—West Virginia University Library, West Virginia & Regional History Collection, P.O. Box 6464, 26506.
Parkersburg—Parkersburg and Wood County Public Library, 3100 Emerson Ave., 26104.

WISCONSIN

Eau Claire—University of Wisconsin at Eau Claire, Library, 105 Garfield Ave., 54702. (area research center for Chippewa Valley history and genealogy)
Green Bay—Brown County Library, 515 Pine St., 54301.
—University of Wisconsin at Green Bay, Library, 2420 Nicolet Dr., 54311-7001. (area history research center, Belgian-American ethnic collection)
Janesville—Rock County Historical Society, Research Library, Ten S. High, P.O. Box 8096, 53547. (local history, family and business papers)
—Seventh Day Baptist Historical Society Library, 3120 Kennedy Rd., P.O. Box 1678, 53547. Open by appointment.
Madison—State Historical Society of Wisconsin, Library, 816 State St., 53706.
—University of Wisconsin at Madison, Memorial Library, 728 State St., 53706. (Local history and Norwegian-American collection)
—Vesterheim Genealogical Center, 415 Main St., 53703-3116. (Norwegian-American research)
—Wisconsin Division of Archives and Manuscripts, 816 State St., 53706.
Milwaukee—Milwaukee Public Library, Local History Room, 814 W. Wisconsin Ave., 53233-2385.
—University of Wisconsin at Milwaukee, Library, 2311 E. Hartford Ave., P.O. Box 604, 53201. (area research center for Wisconsin history)
Oshkosh—Oshkosh Public Library, 106 Washington Ave., 54901.
Platteville—University of Wisconsin at Platteville Library, 1 University Plaza, 53818-3099. (Southwest Wisconsin area research center, archives)
Racine—Racine County Historical Society and Museum, Reference Library of Local History and Genealogy, 701 Main St., 53401-1527.
Superior—University of Wisconsin at Superior, Hill Library, 1800 Grand Ave., 54880. (area research center)
Whitewater—University of Wisconsin at Whitewater Library, 800 W. Main St., 53190. (area research center)

WYOMING

Cheyenne—Laramie County Library System, Genealogy Collection, 2800 Central Ave., 82001.
—Wyoming State Archives, Barrett Bldg., 2301 Central Ave., 82002.
—Wyoming State Library, Supreme Court-Library Bldg., 82002. (area history, documents)
Laramie—University of Wyoming Library, University Station, P.O. Box 3334, 82071-3334.

CANADIAN LIBRARIES AND ARCHIVES

ALBERTA

Edmonton—Alberta Department of Culture, Provincial Archives, 12845 102nd Ave., Edmonton, Alberta, T5N 0M6 Canada.
—Alberta Genealogical Society, P.O. Box 12015, T5J 3L2. (Branches in Brooks, Grande Prairie, Red Deer, and Wetaskiwin)
—City of Edmonton Archives and Library, 10105 112th Ave., T5G 0H1.

BRITISH COLUMBIA

Surrey—Surrey Public Library, 14245 56th Ave., Surrey, British Columbia, V3W 1J2 Canada.

Victoria—British Columbia Archives and Records Service Library, 655 Belleville, V8V 1X4.

MANITOBA

Winnipeg—Jewish Historical Society of Western Canada Archives, 404-365 Hargrave St., Winnipeg, Manitoba, R3B 2K3 Canada.
—Legislative Library of Manitoba, 200 Vaughan St., R3C 1T5. (regional history)
—Manitoba Genealogical Society Library, 420-167 Lombard Ave., R3B 0T6.
—Provincial Archives of Manitoba, 200 Vaughan St., R3C 1T5.

NEW BRUNSWICK

Fredericton—New Brunswick Legislative Library, Queen St., Legislative Building, P.O. Box 6000, Fredericton, New Brunswick, E3B 5H1 Canada.
—New Brunswick Provincial Archives, P.O. Box 6000, E3B 5H1.
—University of New Brunswick Library, P.O. Box 7500, E3B 5H1. (regional history, newspapers)
Newcastle—Old Manse Library, 225 Mary St., E1V 1Z3.

NEWFOUNDLAND

St. John's—Provincial Public Library Services, Arts and Culture Center, Provincial Reference and Resource Division, Allandale Rd., St. John's, Newfoundland, A1B 3A3 Canada.
—Public Archives of Newfoundland and Labrador, Colonial Bldg., Military Rd., A1C 5E2.

NORTHWEST TERRITORIES

Yellowknife—Northwest Territories Archives Branch, Government of Northwest Territories, Yellowknife, Northwest Territories, X1A 2L9 Canada.

NOVA SCOTIA

Halifax—Legislative Library of Nova Scotia, Province House, Hollis St., Halifax, Nova Scotia, B3J 2P8 Canada. (provincial history)
—Public Archives of Nova Scotia, 6016 University Ave., B3H 1W4.
Wolfville—Acadia University Library, Acadia St., Box D, B0P 1X0. (Acadia archives, Baptist history)
Yarmouth—Yarmouth County Historical Society Library, P.O. Box 39, B5A 4B1.

ONTARIO

A number of public libraries have local history and/or genealogy collections.

Hamilton—Canadian Baptist Archives, McMaster Divinity College, Hamilton, Ontario, L8S 4K1 Canada.
Kingston—Archives of the Anglican Diocese of Ontario, 90 Johnson St., K7L 1X7.
—Kingston Public Library, 130 Johnson St., K7L 1X8. (genealogy and local history)
London—University of Western Ontario Library, 1151 Richmond St. N., N6A 3K7.
North York—North York Public Library, 5120 Yonge St., M2N 5N9.
Oshawa—Oshawa Historical Society Archives, P.O. Box 2303, L1H 7V5.
Ottawa—Canadian Historical Association, National Library of Canada, and Public Archives of Canada (all three institutions), 395 Wellington St., K1A 0N4.
St. Catharines—St. Catharines Historical Museum, Library and Archives, 1932 Canal Rd., P.O. Box 3012, L2R 7C2.
Toronto—Ontario Genealogical Society Library, 40 Orchard View Blvd., Suite 251, M4R 1B9.
—Archives of Ontario Library, 77 Grenville St., Queen's Park, M7A 2R9.
—The United Church of Canada Archives, Victoria University, 73 Queens Park Crescent East, M5S 1K7.
—United Empire Loyalists' Association of Canada, Library, 50 Baldwin St., M5T 1L4.
Willowdale—Toronto Jewish Congress, Jewish Public Library, 4600 Bathurst St., M2R 3V3.

PRINCE EDWARD ISLAND

Charlottetown—Prince Edward Island Museum and Heritage Foundation Library, 2 Kent St., Charlottetown, Prince Edward Island, C1A 1M6 Canada. (local history)
—Prince Edward Island Provincial Library, Enman Cres., P.O. Box 7500, C1A 8T8. (local history)
—The Public Archives of Prince Edward Island, P.O. Box 1000, C1A 7M4.

QUEBEC

A number of public libraries have local history and/or genealogical collections.

Longueil—Bibliothèque Municipale de Longueil, 100 rue St. Laurent Ouest, CP 5000, Longueil, Quebec, J4K 4Y7 Canada. Consult also the Grignon Branch

of the Longueil Library, 1660 Bourassa, J7J 3A5.
Montreal—Anglican Church of Canada, Diocese of Montreal Archives, 1444 Union Ave., H3A 2B8
—Archives National du Quebec, 100 rue Notre Dame est, H2Y 1C1.
—Bibliothèque Publique Juive, Jewish Public Library, 5151 Ste. Catherine Rd., H3W 1M6.
—Canadian Jewish Congress, Archives, 1590 Docteur Penfield Ave., H3G 1C5.
Sainte Foy—Archives Nationales de Quebec, Section de Généalogie, Quebec, CP 10450, G1V 4N1. (located at 1210 Avenue Du Séminaire)

SASKATCHEWAN

Regina—Saskatchewan Archives Board, 3303 Hillsdale St., Regina, Saskatchewan, S4S 0A2 Canada.
—Saskatchewan Genealogical Society Library, 1870 Lorne St., S4P 2L7.

YUKON TERRITORIES

Whitehorse—Government of Yukon Libraries and Archives Branch, 2071 Second Ave., P.O. Box 2703, Whitehorse, Yukon Territories, Y1A 2C6 Canada. (regional history)

BRITISH ISLES LIBRARIES AND ARCHIVES

ENGLAND

Many genealogical sources, such as parish registers, wills, marriage records, deeds, apprenticeship records, manorial records, some census returns, and nonconformist (Congregational Presbyterian, Methodist, Quaker, Catholic, etc.) registers, are located in the county record offices. An excellent reference for their locations and holdings is *In Search of Your British and Irish Roots*, by Angus Baxter (Baltimore: Genealogical Publishing Company, 1991 reprint of 1982 original).

Baptist History Society, 4 Southampton Row, London WC1B 4AB, England.
British Library, Great Russell St., London WC1B 3DG, England. (formerly British Museum)
British Newspaper Library, Colindale Ave., London NW9 5HE, England.
Catholic Record Society, Secretary, 114 Mount St., London W1Y 6AH, England.
Congregational Library, Memorial Hall, 2 Fleet Lane, London EC4, England.
General Register Office, St. Catherine's House, 10 Kingsway, London, WC2B 6JB, England. Mailing address: Smedley Hydro, Southport, Merseyside, PR8 2HH, England. (Births, deaths, marriages after 1837, England and Wales)
Greater London Records Office, County Hall, London, SE1 7PB, England.
Guildhall, Library of the Corporation of London, Aldermanbury, London EC2P 2EJ, England.
Huguenot Society, % Secretary, 67 Victoria Rd., London W8 5RH, England.
(The) Irish Genealogical Research Society, 82 Eaton Square, London SW1, England.
Jewish Museum and United Synagogue Archives, Woburn House, Tavistock Square, London WC1H 0EP, England.
Lambeth Palace Library, Lambeth, London SE1 7JU, England.
Liverpool Palace Library, William Brown St., Liverpool, L38EW, England.
Manchester Central Library, St. Peter's Square, Manchester M2 5PD, England.
Methodist Archives, Central Hall, Oldham St., Manchester M1 1JQ, England.
Presbyterian Historical Society of England, 86 Tavistock Pl., London WC1, England.
Public Record Office, Chancery Lane, London WC2A 1LR, England. (Will not do searching for a correspondent but will provide names of qualified researchers)
Public Record Office Branch, Ruskin Ave., Kew, Richmond, Surrey TW9 4DU, England.
Religious Society of Friends, Friends House, Euston Road, London NW1 2BJ, England.
Society of Genealogists, 14 Charterhouse Buildings, London EC1M 7BA, England. (Can suggest sources or course of action for a search in the U.K.)

NORTHERN IRELAND

Belfast Library and Society for Promoting Knowledge, 17 Donegall Square North, Belfast BT1 5GD, Northern Ireland.
General Register Office, Department of Health and Social Services, Oxford House, 49-55 Chichester St., Belfast BT1 4HL, Northern Ireland (1922 to the present)
General Register Office, Joyce House, 8-11 Lombard St. E., Dublin 2, Republic of Ireland. (Vital records before 1922)

Presbyterian Historical Society, Church House, Fisherwick Pl., Belfast 1, Northern Ireland.

Public Record Office for Northern Ireland, 66 Balmoral Ave., Belfast BT9 6NY, Northern Ireland.

Society of Friends Meeting House, Railway St., Lisburn, County Antrim, Northern Ireland.

Ulster Historical Foundation, 66 Balmoral Ave., Belfast BT9 6NY, Northern Ireland.

REPUBLIC OF IRELAND (EIRE)

The Genealogical Office, 2 Kildare St., Dublin 2, Eire.

General Register Office, Joyce House, 8-11 Lombard St. E., Dublin 2, Eire. (Vital records, 1845 to present for Eire, 1845-1922 for Northern Ireland)

National Archives of Ireland, Kildare St., Dublin 2, Eire.

National Library of Ireland, Kildare St., Dublin 2, Eire.

Public Record Office of Ireland, Four Courts, Dublin 7, Eire.

Registry of Deeds, Henrietta St., Dublin 1, Eire.

Religious Society of Friends, Historical Library, 6 Eustace St., Dublin, Eire.

Royal Irish Academy, 19 Dawson, Dublin 2, Eire.

Trinity College Library, College St., Dublin 2, Eire.

SCOTLAND

Aberdeen City Libraries, Central Library, Rosemount Viaduct, Aberdeen AB9 1GU, Scotland.

Edinburgh City Archives, City Chambers, Edinburgh EH1 1YJ, Scotland.

Episcopal Church in Scotland, Theological College, Rosebery Crescent, Edinburgh, Scotland.

General Register Office for Scotland, New Register House, Edinburgh EH1 3YY, Scotland. (Vital records, nineteenth-century censuses, parish registers)

Glasgow City Archives and Strathclyde Regional Archives, City Chambers, Glasgow G2 1DU, Scotland.

Glasgow Public Library, Mitchell Library, North St., Glasgow G3 7DN, Scotland.

National Library of Scotland, George IV Building, Edinburgh EH1 1EW, Scotland.

Orkney Library, Laing St., Kirkwall, Orkneys, Scotland. (Archives of the Orkney Islands)

Scots Ancestry Research Society, 3 Albany St., Edinburgh EH1 3PY, Scotland.

Scottish Catholic Archives, Columba House, 16 Drummond Place, Edinburgh EH3 6PL, Scotland.

Scottish History Society, % Department of History, University of Aberdeen, Aberdeen AB9 2UB, Scotland.

Scottish Record Office, P.O. Box 36, H.M. General Register House, Princes St., Edinburgh EH1 3YY, Scotland.

Scottish Records Association, % The Archivist, The University, Glasgow G12 8QQ, Scotland.

Shetland Islands Archives, Council Offices, 93 St. Olaf St., Lerwick, Shetlands, Scotland.

West Register House, Charlotte Square, Edinburgh EH2 4DF, Scotland.

Western Isles Archives, Public Library, Stornoway, Isle of Lewis, Scotland.

WALES

National Library of Wales, Aberystwyth, Dyfed SY23 3BU, Wales.

APPENDIX D

National Archives

National Archives, Pennsylvania Ave. at Eighth St. NW, Washington, DC 20408. Tel: (202) 501-5400.

National Archives II, 8601 Adelphi Rd., College Park, MD 20740.

REGIONAL BRANCHES OF THE NATIONAL ARCHIVES

Anchorage—National Archives, Alaska Region, 654 W. 3rd Ave., Anchorage, AK 99501. Tel: (907) 271-2441. Serving Alaska.

Atlanta area—National Archives, Southeast Region, 1557 St. Joseph Ave., East Point, GA 30344. Tel: (404) 763-7477. Serving Alabama, Florida, Georgia, Kentucky, Mississippi, North Carolina, South Carolina, Tennessee.

Boston area—National Archives, New England Region, 380 Trapelo Rd., Waltham, MA 02154. Tel: (617) 647-8100. Serving Connecticut, Maine, Massachusetts, New Hampshire, Rhode Island, Vermont.

Chicago—National Archives, Great Lakes Region, 7358 S. Pulaski Rd., Chicago, IL 60629. Tel: (312) 581-7816. Serving Illinois, Indiana, Michigan, Minnesota, Ohio, Wisconsin.

Denver—National Archives, Rocky Mountain Region, Bldg. 48, Denver Federal Center, P.O. Box 25307, Denver, CO 80225. Tel: (303) 236-0817. Serving Colorado, Montana, North Dakota, South Dakota, Utah, Wyoming. Also has most New Mexico records.

Fort Worth—National Archives, Southwest Region, 501 W. Felix, P.O. Box 6216, Fort Worth, TX 76115. Tel: (817) 334-5525. Serving Arkansas, Louisiana, New Mexico, Oklahoma, Texas. Most New Mexico records are in Denver.

Kansas City—National Archives, Central Plains Region, 2312 E. Bannister Rd., Kansas City, MO 64131. Tel: (816) 926-6272. Serving Iowa, Kansas, Missouri, Nebraska.

Los Angeles area—National Archives, Pacific Southwest Region, 24000 Avila Rd., Los Angeles, CA 92656, or P.O. Box 6719, Laguna Niguel, CA 92607-6719. Tel: (714) 643-4241. Serving Southern California, Arizona, and Clark County, Nevada.

New York—National Archives, Northeast Region, 201 Varick St., New York, NY 10014. Tel: (212) 337-1300. Serving New Jersey, New York, Puerto Rico, Virgin Islands.

Philadelphia—National Archives, Mid-Atlantic Region, 9th and Market Sts., Room 1350, Philadelphia, PA 19107. Tel: (215) 597-3000. Serving Delaware, Pennsylvania, Maryland, Virginia, West Virginia.

Pittsfield—National Archives, Pittsfield Region, 100 Dan Fox Dr., Pittsfield, MA 01201. Tel: (413) 445-6885, ext. 26. A microfilm reading room, serving primarily the Northeast but with census, military, and other records with national coverage.

San Francisco area—National Archives, Pacific Sierra Region, 1000 Commodore Dr., San Bruno, CA 94066. Tel: (415) 876-9009. Serving Hawaii, Nevada except for Clark County, Northern California, American Samoa, Trust Territories of Pacific Islands.

Seattle—National Archives, Pacific Northwest Region, 6125 Sand Point Way NE, Seattle, WA 98115. Tel: (206) 526-6507. Serving Idaho, Oregon, Washington.

APPENDIX E

Territorial and State Census Records

GENERAL SOURCES FOR LOCATING STATE CENSUS RECORDS

State census records are usually found at the state archives or state historical society. Some have been published by these institutions or commercial publishers. Microfilm copies of some are available from (1) the Family History Library, Salt Lake City, through its branch family history centers or (2) the American Genealogical Lending Library, P.O. Box 244, Bountiful, UT 84011. See Appendix B, chapter eleven, for books useful in locating state censuses.

The territories did participate in the federal decennial censuses. The federal territorial censuses marked *National Archives* in the following chart are readily available on microfilm from rental libraries and in many libraries nationwide. Before a territory was organized under its own name and government, it was often a county within a parent territory and thus was enumerated with the census of that parent region. The following chart below will help you find the censuses that are part of the parent schedules. For more detail on these territorial censuses, consult *Map Guide to the U.S. Federal Censuses, 1790-1920,* by William Thorndale and William Dollarhide (Baltimore: Genealogical Publishing Company, 1987).

Although lost censuses cannot be fully replaced, residents lists, such as tax rolls, petitions, and jury and voter lists, can help genealogists identify part of the population of a given place at a given time. Such lists are often published in genealogical periodicals. Another major source of such documents is the *Territorial Papers of the United States,* pertaining to states that were first territories. The *Territorial Papers* are available in many large libraries and from the American Genealogical Lending Library.

The following information is arranged by: **STATE NAME—DATE OF ENTRY INTO THE UNION—DATE AND SOURCE OF CENSUS**

ALABAMA—1819

- Eighteenth-century scattered censuses—Published in *Deep South Genealogical Quarterly* of the Mobile Genealogical Society, vols. 1-3, 5.
- 1801, 1808, 1810 Washington County and 1819 residents of northern Alabama—Published in *Alabama Genealogical Register* of Tuscaloosa, vol. 9. See also pre-1817 Mississippi schedules.
- 1820 territorial census—State archives; published by Genealogical Publishing Company, Baltimore, 1967; published by *Alabama Historical Quarterly* of the state archives, vol. 6, pp. 339-515.
- 1855, 1866 state censuses—State archives.

ALASKA—1959

- Federal territorial censuses of Alaska began in 1900.
- Other early censuses from 1870 to at least 1907 include Sitka (1870, 1880, 1881), Cape Smyth-Pt. Barrow (1885), and St. George and St. Paul Islands (1890-1895, 1904, 1905, 1907). These are published in the Serial Set in reports to Congress. The three Sitka reports are found in House Executive Document 5 (42d Cong., 1st Sess.) Serial 1470, pp. 13-26; Senate Executive Document 71 (47th Cong., 1st Sess., Vol. 4) Serial 1989, p. 34; and House Executive Document 81 (47th Cong., 1st Sess.) Serial 2027, pp. 14-23. The Serial Set is available at U.S. government documents depositories in many public and university libraries. For further information

see *The Genealogist's Companion & Sourcebook*, by Emily Croom (Cincinnati: Betterway Books, 1994).

ARIZONA—1912

- 1864, 1866, 1872, 1876, 1882 territorial censuses—State archives. Not available for all counties.
- 1860, 1864, 1870—Printed as Senate Document 13 (89th Cong., 1st Sess.) Serial 12668-1.
- 1850-1910 federal territorial censuses—National Archives.

ARKANSAS—1836

- 1823 (Arkansas Co.) and 1829 sheriff censuses (incomplete)—State archives and Southwest Arkansas Regional Archives.
- 1830 federal territorial census—National Archives.

CALIFORNIA—1850

- 1852—State library and state archives.

COLORADO—1876

- 1860 federal territorial census included with Kansas—National Archives.
- 1885—National Archives, state archives, state historical society.

CONNECTICUT—1788

- Seventeenth-century residents lists—Published in the *New England Historical and Genealogical Register.*
- 1776 census of Newington County—*A Census of Newington, Connecticut Taken According to Household in 1776.* Josiah Willard. Hartford: Frederic B. Hartranft, 1909.

DELAWARE—1787

- Seventeenth-century residents lists—(1) *Documents Relative to The Colonial History of New York.* E.B. O'Callaghan, comp. Albany, 1856; (2) National Genealogical Society *Quarterly*, Vol. 53; (3) *Early Delaware Census Records, 1665-1697.* Ronald Vern Jackson, ed. North Salt Lake, UT: Accelerated Indexing Systems, 1977.
- None after 1790.

FLORIDA—1845

- 1825 territorial census; 1855, 1867, 1875 state censuses—State archives. None are complete.
- 1830, 1840 federal territorial censuses—National Archives.
- 1885 state census—National Archives and state archives.
- 1895, 1905, 1915, 1925—Originals destroyed.
- 1935, 1945—State archives.

GEORGIA—1788

- Fragments of septennial state censuses, 1799, 1804-1859—State archives.
- *Indexes to Seven State Census Reports for Counties in Georgia, 1838-1845.* Brigid S. Town-send, comp. Atlanta: R.J. Taylor, Jr., Foundation, c1975. Also *Censuses for Georgia Counties: Taliaferro, 1827, Lumpkin, 1838, Chatham, 1845.* Atlanta: R.J. Taylor, Jr., Foundation, 1979.

HAWAII—1959

- Fragments of the 1866, 1878, 1890, 1896 pre-territorial censuses—State archives.
- Federal territorial censuses, 1900-1920—National Archives.

IDAHO—1890

- 1870, 1880 federal territorial censuses—National Archives; state historical society; *Idaho Territory: Federal Population Schedules and Mortality Schedules, 1870* published by Idaho Genealogical Society, 1973; 1880 population and mortality schedules published by the society, 1976. For 1860, consult Utah and Washington censuses.
- None after statehood.

ILLINOIS—1818

- 1810, 1818 territorial censuses—State archives; in *Illinois Census Returns, 1810 and 1818.* Margaret Cross Norton, ed. Collections of the Illinois Historical Library, Vol. 24, c1935.
- 1825, 1835, 1845, 1855, 1865—State archives. Existing records are incomplete.

INDIANA—1816

- 1807—State historical society and Allen County Public Library.

- Partial 1810 federal territorial census—National Archives.
- No state censuses. Enumerations of eligible voters may be in county auditor's office.

IOWA—1846

- 1836-1897 heads of household censuses, various counties in various years—State historical society and Iowa Genealogical Society. Some have been published.
- 1840 federal territorial census—National Archives. (Part of Clayton County enumerated with Minnesota).
- 1856, 1885, 1895, 1905, 1915, 1925 state censuses—State historical society. These name all family members. Interlibrary loan available for 1856, 1885, 1915.

KANSAS—1861

- 1855-1859, 1865, 1875, 1885, 1895, 1905, 1915, 1925 state censuses—State historical society. Contact historical society for interlibrary loan of 1865-1925 censuses.
- 1855—*The Census of the Territory of Kansas, February, 1855.* Willard Heiss, comp. Knightstown, IN: Eastern Indiana Publishing Company, 1968.
- 1860 federal territorial census—National Archives.

KENTUCKY—1792

- No state censuses. For evidence of pre-statehood residents, see county records and published census substitutes for Kentucky and Virginia.

LOUISIANA—1812

- *The Census Tables for the French Colony of Louisiana from 1699 through 1732.* Charles R. Maduell, comp. Baltimore: The Genealogical Publishing Company, 1972. From Library of Congress, microfilm copies of manuscripts in Archives des Colonies in Paris.
- *Louisiana Census and Militia Lists, 1770-1789.* Albert J. Robichaux, comp. Harvey, Louisiana, 1973. Originals in General Archives of the Indies, Seville, Spain.
- *Some Late-Eighteenth-Century Louisianians, Census Records, 1758-1796.* Jacqueline K. Voorhies, comp. University of Southwestern Louisiana, 1973.
- Eighteenth-century censuses of New Orleans and other areas of Louisiana have been published in the Louisiana Historical Society *Quarterly*, Vols. 1-6.
- 1804 list of free black residents—*Territorial Papers of the United States*, Vol. 9.
- 1810 federal territorial census—National Archives.
- No state censuses that name heads of household or family members.

MAINE—1820

- 1790 federal territorial census—National Archives.
- No statewide censuses. State archives and historical society have fragments of an 1837 census of some towns.

MARYLAND—1788

- Seventeenth-century residents lists—Published by Maryland Historical Society, *Archives of Maryland*, Vols. 1, 5, 7, 8, 13, 20.
- 1710 residents—Calendar of Maryland State Papers, Vol. 1, 1943.
- No statewide censuses taken.

MASSACHUSETTS—1788

- 1779 census—National Genealogical Society *Quarterly*, Vols. 49-51.
- 1855, 1865 state censuses—State archives.

MICHIGAN—1837

- *Early Michigan Census Records, 1799, 1806, 1827.* Ronald Vern Jackson, ed. Salt Lake City: Accelerated Indexing Systems, 1976.
- Detroit censuses between 1750 and 1810—Detroit Public Library.
- 1827 Wayne County—Detroit Public Library. See also *Michigan Censuses 1710-1830 Under the French, British and Americans*, Detroit Society for Genealogical Research, 1982.
- 1845, 1854, 1864, 1874, 1884, 1894—State archives.
- 1894, 1904 state censuses—State library.
- Check the county courthouses and local libraries for others.

MINNESOTA—1858

- 1830 (in Michigan territory), 1840 (in Wisconsin and Iowa territories), 1850 federal territorial censuses—National Archives.
- 1849, 1857, 1865, 1875, 1885, 1895, 1905 censuses—State historical society.
- 1857—National Archives.
- See also 1836 Iowa Territory census.

MISSISSIPPI—1817

- French, English, Spanish provincial records, record groups 24, 25, 26 in the State archives.
- 1792, 1837 Natchez census, 1908 Centreville census, 1920 Hattiesburg census—State archives.
- 1805, 1808, 1810, 1813, 1816, 1822, 1823, 1825, 1833, 1837, 1841, 1845, 1853, 1866 state censuses—State archives, record group 2 and 28. Scattered counties and towns. Some 1805 and 1810 schedules published in *Journal of Mississippi History*, Vols. 10, 11, 13, 14, 15.
- 1809 Madison and Washington Counties—*Territorial Papers of the United States.* Vol. 5.
- 1816 state census—*Early Inhabitants of the Natchez District.* Norman E. Gillis. Baton Rouge, 1963.
- 1831-1832, 1837, 1839, 1855, 1856, 1926-39 federal Indian censuses—State archives.
- 1907, 1925-33 enumeration of Confederate soldiers and widows—State archives, record group 29.

MISSOURI—1821

- 1787, 1791, 1803 censuses of early towns and 1845 St. Louis census—State historical society.
- 1840 state census (New Madrid, Newton, Pike, Randolph, Ray, Rives (later Henry), Shelby, Stoddard, and Warren counties only)—State archives.
- 1844 state census (Callaway County) and 1868 (Cape Girardeau County)—State archives.
- 1876 state census (Benton, Calloway, Cape Girardeau, Christian, Greene, Holt, Howard, McDonald, Montgomery, Osage, Phelps, Reynolds, and St. Francis counties)—State archives.

MONTANA—1889

- A state census was apparently approved but never taken.
- 1860 federal territorial census—National Archives. Eastern part of Montana included in the unorganized part of Nebraska Territory. Western part of Montana included in Washington Territory.
- 1870, 1880 federal territorial censuses—National Archives.

NEBRASKA—1867

- 1854-1856 state census (eastern counties)—State historical society; also published by Nebraska Genealogical Society.
- 1854-1856—*Nebraska State Censuses.* Evelyn M. Cox. Ellensburg, WA, 1973.
- 1860 federal territorial census—National Archives.
- 1865 and 1869 (2 counties each) state censuses—State historical society.
- 1885 state census—National Archives.

NEVADA—1864

- 1850 and 1860 federal territorial censuses included in Utah Territory—National Archives.
- 1861-1863 state census—State archives and historical society. Not all counties.
- 1875 inhabitants—State archives and historical society.

NEW HAMPSHIRE—1788

- 1786 heads of families in Peterborough—*State Papers*, Vol. 10.
- No state censuses.

NEW JERSEY—1787

- 1693 census of New Sweden—*Genealogical Magazine of New Jersey*, Vol. 13. Newark: Genealogical Society of New Jersey.
- 1855, 1865, 1875, 1885, 1895, 1905, 1915 state censuses—State library and state archives. 1855-1875 are incomplete.

NEW MEXICO—1912

- 1790, 1823, 1845 censuses—*Spanish and Mexican Colonial Censuses of New Mexico, 1790, 1823, 1845.* Virginia L. Olmsted. Albuquerque: New Mexico Genealogical Society, 1975. Vol. 2 contains 1750, 1790, 1830.
- 1850-1910 federal territorial censuses—National Archives.
- 1885 state census—National Archives and state archives.

NEW YORK—1788

- *An Inventory of New York State and Federal Census Records, 1825-1925*, New York State Library, 1942.
- *Search and Research*. Noel C. Stevenson. Salt Lake City: Deseret Book Company, 1959. County by county listing of where the state censuses of New York are: county clerks' offices, New York State Library, public and historical libraries.
- 1698 census, Westchester County—*New York Genealogical and Biographical Register*. Vol. 38.
- 1825, 1835, 1845, 1855, 1865, 1875, 1892, 1905, 1915, 1925 state censuses—State library has considerable records.

NORTH CAROLINA—1789

- 1701 residents—National Genealogical Society *Quarterly*, Vol. 53.
- 1741-52 colonial census—*Journal of North Carolina Genealogy*, Raleigh.
- 1785-87 state census (incomplete)—State archives.
- None after 1790.

NORTH DAKOTA—1889

- 1850 federal territorial census (Pembina County, North Dakota) included with Minnesota—National Archives, and has been published.
- 1857 (Pembina County), 1885, 1915, 1925 state censuses—State historical society.
- 1860, 1870, 1880 federal territorial censuses under Dakota Territory—National Archives.
- 1900 federal census was first to designate North Dakota and South Dakota instead of simply Dakota.

OHIO—1803

- 1790-1810 censuses lost. Some census lists and other evidence of early Northwest Territory residents are found in the *Territorial Papers of the United States*, Vols. 2 & 3.
- 1800, 1803 Washington County only—State historical society. Microfilm copy at National Archives.

OKLAHOMA—1907

- 1860 federal territorial census, under Arkansas as Indian lands west of Arkansas—National Archives. Enumerates whites and free blacks. See corresponding slave schedule for list of slave owners, including Indians.
- 1890 territorial census—State historical society and microfilm copy in Stillwater Public Library. Counties available: Logan, Oklahoma, Cleveland, Canadian, Kingfisher, Payne, Beaver.
- 1900 federal territorial census—National Archives.
- 1907 Seminole County census—National Archives.

OREGON—1859

- 1842-1845, 1849, 1850-1859, 1865, 1875, 1885, 1895, 1905 territorial and state censuses of scattered counties—State archives.
- 1842-1859, various territorial censuses—State historical society.
- 1850 federal territorial census—National Archives.

PENNSYLVANIA—1787

- 1693 census along the Delaware River—*Genealogical Magazine of New Jersey*, Vol. 13, of the Genealogical Society of New Jersey, Newark.
- 1761 census of Pittsburgh—*Pennsylvania Magazine of History and Biography*, Vol. 6, of the Historical Society of Pennsylvania, Philadelphia.
- No real state censuses. Contact historical society and state library for any of scattered counties.

RHODE ISLAND—1790

- 1747 freemen list, 1774 and 1782 censuses, 1777 military census—State historical society. All available as published works as well.
- Various residents lists—*New England Historical and Genealogical Register*.
- 1865, 1875, 1885, 1915, 1925, 1935 state censuses—State archives.

SOUTH CAROLINA—1788

- 1829, 1839, 1869, 1875 state censuses of scattered counties—State archives.

SOUTH DAKOTA—1889

- 1860 federal territorial census—National Archives. Western part included with Nebraska Territory; eastern part as Dakota Territory.

- 1870, 1880 federal territorial censuses, as Dakota Territory—National Archives.
- 1885, 1895, 1905, 1915, 1925, 1935, 1945 state censuses—State historical society.

TENNESSEE—1796

- 1770-1790 settlers on the Cumberland River—*Census of the Cumberland Settlements, 1770-1790.* Richard Fulcher. Baltimore: Genealogical Publishing Company, 1987. See also Vol. 16, *Ansearchin' News* (address below).
- 1798 slaves and their owners—*Ansearchin' News*, Vol. 8, No. 3. Quarterly of the Tennessee Genealogical Society, P.O. Box 111249, Memphis, TN 38111-1249.
- 1800 census reconstructed from tax records—*Early East Tennessee Tax Payers.* Pollyanna Creekmore, comp. Easley, SC: Southern Historical Press, 1980.
- No state censuses extant.

TEXAS—1845

- 1819-1826 census of Austin's Colony—National Genealogical Society *Quarterly*, Vol. 45, printed as a book, 1959.
- 1829-1836 censuses—State archives; *The First Census of Texas 1829-1836.* Marion Day Mullins. Washington, DC: National Genealogical Society, 1976; National Genealogical Society *Quarterly*, Vols. 40-44.
- 1830 (San Antonio, Nacogdoches)—included in *1830 Citizens of Texas.* Gifford E. White. Austin: Eakin Press, 1983.
- 1840 Republic census—*The 1840 Census of the Republic of Texas.* Gifford E. White, ed. Austin: The Pemberton Press, 1966.
- No state censuses.

UTAH—1896

- 1850-1880 federal territorial censuses—National Archives.
- 1851 territorial census for scattered counties—*Utah Genealogical and Historical Magazine*, Vols. 28-29, Genealogical Society of Utah. Census has been published: *Genealogical Researchers Records Roundup*, Vols. 1-2. Rowene Obert and Helen Blumhagen, eds. Salt Lake City, 1968.
- 1856 territorial census and index—Family History Library, Salt Lake City.

VERMONT—1791

- Censuses of scattered towns—State historical society.
- Vermont has never taken a state census.

VIRGINIA—1788

- Seventeenth-century residents—(1) *The William and Mary Quarterly*, Vol. 24; (2) *New England Historical and Genealogical Register*, Vol. 31; (3) *Virginia Magazine of History and Biography*, Vol. 16, of the Virginia Historical Society; (4) *The Original Lists of Persons of Quality.* John Camden Hotten. New York, 1880.
- 1758 residents of some counties—Hening's *Statutes at Large*, Vol. 7.
- 1782-1787 heads of families—Compiled from state censuses and tax lists, the following books are often used together as a substitute for the missing 1790 federal census for the present states of Virginia, West Virginia, and Kentucky. (1) *Heads of Families at the First Census of the United States Taken in the year 1790: Virginia.* Washington, DC: Bureau of the Census, 1908. (2) *Virginia Tax Payers, 1782-1787: Other Than Those Published by the United States Census Bureau.* Augusta B. Fothergill and John Mark Naugle, comps. Baltimore: Genealogical Publishing Company, 1978. (3) *The 1787 Census of Virginia*, 2 vols. Netti Schreiner-Yantis and Florene Speakman Love, comps. Springfield, VA: Genealogical Books in Print, 1987.

WASHINGTON—1889

- 1850 federal territorial census under Oregon Territory, 1860-1880 as Washington Territory—National Archives.
- 1871-1892 Auditor censuses—State library, state archives, Seattle Public Library. Various counties, various years. Compiled by county assessors.

WEST VIRGINIA—1863

- No state censuses. See sources listed under Virginia.

WISCONSIN—1848

- 1820, 1830 territorial censuses under Michigan Territory—National Archives.
- 1840 territorial census as Wisconsin Territory—National Archives.
- 1839 residents of Southwestern Wisconsin—National Genealogical Society *Quarterly*, Vol. 58.
- 1836, 1838, 1842, 1846, 1847, 1855, 1865, 1875, 1885, 1895, 1905 state censuses—State historical society. (1905 state census is the only one to name all family members.)

WYOMING—1890

- 1850 federal territorial census with Utah; 1860, with Nebraska; 1870, 1880 as Wyoming Territory—National Archives.
- 1869 territorial census—State archives.

1910 SOUNDEX AND MIRACODE

Soundex available for these states:

Alabama
Georgia
Louisiana
Mississippi
South Carolina
Tennessee
Texas

Miracode (gives family visitation number instead of page number but uses the same coding system as Soundex) available for these states:

Arkansas
California
Florida
Illinois
Kansas
Kentucky
Michigan
Missouri
North Carolina
Ohio
Oklahoma
Pennsylvania
Virginia
West Virginia

THE FIRST FEDERAL CENSUS AVAILABLE FOR EACH STATE*

State	Year	State	Year
Alabama	1830	Montana	1860
Alaska	1900	Nebraska	1860
Arizona	1850	Nevada	1870
Arkansas	1830	New Hampshire	1790
California	1850	New Jersey	1830
Colorado	1860	New Mexico	1850
Connecticut	1790	New York	1790
Delaware	1800	North Carolina	1790
District of Columbia	1800	North Dakota	1860
Florida	1830	Ohio	1820
Georgia	1820	Oklahoma	1860, then 1900
Hawaii	1900	Oregon	1850
Idaho	1870	Pennsylvania	1790
Illinois	1810	Rhode Island	1790
Indiana	1820	South Carolina	1790
Iowa	1840	South Dakota	1860
Kansas	1860	Tennessee	1820, 1810 (fragments only)
Kentucky	1810	Texas	1850
Louisiana	1810	Utah	1850
Maine	1790	Vermont	1790
Maryland	1790	Virginia	1790 (substitute), 1810
Massachusetts	1790	Washington	1860
Michigan	1820	West Virginia	1870
Minnesota	1850	(part of Virginia until 1863)	
Mississippi	1820	Wisconsin	1820
Missouri	1830	Wyoming	1870

*Censuses may be missing for several reasons:

1. State or territory not yet organized, or enumerated with parent territory. See previous pages.
2. Census was taken but schedule misplaced, not turned in, ruined, or destroyed.

FAMILY RECORD OF THE ____________

Birth date
Birth place
Death date
Burial place
Religion
Politics
Occupation
Education

Birth date
Birth place
Death date
Burial place
Religion
Politics
Occupation
Education

Other spouses (his or hers)

CHILDREN O

#	Full Name
1	
2	
3	
4	
5	
6	
7	
8	

FIVE-GENERATION CHART # ______

Compiled by ______
Address ______

b = birth date & place
m = marriage date & place
d = death date & place

1 b m d
Spouse ______

2 b m d
3 b d

4 b m d
5 b d
6 b m d
7 b d

8 b m d
9 b d
10 b m d
11 b d
12 b m d
13 b d
14 b m d
15 b d

16
17
18
19
20
21
22
23
24
25
26
27
28
29
30
31

See Chart #

#1 on this chart is the same as # ______ on Chart # ______.

1920 CENSUS

Local Community ______________ **County** ______________ **State** ______________

Ward ______________ **Supervisor's District No.** ______________

Enumerator ______________ **Date Census Taken** ______________ **Enumeration District No.** ______________

Page No.	Street	House No.	Dwelling No.	Family No.	Name of each person whose place of abode on 1 Jan 1920 was in this family	Relationship	Own or rent home	Owned free or mortgaged	Sex	Color or race	Age	Marital status	Immigration year	Naturalized or alien?	Naturalization year	School since 1 Sept 1919	Can read	Can write	Birthplace of: This person	Mother tongue	Father	Mother tongue	Mother	Mother tongue	Speaks English?	Profession or Occupation & nature of business	Employer, wage earner, or self-employed	No. of farm schedule
	1	2	3	4	5	6	7	8	9	10	11	12	13	14	15	16	17	18	19	20	21	22	23	24	25	26 27	28	29

INDEX

Abstracting records. *See* Research, techniques
Adams, 10
African-American genealogy, 22, 32-33, 70-71, 149
  bibliography of resources, 70
  military records, 70
  slaves, 33, 52, 71
Age information, 75-77
Alabama, automated land records, 106
Allen, 8, 10, 77, 78, 89, 91, 111
American Genealogical Lending Library (AGLL), 60, 64, 68, 71, 74
  computer bulletin board, 106-107
American State Papers: Public Land Series, 69
Archer, 7-8
Archival-quality supplies, 110
Archives and libraries, addresses, 125-146
Archives, sources in, 45, 49, 60, 62, 63, 64, 70, 73
  See also National Archives; State archives
Arkansas, automated land records, 106
Arnold, 10
Atchison, KS, Public Library Bulletin Board System, 107
Austin, 81
Automated Archives, Inc., 107

Baptism, sources of information, 77
Bibles, *See* Family Bibles
Bibliographies,
  additional references, 83-84, 121-123
  African-American sources, 70-71
  choosing computer software, 103-104
  church records, sources for, 57-58
  dictionaries, 116
  directories of libraries, archives, organizations, 125
  early landholders, 83-84
  foreign research, 87
  immigration, 85-86
  Loyalists, 83
  Native American sources, 72
  passports (early), 83
  property and inheritance, 53
Bird, 65
Birth information
  birth records, 54, 63, 75
  estimating birth dates, 76-77
  interviewing for, 12
  sources of information, 4-5, 36, 75-77
  See also Vital statistics
Bishop, 14
Black (surname), 19, 110
Black genealogy. *See* African-American genealogy
Blalock, 10, 14, 18, 19, 40, 61, 79
Bland, 48
Bounty land warrants, 68, 69
Breslford, 19, 51-52, 53, 80, 110
Buford, 61
Bureau of Land Management, 62, 69, 70
  automated records, 70, 106, 107
  regional offices, 70

Calendars, Julian and Gregorian, 57-58, 88-89
Campbell, 5, 90-91
Canada,
  census (1871), 106
  libraries and archives, 142-144
Cemeteries, 46-48, 59
Census, federal, 63-66
  1885 optional census, 64
  age information in, 75-76
  census check form, 66-67, 162
  census day, 64
  forms, 163-176
  indexes on CD-ROM, 106
  indexes via computer bulletin board, 106
  marriage information in, 77-78
  mortality schedules, 64
  property information in, 85
  slave schedules, 64
  Soundex, 65, 66
  supplemental census schedules, 64
  Union Army veterans and widows (1890), 64
  using, 2, 6, 45, 46, 65-66, 75-76, 77-78, 79-80, 81, 82, 85, 95, 96
Census, state, 62, 80, 147-153
Checklists of sources for
  education information, 56
  finding church records, 57-58
  finding distant relatives, 38-39
  local sources, 58-59
  religious affiliation information, 58
  state sources, 62-63
Children, sources for identifying, 79-80
Church records, 56-58
Citizenship. *See* Naturalization
Civil service employee records (federal), 74
Civil War, military service records, 63, 68, 70, 108
Cluster genealogy, 2, 6, 9, 36, 45, 48, 50, 79, 81, 85
Collier, 96, 98
Coleman, 2, 7, 8-9, 10, 36, 41-44, 47, 48, 51, 53, 77, 78, 79, 82, 84, 111
Colvin, 80
Compiled service records. *See* Military service records
Computers and genealogy, 2, 103-108
  bulletin boards, 105-107
  Bureau of Land Management automated records, 106, 107
  CD-ROM records, 50, 106-107
  computer interest groups, 105
  databases, 106-108
  genealogy and utility software, 103-104
  Internet, 105, 107
  library use of, 105, 107
  remote access research, 105-107
  word processing, 104-105
Confederate pensions, 62, 68
Confederate records, 63
Cooper, 18
County courthouse records, 45, 49-55
  birth and death records, 54
  court records, 54, 73
  deeds, 51-54
  indexes, 49, 52
  marriages, 49-50
  miscellaneous, 53, 54
  tax records, 54
  wills, probate and estate records, 50-51, 78-79
County courthouses, research in, 5

County histories, 39
Court records, 54, 73
Cravens, 53
Croom, 2, 20, 43-44, 79, 82
Cummings, 79, 80-81, 96-98

Daniel, 8, 91, 111
Databases, computerized, 106-108
Dates,
  approximating, 12, 76-77, 78-79
  Old Style and New Style, 88-89
  reading and writing, 88-89
  using or evaluating, 89, 90-91
  See also Day of the week
Daughters of the American Revolution, National Society, 39
Daughters of 1812, National Society, United States, 39
Day of the week, formula for finding, 90
Death information,
  death records, 54, 63
  interviewing for, 12
  sources of, 36, 50, 78-79
  See also Vital statistics
Declaration of Intention, 73
Deed records, 51-54
Depression era (1930s), 28, 29
Dick, 52
Discrepancies. *See* Evidence, evaluating
Documenting sources, 4, 9, 49, 109. *See also* Research
Donation land entries, 69
Dower rights, 51, 52, 53, 91
Draft cards. *See* World War I draft registrations

Education information, 36, 56
Ellis Island immigration database, 108
England,
  books on immigrants from, 85-86
  calendar change, 88-89
  census (1851), 106
Estate inventories, 51
Everett, 80-81, 98
Everton's On-Line Search, 106
Evidence, evaluating, 4-5, 9, 13, 20, 45, 76-80, 89, 90-91, 95-98.
    See also Research

Family associations, 37-38
Family Bibles, 36
Family group sheets, 9, 10, 111, 112
Family History Library and centers, 39, 60, 64, 74, 86, 107, 108
Family history projects, 109-110, 111-112
Family histories, published, 39
Family Periodicals (Ganier), 37-38
Family reunions, 23, 37, 113
Family sources, 12, 36-43, 45, 63, 112-113
Family traditions. *See* Oral tradition; Traditions
Federal census. *See* Census, federal
Federal sources, 45, 63-74
Field, 8
Fire insurance maps. *See* Sanborn Company
First papers (naturalization), 73
Fisher, 10
Five-generation chart, 7, 8
Florida,
  automated land records, 106
  donation land grants, 69-70
Forms,
  census, 163-176
  census check, 66, 67, 162
  family group sheet, 9, 10, 156, 157
  five-generation chart, 7, 8, 155
  map, United States, 43, 44, 161
  outline of a life, 91, 93, 158
  problem search record, 92, 94, 159
  quick reference, 59, 61, 160
Freedmen's Bureau, 70
Freedmen's Savings and Trust Company, 70

Galveston (Texas), Texas Seaport Museum, 86, 107-108
Garner, 51-52
Genealogical societies, 38
Geographic Names Information System (GNIS), 107
Glossary, 116-119
Godwin, 76, 80
Government records. *See* Federal sources; Local sources;
    State sources
Grassroots of America (McMullin), 69, 70
Guestroom exchange network, 60

Handwriting, 41, 66, 99-102, 113
  examples, 42, 99-102
Harrison, 3, 46-47, 78, 79, 92-94
Hazelgrove, 51
Hereditary societies, 39
Hester, 76-77
Historical societies, sources in, 49, 60, 64, 70, 71
Hitchcock, 61
Hodge, 48
Holmes, 66-67, 82
Holt, 79
Homestead Act (1862), 70
  land grants and records, 70, 73
Housing and living conditions, sources of information, 85
Huston, 19, 22-23, 80-81, 98

Illinois,
  automated land records, 106
  Chicago 1870 census index, 106
Immigrant ancestors, 32, 85-87
Immigration, 72-73, 85-86, 108
  bibliography, 85-86
  interview questions, 32
Indian records, 62, 71-72
Indiana, land records, 84, 106
Interlibrary loan, 49, 60, 74
International reply coupons, 87
Internet, 105, 107
Interviews, 12, 24-32, 113
  examples, 5, 12, 96-98
  questions, 24-35
  taping, 15-16, 113
  techniques, 5, 12-13, 15, 96-97
  vital statistics from, 12, 13, 96-97
Inventories of estates, 51, 85
Iowa, automated land records, 106
Ireland,
  census records, 106
  libraries and archives, 144-145

Jackson, 10
Jaggers, 61
Judah, 61

Kansas, Atchison Public Library Bulletin Board System, 107
Keahey, 80

Kentucky death index, 106
King, 19, 104

Land records,
bibliography, early land grants, 83-84
Bureau of Land Management (BLM), 62, 69, 70
BLM, Automated Records System, 70, 106, 107
cash and credit entry case files, 70, 73, 106
deeds, 51-54
federal (public domain), 63, 69-70
Lee, 61
Lending libraries, 60, 74
Letters, 37
as sources, 36, 41, 43, 62
sending, overseas, 87
writing, 9, 11, 13
Libraries, 45, 55-56
addresses, by state, 125-145
lending, 46, 60
use of, 55-57
interlibrary loan, 60, 74
sources in, 46, 49, 55, 62, 64, 65, 73
Library catalogs,
using, 56
computerized, 105, 107
Library of Congress, 74
catalog, computer access, 105-106
Local sources, 45-60
checklist, 58-59
Lockhart, 52
Louisiana,
automated land records, 106
New Orleans notarial archives, 55, 85
Loyalists, bibliography, 83

MacFarlane, 61
Maiden names, 80-81
Manuscript collections, 63
Map, United States, 43-44, 161
Maps, as research aids, 43, 46
Marriage information,
estimating dates, 77-78
interviewing for, 5, 12
marriage agreements, 78
marriage records, 49-50, 51
sources for, 36, 77-78, 106
See also Vital statistics
Mary and John (ship) immigrants, 86
Maryland,
Baltimore 1870 census index, 106
Baltimore passenger arrivals, 1820-1834, 86
McAlpin, 6
McBride, 61
McCain, 104
McFadden, 10, 50-51, 52, 61, 79
McKennon, 61
Medical history, 35
Metcalf, 41
Metcalfe, 19, 28
Michigan, automated land records, 106
Microfilm rental and purchase, 60, 64, 68, 71, 74
Military pension records, 62, 63, 67, 68
Military service records, 68
African-Americans, 70-71
on CD-ROM with graphic imaging, 107
Civil War Soldiers database, 108
Confederate, 63, 68
copies of, 68
Korean War and Vietnam death index, 107
Native Americans, 71-72
Miller, 41, 111
Minnesota, automated land records, 106
Mississippi, automated land records, 106
Missouri,
automated land records, 106
St. Louis 1870 census index, 106
Montgomery, 10
Mood, 17
Moore, 6
Mortality schedules, 64, 107

Names, 17-20, 79
abbreviations, 18
middle, 18, 19, 80
nicknames, 17-18
variant spellings, 17
Naming patterns, 18-20
National Archives,
guides to, 63
records, 63, 68-74, 83, 106, 108
regional branches, 70, 71, 146
National Archives Microfilm Rental Program, 60, 74
National Genealogical Conference (computer bulletin board), 105
National Personnel Records Center, 68
National Union Catalog of Manuscript Collections, 75
Native American records, 62, 71-72
Naturalization (citizenship), 73
New Orleans Notarial Archives, 55, 85
Newspapers, 48-49, 54, 55
union catalogs, 49
Newton, 22, 81, 98
New York,
Ellis Island immigration project, 108
New York City 1870 census index, 106
passenger arrivals, 86
Nicknames. *See* Names
Non-population census schedules. *See* Supplemental census schedules
North Carolina,
land grants, 69
Revolutionary War claims, 83
Notebooks,
organizing, 1-3
versus computers, 2
NUCMC (nuck-muck). *See* National Union Catalog of Manuscript Collections

Occupation information, source, 84
Ohio,
automated land records, 106
Virginia Military District of, 69
Oklahoma, Indian records, 71
Oldham, 6
Oral tradition, 21-23, 24, 112
Oregon, donation land grants, 69-70
Orgain, 2, 3, 6, 19, 46
Organizing. *See* Research

Parents, sources for identifying, 79-81
Passenger lists, 72-73, 86, 108
Passports, 74, 83

Patton, 10, 61, 79
Pedigree chart (five-generation chart), 7, 8
Pennington, 10
Pennsylvania,
Philadelphia 1870 census index, 106
Philadelphia passenger arrivals, 86
Pension records (military), 62, 63, 67, 68
Phillips, 7, 8, 10, 18, 51, 78, 79, 111
Philpot, 19
Photographs, 37, 39
Figure 8, Photos and handwriting samples, 42
Political affiliation, sources, 84
Preservation Emporium, 110
Preuss, 104
Primary sources, 4, 5
Privacy law (1974), 56
Probate records, 50-51, 76-77, 78-79
See also Glossary pages 117-118
Problem search form, 92, 94
Prusler, 104
Public domain, 69. *See also* Public land states
Public land records, 69-70
computer access to, 106, 107
Public land states, 54, 62, 69, 106
Public libraries, 55-56, 125-145. *See also* Libraries
Publishers, addresses, 123-124

Quakers, records and use of dates, 57-58
Queries, 38
Questions for interviews. *See* Interviews
Quick reference chart, 59, 61

Records. *See* County courthouse records; Family sources; Research; and specific kinds of records, such as census, church, court, land, military, school
Relationship chart, 119-120
Reliability of data, 75
Religious affiliation, 58. *See also* Church records
Rental libraries. *See* Lending libraries
Research,
abstracting records, 50, 52, 53
documenting sources, 4, 9, 49, 109
materials needed, 1-2
note taking, 2-3, 49, 50
organizing, 1-2, 5, 9, 56
original records, using, 5, 49-55, 62-66, 68-74, 75-82, 106, 107
rules and strategies, 4-6, 53
techniques, 4, 12, 50, 52, 75, 82
See also Cluster genealogy; Evidence, evaluating; Interviews; Primary sources; Reliability of data; Secondary sources; Transcriptions
Revolutionary War,
pensions, 62
records, 63
Richardson, 47, 61
Robertson/Robberson, 82
Rock, 104
Rules and strategies of research. *See* Research

Sanborn Co. fire insurance maps, 85
Scholarly Resources, 74
School records, 36, 56
Scotland,
books on immigrants from, 85
libraries and archives, 145
Secondary sources, 4, 5
Shaw, 84
Shelby, 6
Signature collection, 115
Slave census schedules (1850-1860), 64
Smith, 77, 79, 104
Social Security death index, 78, 81, 106, 107
Societies,
genealogical, 38
hereditary, 39
historical, sources in, 49, 60, 64, 70, 71
Soundex, 65, 66
1880, 65
1910 availability, 153
code chart, 65
South Carolina, Audited Accounts (Revolutionary War claims), 83
Southern Claims Commission, 83
State archives and libraries,
addresses, 125-145
sources in, 60, 62, 63, 70, 73
State censuses, 62, 80, 147-153
State land states, 54, 62
State sources, 62-63, 83-84. *See also* State censuses
Steele, 10, 61
Stories. *See* Oral tradition; Traditions
Stuart, 53
Sturdivant, 5
Successions. *See* Probate records
Supplemental census schedules, 1850-1880, 64
Swem Index, 84

Taping interviews, 15-16, 113. *See also* Interviews
Tax records, 6, 54, 73
Techniques for research. *See* Research
Tennessee, Civil War Direct Tax, 73
Territorial censuses, 147-153
Territorial Papers of the United States, 73, 147, 149, 150
Texas Seaport Museum (Galveston), 86, 107-108
Tisdale, 3
Tombstones, 46-48, 90-91
Tract books, 54, 70
Traditions and customs, 23, 112. *See also* Oral tradition
Transcriptions, caution in using, 48, 50
Turley, 20, 80

United States Geological Survey, GNIS, 107
University libraries. *See* Libraries

Vaughan, 78, 79
Virginia, Revolutionary War claims, 83
Virginia Historical Index (Swem), 84
Virginia Military District of Ohio, 69
Visiting Friends, Inc., 60
Vital statistics, 7, 63
interviewing for, 12-13
records, 54, 63
sources for, 36, 46, 49, 54, 56, 68, 70, 75-79

Wales, National Library, 145
Walton, 77
Washington (state), donation land grants, 69-70
Watkins, 7, 8
White, 82, 95-96, 97
Whitesides, 52
Wills and probate records, 50-51, 76-77, 78-79
Wisconsin, automated land records, 106
Women, property rights. *See* Dower rights
Works Progress Administration, inventories, 58
World War I draft registrations, 68
Writing a family history, 109